O Metaphors of Identity

SUNY Series, Human Communication Processes

Donald P. Cushman and Ted J. Smith III, Editors

O Metaphors of Identity

A Culture-Communication Dialogue

THOMAS K. FITZGERALD

Foreword by George and Louise Spindler

STATE UNIVERSITY OF NEW YORK PRESS

Published by
State University of New York Press, Albany

For information, address State University of New York Press,
State University Plaza, Albany, N.Y. 12246

Production by M. R. Mulholland
Marketing by Bernadette LaManna

Library of Congress Cataloging-in-Publication Data

Fitzgerald, Thomas K.
    Metaphors of identity : a culture-communication dialogue / Thomas
K. Fitzgerald ; foreword by George and Louise Spindler.
        p.   cm. — (SUNY series, human communcation processes)
    Includes bibliographical references (p.   ) and index.
    ISBN 0-7914-1595-3 (CH : Acid-free). — ISBN 0-7914-1596-1 (PB :
Acid-free)
    1. Identity (Psychology)   2. Intercultural communication.
3. Interpersonal relations.   4. Group identity.   5. Personality and
culture.   I. Title.   II. Series: SUNY series in human communication
processes.
GN512.F57   1993
155.2—dc20   92-27080
                                                             CIP

10 9 8 7 6 5 4 3 2 1

For
FRANK L. SAUNDERS
friend and companion

CONTENTS

FOREWORD

This remarkable book attends to communication, culture, and identity in a consistent framework of metaphoric analysis. There is nothing like it in the existing literature. Though there are hundreds of articles and books that take steps toward such a holistic interpretation, and dozens that pursue quite different lines of analysis and interpretation of related processes, Fitzgerald's bibliography is virtually all-encompassing; and the reader is guided to and through this bibliography by his sophisticated and fair-handed discussions.

Identity is posited as the academic metaphor for self-in-context, which immediately calls attention to a current preoccupation on the part of social analysts—the multiplicity and diversity of cultures, contexts, and selves in the perceived world we live in. In the United States, as Fitzgerald points out, psychiatrists and psychologists are fascinated by multiple personalities that presumably reside in one psyche. We could also cite sociological descriptions of multiple contexts for emerging selves. Educational psychologists, too, talk about distinctive selves and a diversified sense of self-efficacy—one for math, one for literature, one for art, and so forth. We, ourselves, have recently applied a distinction between an "enduring" self and a "situated" self (as well as an "endangered" self) to the analysis of adaptations by ethnic minority students to school-imposed tasks and criteria for academic success.

In all of this perception of multiplicity, there is a pervasive theme of "construction." Humans are constructing selves to fit contexts and constructing contexts to fit selves. Prometheus seems to have been unbound, in contrast to the more mechanistic "society determines everything" model that dominated the social and behavioral disciplines until about the 1960s.

All of us who do research in contemporary, complex societies have faced both the problems and opportunities inherent in this promethean perspective on action and self-identification. Those of us whose youth and early training are in another age, one where communities existed (or so we thought), where people had character (so it seemed), and where identity was taken for granted, find the modern scene both academic and "real"—perplexing, threatening, and immensely exciting.

Everyone, everywhere, seems caught up in a desperate search for self, for identity, and for recognition. Native Americans reaffirm an identity that they feel is about to slip away forever. Modern Indian "pow-wows," replete with costumes, dancing, and drumming, attract not only Indians but many others who look upon Native American traditions with a certain, perhaps "imperialist," nostalgia. American blacks search for their African roots. White ethnics revive Rosemaling (a form of painting), cookery, and clothing styles as a way of recognizing their own ancestors. White mainstreamers celebrate their historical Americanness while, at the same time, looking for ways to exclude others from full participation. Youths invent languages, mannerisms, music, and style to distinguish themselves from their elders as well as from each other.

This promethean creation of separatist identities seems harmless most of the time. Occasionally, however, we are reminded—with a jolt—that separate identities in America can have serious results, a poignant example being the 1992 Los Angeles riots. All the participants—whether the jurors, the police, or the rioters—were in a real sense acting out separate and confrontational identities.

Those of us who are trying to make sense of the modern world apply analytic concepts that transcend immediate reality. We have used the concept of "dialogue" to create a partial theory of American culture (G & L Spindler 1990). Fitzgerald—with the consistent use of metaphor as a guiding construct—also uses dialogue as an analytic concept, but moves his analysis closer to self and identity than to culture in process (as we think we do).

In viewing the current *Zeitgeisten* of the academic disciplines, Fitzgerald takes a measured stance. Consequently, he has written a book that is potentially useful in all of them. We will certainly use *Metaphors of Identity* as text or reference in several of our courses, including Cultural Transmission, Psychological Anthropology, Education and Cultural Process, as well as in Ethnography of Schooling, and Perspectives on American Culture. We heartily recommend it to others.

George and Louise Spindler
Stanford University

ACKNOWLEDGMENTS

Concerned with what is now known across disciplines about identity, this study opens up an exciting multidisciplinary "dialogue" that grapples with issues of interpersonal and intercultural communication. Because of the book's transdisciplinary nature, many ideas are interpretations of the writings of other individuals.

I sincerely wish to thank these scholars (from disciplines are far-flung as religion and philosophy, history, sociology, psychology, anthropology, and of course the communication sciences) for providing me with fundamental insights into the complex workings of culture, identity, and communication. Although some scholars undoubtedly stand out as more influential than others, it would be foolish to try to list all the important researchers that left a lasting theoretical impression on this study. I am humbly indebted to them all.

I was fortunate to have had access to the Pacific collection at the Macmillan Brown Centre for Pacific Studies (University of Canterbury, New Zealand), where I was gently guided by Dr. Malama Maleisea and his staff for three weeks in March 1992. As for financial help, I gratefully acknowledge a Research Council grant (UNCG) and a Southern Regional Education Board travel award, both of which allowed me to accept the position of Research Fellow at the Macmillan Brown Centre, where I did the final reworking of the ethnographic material.

As chapter 5 is a revised version of the article "Media and Changing Metaphors of Ethnicity and Identity," which first appeared in *Media, Culture & Society* (SAGE: London, 1991), and subsequently in the Paddy Scannell, et al. edition of *Culture and Power* (SAGE: London, 1992), special thanks go to the editors at SAGE, London, for allowing me to reprint this material. I also acknowledge permission to quote extensively from Diane Ravitch's article "Multiculturalism: E Pluribus Plures," in *The Key Reporter* (vol. 56, no. 1, Autumn 1990). Parts of chapter 7 are adapted from a chapter written in 1983 for a sociology textbook by R. C. Federico and J. S. Schwartz, eds. *Sociology* (Reading, Mass.: Addison-Wesley Co); permission to reuse this material was granted by McGraw-Hill, now owner of the rights to this text.

Fortunately, I have had the steady support and encouragement from both friends and colleagues, among whom I would like especially to mention my companion, Frank L. Saunders, to whom this volume is dedicated. I would like to recognize my ever-faithful friends Susan Dorn, Cyndy and Don Adams, Gretchen L. Biddix, Richard Webb, Marty and Andrew Sykes, as well as my secretary Pattie Barlow. Colleagues who advised me throughout the writing of this book include Dr. Elizabeth Natalle, Dr. John Altrocchi, Dr. Jack Bardon, Dr. Carole Hill, Dr. Ronald Federico and Jay Wilson; Dr. Richard Robbins, Drs. George and Louise Spindler, Dr. Maria Tsiapera, Dr. Amy Webb, Dr. Mary Kay Sanford, Dr. Tom Scullion, and Dr. Willie Baber. I have been blessed with a competent and efficient editor at SUNY, Megeen Mulholland, whose prompt assistance during the last months of rewriting made the task easier and more fruitful. Thanks go to these generous friends and colleagues for their indispensable help.

1

◯ Conceptions of Identity in the Culture-Communication Dialogue

The most significant intellectual movements of the last two decades...have placed cultural analysis at the center of the human and literary disciplines. The most significant political and moral strategies of the time, at least in the industrial West, focus on cultural issues concerning personal identity, community building and social legitimation and inclusion, moral order, and everyday ethics.

—Jeffrey C. Alexander and Steven Seidman,
Culture and Society

Goals and Objectives/Concepts and Definitions

In their encyclopedic book, *Managing Cultural Differences*, Harris and Moran (1989: 53) argue convincingly that Americans must learn to improve interpersonal and intercultural communication skills in order to become more effective performers in an increasingly global and plural environment. Western business leaders, they point out, could benefit from training in cultural awareness if we expect to succeed in our social and commercial relations in other parts of the world.

This cultural awareness might involve recognizing values and attitudes that differ from our own or simply becoming more sensitive to taken-for-granted social customs that signal a different sense of time, privacy, tradition, status, and the role of women in culture. Maintaining successful encounters with minority groups living within the boundaries of a nation, such as the handicapped or the elderly, can also be problematic (Harris & Moran 1989: 345). Failure to recognize the social distinctions of minorities, then, can have serious implications for intergroup harmony. Even when such differences are not primarily cultural, the communication styles of group members may differ in part from those of mainstream Americans.

Clearly, communication is at the heart of international, intercultural, and interpersonal relations. If we are to become better global communicators, we must learn new competencies, skills, and sensitivities not the least of which involve new ways of looking at self, or identity, as this construct relates to communication. A primary goal of *Metaphors of Identity* is to use the bridging concept of identity to gain insight into the contemporary debates about culture and communication—what I call *"the culture-communication dialogue."*

In recent years, psychologists and anthropologists have witnessed the revival of interest in the concept of self and its relationship to both social and cultural variability. Advances in travel and mass media have demonstrated the reciprocal influences of culture and communication. The growing and impressive communication literature attests to this emphasis. In the Western world, we live in a veritable information society that affects the nature of work, the use of time, power relations, systems of stratification and values as well as, more fundamentally, the way we conceive of self (McQuail 1989: 77; Markus & Kitayama 1991: 224).

Few books, however, have attended to how the self-concept relates to culture and the communication processes. Work in this area, though exciting, is still somewhat exploratory; and definitions of communication, even in the communication sciences, remain variable (Hall 1992: 51).[1] There is an urgent need for clarification of theoretical concepts, such as culture versus society; change (social and cultural change[2]); community as it relates to communication; and, finally, metaphorical conceptualizations of all these interrelated abstractions.

Identity, a central construct of the social sciences, can provide the bridge between studies of interpersonal and mass communication. Since both personal and group identity are, to some extent, always mutually involved in communication encounters, the identity model presented in this volume attempts to integrate both interpersonal and intergroup levels of communication, thus dealing with the "microworld" of interpersonal communication and the "macroworld" of mediated mass communication, to borrow—with minor alteration—Thomas Scheff's terminology (1990). Both are necessary for a full understanding of human relationships. The focus, then, is on understanding the impact of social and cultural factors on behavioral communication, specifically how identity is crucial in situations of interpersonal and cross-cultural communication.

Erikson ([1950]1963: 282), the first to use the term *identity* in its presently accepted scientific sense, felt that the study of identity would become as strategic in our times as the study of sexuality was in Freud's. Certainly this volume gives special prominence to the academic construct of identity. While teaching ideas from this book for a graduate seminar, I made a surprising discovery. Midway through the semester, students suddenly realized that identity was something they had been studying all along, only under different labels in diverse fields. Philosophy, they began to recognize, typically considers personhood. Psychologists study ego, personality, and self-actualization. Sociologists tend to talk about social identities in group contexts, while anthropologists write about cultural identity. Self-concept, on the other hand, dominates recent work in both education and psychology. Evoking the familiar blindmen-and-elephant imagery, ultimately we were all talking about the same animal: self-in-context; the emphases were merely on different parts of this same metaphoric elephant.

In the identity literature, Phinney and Rotheram (1987) remind us, researchers too often limit themselves to single components of the identity pool, thus making the results of such studies seem more concrete and definitive than they really are. The principal players in the ongoing culture-communication dialogue have been anthropology, psychology, and the communication sciences; but this volume does not confine itself to these three. Obviously many disciplines have been concerned with understanding significant aspects of this multifaceted construct.

In this book, identity is defined as *the academic metaphor for self-in-context*. Each chapter addresses a different, often neglected, context for the expression of this many-sided abstraction. Furthermore, the book explores the implications of identification for a better understanding of culture and communication. Identity cuts across almost all academic boundaries; hence it is one of those truly transdisciplinary ideas that touches all of us in myriad ways and is interpreted and understood differently by individuals and groups. There is ample evidence of the complexity of this multi-dimensional concept; the range of identity topics is extremely wide, overlapping areas such as mental health, ethnicity, gender, education, social conflict, and change. However, the far-reaching applicability of the construct may be one of its major strengths.

In general, *Metaphors of Identity* traces the relation of identity to its biological roots, briefly outlines the history of the concept, and considers its relationships to communication, education, ethnicity, gender, and age. As the search for identity has been described as a "modern existential dilemma," some philosophical speculations on the adaptive functions of identity for human survival are offered as well (Weigert, Teitge & Teitge 1990: 14).

The number of philosophers, psychologists, anthropologists, and others that have tried to make sense of identity is enormous; and the scientific literature on specialized aspects of this subject (person, self, self-concept, ego, and so forth) is equally extensive. I have attempted in this volume to achieve some academic holism, or integration of ideas. The need for synthesis in this field is great; and, among the social sciences, anthropology may be best suited for such a multidisciplinary effort. Certainly the transdisciplinary nature of the identity construct forbids any slavish respect for academic boundaries.

Specifically, the book attempts to use ideas from various disciplines for a multi-interest audience. Drawing upon many disciplines to get a picture of identity in its full complexity is, nevertheless, a daunting task. For one thing, as the book has multiple audiences in mind, certain chapters reflect mixed levels of writing consistent with this aim. I have also tried to reduce jargon to a minimum. For clarity's sake, *principal points* are included at the end of each chapter to highlight central debates in the culture-communication dialogue.

Although there have been attempts to study identity before, the results generally have been highly specialized or do not really deal with the relationships between culture and communication (White & Kirkpatrick 1985; Carrithers, et al. 1987). Books from the science of communication, including the excellent examples mentioned in the bibliography, underscore the importance of understanding the diversity of cultural and social outlooks by different human groups, but have tended to neglect the construct of identity even when narrowly focused on interpersonal communication. As a case in point, Gudykunst and Ting-Toomey (1988) address some salient issues of identification, although naturally their central concern was with the communication process itself. The present volume takes a broader perspective.

What many previous books have demonstrated is that serious scholarship dealing with culture is still possible and fruitful, especially studies concerned with how the concept relates to identity and change. Much of the current intercultural communication literature is still inconsistent and contradictory in its definition and application of the culture concept. Confusion of the constructs *culture* and *society* typifies this problem. Although there is often an interdependence between culture and society, the two can and do exist separately. The notion of culture can be problematic at several levels. Although not suggesting that the term be dropped, *Metaphors of Identity* calls for a better understanding of its underlying meanings. Certainly a secondary focus of this volume has been to examine and critique the uses and abuses of the culture concept, while attempting to clarify culture's impact on identity and communication.

The concept of culture has helped us greatly in understanding the diversity of human behavior; but, according to Alexander and Seidman (1990: 235), it has become a theoretically, as well as politically, contested terrain in contemporary scientific discourse. Consider the modern debates over so-called multiculturalism in the schools and their implications for hindering or improving minority relationships. Identity is surely at the core of these contemporary dialogues. The American intellectual tradition, Marcus and Fischer (1986: 35) assert, is biased toward downplaying the importance of cultural differences for a more general, egalitarian humanism. According to these authors, we accept cultural differences but play down their consequences. These tendencies are further reinforced by the widespread diffusion of communication technologies. At the very least, identity changes are speeded up by telecommunication influences.

Identity remains a good construct for interdisciplinary use, one of the central and characteristic issues in modern pluralistic societies. However, a major factor largely ignored in studies of identity is the mediated reality of the contemporary social order, i.e., the influence of media, and mass communication in general, on the identification process. Bergheim states boldly that the electronic world has become "as American as microwaved apple pie and video baseball" (1990:94). It is precisely the implication of mediated communication in the institutionalization of human selfhood that is a primary concern of the present volume. Definitions of self are today the work of mediated experiences as well as culturally and socially constructed beliefs and values (Weigert, et al. 1990: 63).

The tripartite theoretical model employed in this book considers self a multi-dimensional, reflexive process involving psychological motivation, cultural knowledge, and the ability to perform appropriate roles. These roles have been shaped by the individual's social positions, but at the same time they are significantly influenced by the mediated environments in which most of us live today. Put another way, social relationships in the contemporary world include mediated cultural and social experiences in ways not true, for example, of nonindustrialized societies. We emerge as human selves through the responses of others. However, these responses, in a modern, Western context, are largely filtered through communication channels that themselves call for further investigation (Altheide 1976, 1985; Snow 1983; Arterton 1987; Dennis 1989).

The important point is that the media shape our lives in ways not always obvious. This book, like others that have placed emphasis on mass communication, stresses the impact of electronic media on social behavior.[3] The link between communication and identity has yet to be completely forged. *Metaphors of Identity*, then, is concerned with understanding the "why" and "how" of managing, or failing to manage, human differences, cultural or social, that can become potential barriers to communication.

As a psychological anthropologist, I have used the concept of identity extensively in the past twenty years: in research and writing that have focused on Canadian Indians, New Zealand Maoris, Cook Island migrants in the South Pacific, sexual minorities in Sweden and Finland, and to a lesser extent racial and ethnic groups in North America (Fitzgerald 1972, 1974, 1975, 1977a, 1977b, 1977c, 1979, 1988, 1989, 1991, 1992). Fieldwork experiences are employed to give a fuller understanding of identity, with the following specific objectives in mind:

1. A substantive overview of identity, from the point of view of several perspectives, is attempted. Including ideas from other disciplines is one way of pointing out areas of identity not previously considered. Although identity always comprises a subset of different parts, it is considered in its various dimensions, including social, cultural, and personal identity. The goal for the first half of the book is to try and achieve academic integration compatible with the more research-oriented second half of the volume. This approach constitutes a more holistic view of self than is characteristic of the contemporary literature on identity.

2. Another objective is to provide a theoretical model that grounds identity in both biology and culture, attempting to explain what it does in terms of its communication functions. Self-consciousness, after all, develops largely through communication with other persons. This integrative, adaptive/growth model views identity as a psychological process that mediates between culture and communication. Cultural, social, and psychological systems have been portrayed, in the past, as operating more or less autonomously. Human action is likely to be seen today as symbolic, social, and motivational all at the same time (Alexander & Seidman 1990: 5).

Although presenting a new definition of identity (the academic metaphor for self-in-context), this book does not offer a new communication theory. Rather, the performance model attempts to show the interrelatedness of culture, identity, and communication. The present volume focuses squarely on culture and identity, with emphasis on the theoretical implications for the communication sciences.

From the point of view of the communicating individual, personality structure is seen as involving three subsystems: psychological motivation, cultural knowledge, and ability to perform socially appropriate roles. Performance, in this integrative scheme, becomes critical in the analysis of meaning and experience. In addition, special attention is paid to the media through which the performance is often realized in contemporary society.[4] In delineating the interrelatedness of these three concepts within a single theoretical system, the book affords a unique opportunity to integrate diverse disciplinary perspectives.

Ideas like culture and identity have been compared to the air we breathe: something taken for granted until there is an external stimulation that forces us to think about them (Brislin, et al. 1986: 22). For some reason, in the past twenty years, life seems to have forced me to want to think about culture and identity. The interest in communication arrived later, but with no less intellectual impact.

3. A further objective is to demonstrate how the model works using specific cultures, or social groups, many chosen from my two decades of anthropological fieldwork. I have tried to pick the best theoretical insights from studies of Indians, Pacific Islanders, sexual minorities, and identity and aging (condensed and summarized, hopefully in an appealing writing style) that illustrate how culture, identity, and communication influence each other. There is need for convergence of disciplinary perspectives, and *Metaphors of Identity* is clearly a book that bridges many academic disciplines.

Identity studies have involved two methodological traditions: one qualitative and interpersonal, the other quantitative and measurement-oriented. These are the so-called "subjective" versus "objective" methodologies (Weigert, Teitge & Teitge 1990: 27). Although studies cited in this volume lean toward the qualitative, effort has been made to include both approaches where appropriate. This book should be especially attractive to students and instructors needing to ground abstract, theoretical discussions of identity in concrete, ethnographic examples.

4. Finally, I consider some of the larger implications of this quest for identity, or the modern search for a more relevant identity in an age of instant communication, especially how identity—cultural, social, or personal—relates to the communication processes. Admittedly, this latter discussion is highly speculative. Identity is certainly a central concern of the social sciences, but there is still lack of agreement on its various levels and meanings. We are reminded that identity, the academic metaphor for self-in-context, is always both a "technical" and a "folk" category, a philosophical inquiry as well as a "cultural cliché" for making sense of everyday realities (Weigert, et al. 1990: 21). My aim was to write a down-to-earth account that tackles both the scientific and some of the more ineffable dimensions of identity in the exciting, contemporary culture-communication dialogue.

The Notion of Dialogue/A Cross-Disciplinary Conversation

The word *dialogue* generally conveys the image of a conversation between two or more people. In fact, it was a conversation that sparked my initial interest in the scientific field of communication. A young colleague at the university, recognizing the significance of the contemporary debates over culture for her own research and teaching, sought an anthropological perspective on this complex and abstract issue. In fact, anthropologists and communication specialists have been more or less sharing intercultural insights since the seminal publication of Edward T. Hall's *Silent Language* in 1959.

Little was I to know the passionate, intellectual ferment that would result from this innocent conversation. For the past three years, I have been avidly reading in the areas of interpersonal and intercultural communication, trying to relate my lifelong fascination with identity to the modern debates over culture and communication. At this juncture, I began to view dialogue less literally as a conversation and more broadly as an exchange of ideas—in this case, an extended, somewhat metaphorical, dialogue between those interested in culture and those specializing in the area of the communication sciences.

Unfortunately, most of the discussions among different disciplines that have concerned themselves with these ideas have been characterized by a series of separate monologues. Each, however, has made distinct and valuable contributions. This book attempts a more dialogic approach, which invites different parties to listen to diverse viewpoints, perspectives, and debates with the aim of trying to unify this complex subject.

Marcus and Fischer, in *Anthropology As Cultural Critique*, suggest that the metaphor of dialogue has become the dominant imagery for expressing the way many contemporary anthropologists inquire about communication within and between cultures (1986: 30). Certainly, a dialogue has developed between those interested in communication and those concerned with social and cultural variability. Hence, my choice of subtitle for this volume: *A Culture-Communication Dialogue*. However, the exchange is not solely between anthropology and the communication sciences; the culture-communication debates extend well beyond these two disciplines. Although clearly a book about identity, the work focuses on the impact of socio-cultural factors on behavioral communication—namely, how identity can be instrumental in improving or hindering interpersonal and cross-cultural communication.

Stimulated by international exchanges and multicultural trade, a unique world culture may be emerging that places immediate and practical emphasis on a global environment (Featherstone 1990). Modern-day assertions of ethnic identity, as well as the political demands of minorities for basic human rights, make a better understanding of the socio-cultural dimensions of communication more and more a daily imperative. The development of knowledge and skills needed to cope with diversity, both social and cultural, are widespread demands that cannot be ignored.

Interpretive anthropology, Marcus and Fischer have reminded us (1986: 25), tries to elucidate how different cultural constructions of reality affect social action or, broadly, communication. Social life, viewed from such a perspective, is nonetheless concerned ultimately with the negotiation of meaning at the personal, psychological level. Clearly, identity is *a* core, if not *the* core, issue in terms of broader communication processes. Dialogue becomes a powerful "image-metaphor" for continuing the discourse on identity in the context of the contemporary culture-communication debates.

Metaphor/The Organizational Frame

Why metaphors of identity? In preparing to write this book, I experienced something similar to what Jeff Greenwald describes in his book, *Shopping for Buddhas*, a funny-serious portrait of a traveler's quest for identity in a strange and exotic land: "No matter what's going on in your life," wrote Greenwald matter-of-factly, "if you walk down the streets in Katmandu you'll run smack into a metaphor for it" (1990: 130).

Greenwald's "shopping for Buddhas" was, of course, the quintessential American metaphor of consumerism, whereas the perennial academic quest for me has been something more abstract, if no less illusive. Everywhere I looked, I discovered metaphors of identity. Even the label "identity" can be seen as the academic metaphor for self-in-context; and the contexts—historical, biological, cultural, and social—are fascinating and intricate in the contemporary culture and communication dialogue. Identity, regarded here as part of the communication process—functioning as metaphor—links the individual to his or her expanding world. Used in this fashion, metaphor is simply a logical way to tie together complicated, abstract data on identification from a culture-communication perspective.

Metaphor, the essence of which is the conceptualization of one thing in terms of another, has always played an extensive role in the dialogues surrounding discussions of identity.[5] In fact, metaphors are ever-present in academic studies. Even the power of research itself has been explained metaphorically, using an analogy of crafts (Johnson & Tuttle 1989: 461). The researcher is likened to a crafts person in that both use imagination (the art) and scientific tools (the science) to create an end product (the craft). Not confined to poetry or esoteric language, metaphors are commonly used in scientific discourse, especially in abstract discussions of identity, culture, and communication. Lakoff and Johnson (1980: 19) argue convincingly: "The intuitive appeal of a scientific theory has to do with how well its metaphors fit one's experience."

One goal of *Metaphors of Identity,* as already stated, is to summarize theoretical approaches to the study of identity, showing how this many-sided construct is related to the culture-communication debates. Another aim is to place these discussions in the context of concrete, ethnographic examples that explore the implications of identity for improving communication in an emerging world culture. Integrating the general summaries (part 1 of the book) and the more specific, ethnographic research (part 2), through the use of metaphor, became an effective way of organizing these debates.

Although not a book about metaphors per se, discussions of identity are linked together in the culture-communication dialogue through metaphorical imagery—whether involving the geographic metaphor of "place," employed extensively in analyses of identity and change throughout the South Pacific, or the various metaphorical representations of the culture construct: culture represented as map, schema, code, script, or text.[6] Visualizations of the communication process itself typically have used, among others, transportation metaphors with mass communication pictured as mediating social relations.

Metaphors of identity in the culture-communication dialogue have evolved from the older, more static images of "person in society," as the mirror of social reality; to the more action-oriented dramaturgical metaphors, suggesting role competence and "on-stage" activity; finally, to more contemporary metaphors that—rightly or wrongly—imply that we humans are in total control of our lives, and hence are potentially constructing, creating, or transforming identities as situations vary. For an excellent example of this approach, one might read Dorinne Kondo's new book, *Crafting Selves*.

The mechanical notion of interactive feedback provides the final metaphorical link in the mutuality between humans and our social and cultural environs. Building metaphors of identity, coupled with the transportation metaphors from the field of communication, afford the reader and the scientist "emotional snapshots" of a complex, multifaceted phenomenon. Certainly *image-metaphors* have played a central role in media presentations and descriptions of media influence on human behavior.

As a brief aside, while researching the literature, it occurred to me that the recent revival of interest in metaphor, the study of this figure of speech being at least two thousand years old, is probably not accidental. The audience for this topic is the generation reared on television, with its thirty-second attention span that, I would argue, is more compatible with image-metaphors as a learning device.

In my generation, people (especially scientists) were skeptical of metaphorical applications in a scientific context, preferring to relegate such emotional snapshots to poetry or art. The present generation (accustomed to making sense of their lives through lyrics, such as Neil Diamond's [1981] "You are the Sun, I am the Moon; You are the Song, I am the Tune, Play Me!") has been literally nurtured on metaphorical images! Television only enhances such visual learning at the expense of more analytic approaches to acquiring knowledge. At least one sociological study has indicated that young television watchers, rather than closely following narrations, tend to pay more attention to distinct, out-of-context images (quoted in Gitlin 1990: 38).

Metaphors, therefore, have been borrowed and used in this text to tie together otherwise disparate and seemingly unrelated parts of a complicated reality. They may be employed also to clarify the parts themselves. On the positive side, metaphors can link multifaceted domains of human experience, providing quick visual images of these realities. Metaphor often enhances a "feeling" for context, thus dealing with interpretive subject matter that is at the very heart of scientific imagination. As a lively "poetry of everyday life," it has been argued that metaphor serves useful, even unavoidable, functions in scientific discourse (Lakoff & Johnson 1980).

Although having the power to "connect, associate and gather together," metaphor undeniably has some potential weaknesses (Harries 1979b: 72). There has been widespread distrust of interpretations of metaphor in scientific discourse. Perhaps rightly so, but it can no longer be claimed that metaphors are absent in science. Correspondingly, contemporary social science has become increasingly interested in subjective thought processes. Culture, in its expressive aspects, Fernandez has claimed (1974: 132), rests upon such metaphoric sign-images.

Consciously or unconsciously, all scientists probably use "guiding metaphors" as fundamental ways of noting similarity and difference. For example, Brown has argued that the image of the world as "organism" is as deeply entrenched in Western thought as the "machine" metaphor which underlies much of our contemporary positivist philosophy (1987: 130). Scientists certainly use guiding metaphors as frameworks for interpreting meaning, but the real issues are how and with what degree of effectiveness. In the broadest sense, all scientific models, or theoretical paradigms, are metaphorical mediating devices "connecting the unconnected and bridging the gaps in causality" (Fernandez 1974: 126).

However, metaphors must be judged as to their aptness, if you will, in given contexts. Although researchers have used metaphor to help conceptualize their ideas, metaphors may limit as well as extend observations. Metaphors are especially difficult in anthropological research (ethnographic comparisons) because they do not easily translate across cultures. A case in point is Harriet Rosenberg's account of the problem of doing cross-cultural research on aging when using "feminized" metaphors to describe her results (1990: 40). Whereas we tend to think of caretakers as women, among the !Kung (Africa) men *and* women frequently cared for the elderly. "Mothering," in this context, was difficult to express in nongendered language, contributing inadvertently to subtle distortions of ethnographic truth. As we shall see in later discussions, misleading emotional imagery in media contexts can even deteriorate into a type of political persuasion (Berger 1990; Solomon 1988).

It is perfectly appropriate, therefore, to discuss identity in terms of metaphor, especially in the context of the culture-communication dialogue. In fact, one of the themes of this book is that the media are constant sources of contemporary images of reality. Metaphor, in this text, is often used synonymously with sign-image, or image-metaphor, since the image concept is especially fruitful for analyzing cultural material involving mediated communication. Identity, it will be argued, helps to establish a sort of metaphoric bridge in comprehending culture and communication.

In short, this book is about no less than the existential question: "Who am I?"—looked at holistically (in terms of the culture-communication dialogue) but also, to some extent, from a personal point of view if the reader can see his or her own life experiences grounded in such fieldwork examples. Hopefully, through this approach, the reader is provided with a solid theoretical, and scholarly, frame for understanding identity. Through concrete, ethnographic descriptions, we shall explore some of the larger implications of identity for improving interpersonal and cross-cultural communication in our emerging world culture.

Social and Cultural Awareness/Instructional Considerations

What are some of the unique features of this book? Basically, the pedagogical concerns of the book fall into three separate categories.

First, using the bridging concept of identity to strengthen our understanding of culture and communication, this volume attempts to be truly multidisciplinary. People talk a lot nowadays about multidisciplinary research—its virtues are endless—but I have not seen much evidence in practice. Such an approach implies a degree of academic risk-taking in its attempts to grasp the whole without always being totally aware of all of its parts.

I am reminded here of Jonathan Glover's apology when writing about personal identity from a multidisciplinary perspective (1988: 11): "I have had the sense of talking about things that others know much more about. . . . [b]ut something is lost if everyone sticks to their own special field and a larger picture is never attempted." This book looks at the larger picture; in fact, it cannot adhere strictly to any special academic turf.[7]

Second, I want to engage the reader in a discovery frame for learning about such abstract ideas as identity, culture, and communication. Each chapter involves the reader in a series of debates that constitute the essence of the culture-communication dialogue. Recall that identity is defined as the academic metaphor for self-in-context; hence, the examination of separate *contexts* acts to highlight major academic debates in this ongoing dialogue. Discussions are largely supported by ethnographic interpretations, an intellectual engagement intended to expand thinking about ourselves in different social and cultural contexts, thus enlarging our sense of diversity. If the goal of creating and sharing information is to reach mutual understanding, this enterprise is at least the beginning of effective communication.

The so-called communication revolution, suggests Dean Barnlund (1989: 139), rather than bringing about a harmonious, McLuhanesque "global village," may have dramatically increased intercultural and intersocietal encounters, hence potentially resulting in more inter-human conflicts. Through telecommunications systems, we are today immediately linked with peoples of vastly differing lifestyles that often sharply contrast with our own. In a real sense, communication has become the major challenge for world harmony. As we move toward this global village, with its increasingly frequent cultural and social contacts, we must learn more about the world views, lifestyles, and communication patterns of our neighbors in order to maintain constructive, rather than conflicting, encounters (Barnlund 1989).

Attribution training is the academic term to describe how people learn judgments and general principles that lie behind observed behavior: In essence, people learn the "how, why, and when of human behavior" through, for example, reading short case studies about socially or culturally different groups (Brislin, et al. 1986: 21–22). Ethnographic evidence offers such attribution training in the present volume. Brislin and associates call this approach the "culture assimilator method" for learning new material about culture (1986: 21–26). They suggest that using such examples can facilitate group discussions, can inform us about individual and group relations, or may simply contribute to individual adjustments to diversity in general. At the very least, the ethnographic approach may help to demonstrate where our previous assumptions have been less than adequate. *Metaphors of Identity* adopts many of these same ideas for "putting ourselves in different cultural shoes," although society, as well as culture, is an important concern of this book.

Focus is on the beliefs that individuals bring with them, often influenced by the media, to evaluate people from other cultural or social contexts. Hence, considered in this volume are the psychological constructs (motivation, knowledge, and ability) that can act on these beliefs and values, ultimately to help or hinder in the development of both social sensitivity and cultural competence. The ultimate goal is to facilitate communication. After all, to communicate may not be just a useful social skill but the very price we pay for evolutionary adaptability (Crowley 1982).

Third, my objective has been to use metaphor as the organizational frame for tying together data on culture, identity, and communication—linking these multifaceted domains of human experience and, at the same time, providing visual images for these same realities. In spite of obvious limitations, metaphor has served some positive functions in scientific discourse. As Fernandez has suggested (1974), we may have overdone analyses of culture using language at the expense of images and impressions. Metaphor, then, allows the reader and the scientist to go beyond mere language in comprehension of this academic abstraction we know as "identity." Image-metaphors, it is further argued, may be especially helpful in analyzing cultural material involving the media.

These objectives are ambitious and challenging. Nonetheless, it has been an exciting prospect pulling together such complex information and sharing a discovery that is, for me, the heart of learning and the proper use of knowledge. In preparing this book, however, I have had to admit that the topic of identity is always multifaceted. It is like trying to make sense of the reflections on a prism, each side offering new and different possibilities. Hopefully, with a judicious use of metaphor to provide some structure to the book, we can unravel some of the mysteries of identity, resolve some conflicting ideas in the culture-communication dialogue, and achieve a unitary whole around this many-sided construct of human identification.

The Book's Format/Parts 1 and 2

Chapter 1 concludes with a brief summary of the book's intended format. *Metaphors of Identity* is divided into two major parts, each section representing a separate theoretical thrust: Part 1 surveys diverse scholarly approaches to the study of identity in the culture-communication dialogue. It proposes that culture is "communicable knowledge" that, through the process of identity, functions to help individuals cope in specific cultural and social contexts. In short, identity functions primarily to help sustain self. Part 2 is more research-oriented. Using my twenty years of inquiry into this subject, I try in this section to elucidate neglected aspects of the identity construct, exploring the social, as well as cultural, implications of theories of identity while linking multiple contexts of identification to concrete ethnographic interpretations.

Identity may be, as Weigert and associates suggest, the essential that transforms biological creatures into human persons (1990: 31). The place of biology in identity formation is examined in chapter 2, "Biology, Culture, and Communication," grounding identity in both culture and biology and offering a functional analysis of the properties of the self-concept which serve to enhance communication— ultimately, human adaptation and survival. Identity is considered in the context of split-brain patients, multiple personality, and other psychological pathologies; and a "doctrine of consistencies" is offered to explain why adaptive fictions often surround the identity construct in the debates over personality unity or diversity. How can we organize our identities successfully in an ever-expanding pluralistic society increasingly influenced by telecommunications and other media?

Questions about where our Western notions of the self originated are the focus of chapter 3, "History, Culture, and the Concept of the Person." Considering both the public and private layers of personhood, this chapter traces the emergence of the modern concept of "individuality," demonstrating how changing forms of self-conception indicate changing cultural configurations. Examples from contemporary research on "naming and identity," a special form of symbolic communication, explore the relationships between identity and communication in cultural context.

The focus of chapter 4, "Culture, Identity, and Communication," is squarely on the interrelatedness of these key constructs, specifically from the point of view of the communication sciences. It critiques major theoretical approaches to the study of identity in the exciting contemporary culture-communication dialogue. Using an adaptive-growth model, the chapter proposes a functional view of identity to explain the relationship between culture and communication. The interpersonal-intergroup distinction, so frequently drawn in the communication sciences, may have oversimplified the complex nature of many communication situations (Gudykunst 1990: 23). Thus, a Japanese example was chosen to highlight the principle of cultural context.

Metaphors, media, and social changes are examined in chapter 5, "Identity of Place or Mis-placed Identity," in an attempt to address complex issues, such as the "new ethnicity" and the social implications of modern-day cultural revivals. The book's theoretical model is demonstrated in light of the author's Fulbright research in New Zealand, which attempted to explain changes in the locus of former "identities of place," at the same time considering major educational challenges of this thesis. The critical question is how can we retain a strong national identity while still recognizing a variety of interest groups, ethnic styles, and the continuing psychological need for separate minority identities in our increasingly pluralistic world.

"Males in Transition" is a much-needed complement to the expanding research on women. Chapter 6, then, looks at the connections between masculine gender, culture, and identity, offering an hypothesis about the cultural construction of an "oppositional identity" that considers gender-learning and its effects on identity and intergroup relations in more informal settings. Media and male imagery are linked through various metaphors of masculinity gleaned from the existing ethnographic literature. Recent research on metaphor analysis is also included, which supports an argument for positive gender-identity transformations. After all, identity is viewed from a performance-growth perspective with individual change at least a potential goal.

Using the "closet" metaphor as symbolic of the inclusion versus exclusion debate, chapter 7, "Homophobia and the Cultural Construction of the Social Stranger," questions the cultural myths that sustain a category of "social stranger" for sexual minorities. People become different when treated differently, not because they are different. To be arbitrarily separated, socially or culturally, from the mainstream may be the real issue. The chapter further explores the psychological and social consequences of an externally imposed identity, examines theoretical issues using the author's Swedish research, and points out some of the limits of media influence on social justice for sexual minorities. What are some creative solutions to the problems of exclusiveness and/or discrimination for sexual minorities?

"Metaphors and Scientific Discourse In Social Gerontology," chapter 8, asks how scholars have viewed aging and the aged metaphorically, as well as some of the social implications of using such theoretical analogies. The major debates in the culture-communication dialogue have been over what aging was like in other times and places and where it might be going in the future. This chapter considers aging and its identity transformations in cultural and social contexts. It reiterates the functional theme of the book, attempts to link individual and society and, through a review of metaphorical imagery in the research literature, offers a bridge to the somewhat more speculative discussions of chapter 9.

The quest for meaningful self-process in an emerging world culture is explored in "Communication: Identity, Community, and Survival." Using the performance model, this chapter examines the concept of a global identity, asking how such a flexible identity structure relates to communication and "cultural competence" as guides for future transformations of self. Technology, after all, is created by human beings and may not be intrinsically opposed to cultural or personal adaptability.

Continuing the dialogue begun in chapter 5, the contemporary debates over multiculturalism in the schools are summarized in chapter 9. Education, by all means, should include attention to cultural difference; but culture may not be the only—even the most important—determinant of human behavior or human communication. Nevertheless, the culture-communication dialogue is far from neutral territory today. The novel idea of community as "romantic metaphor" is critiqued in light of contemporary theories of communication and culture. These debates typically have centered around so-called media effects. However, as Anderson and Meyer (1988: 160) point out, trying to predict "effects" (directly or indirectly) has been a contradictory business. Is mass communication still a useful concept in this dialogue?

Chapter 10, "Limits of Metaphor in the Culture-Communication Dialogue," sketches major theoretical conclusions while, at the same time, summarizing the critical debates of the book. Since metaphor has been used as the organizational frame for this dialogic analysis, some brief discussion of the intent of metaphor in scientific discourse is addressed. How helpful have metaphors been in scientific conceptualizations of identity in the contemporary culture-communication dialogue?

Principal Points

Identity is defined as the academic metaphor for self-in-context, and the contexts are examined chapter by chapter to show its many-sidedness. *Culture* is viewed as "communicable knowledge" that, through processes such as identity, "helps individuals to cope within a particular environment" but, furthermore, must be passed on from generation to generation (Harris & Moran 1989: 107). This approach avoids the contemporary tendency to equate culture with subjective cognition, thereby reducing culture to identification. *Communication* is a dynamic process of human interaction involving symbolic transactions between individuals or groups *and*, in today's world, mediated experiences as well. *Metaphor*, the figurative conceptualization of one thing in terms of another, constitutes a didactic device for organizing the debates in the culture-communication dialogue.

Notes

1. Communication is defined as a dynamic process of human interaction involving symbolic transactions between individuals and groups—in short, the way people relate in social groups and through mediated social experiences. Stressing human interaction, potential relationship development, and exchanges of information, this approach is not essentially different from Rogers and Kincaid's definition of communication as "a convergence of meaning achieved by symbolic interaction" (1981: 31).

2. Culture change is often slow, cumulative, and conservative; hence, cultural identities stress continuity over transformation. Social identities, by contrast, facilitate change and adaptation (Fitzgerald 1974: 3).

3. Altheide 1985; Meyrowitz 1986; Real 1989; Littlejohn 1989; McQuail 1989; Dennis 1989; Berger 1990; and Brody 1990.

4. *Media* refer to explicit communication media, including newspapers, telephone, radio, computer terminals, VCRs, cable and, of course, the ever-present TV. The distinction between print media and electronic media is less frequently made as both increasingly resemble television in terms of media format. Altheide believes that all cultural activities today share a media component (1985: 232).

5. Metaphors fall into the larger category of semiotics, the science of signs. Metaphors are only specific types of images derived through analogy. Hence, Berger claims that various aspects of culture can be analyzed in much the same way one might analyze signs (1990: 144).

6. Figurative language, normal to both human thought and discourse, comes in a variety of forms: imaginative, emotional, and cognitive (Sacks 1979). The present text is primarily concerned with deliberate attempts to use *image-metaphors* in the conceptualization of research ideas. Questions, such as the following, have recently been the subject of intense research in psychology and linguistics: "Is cognition shaped by metaphor or is metaphor an illustration of cognition?" (Cohen 1979: 14); "Is metaphoric skill a linguistic ability or a broader perceptual capacity of human beings?" (Gardner

& Winner 1979: 123); or, "What happens in the brains of metaphorizing individuals (e.g., during strokes)?" (1979: 134). Although fascinating, these inquiries go beyond the intent of the present volume.

7. Kenneth Boulding, commenting on McLuhan's ideas: "It is perhaps typical of very creative minds that they hit very large nails not quite on the head" (quoted in Rogers & Kincaid 1981: 256). Multidisciplinary approaches are inevitably subject to this charge!

I

CULTURE AS COMMUNICABLE KNOWLEDGE: A FUNCTIONAL MODEL OF IDENTITY

A review/synthesis, part 1 attempts to integrate what is now known across disciplines about identity in order to achieve a clearer understanding of who we are and why we are what we are. Not intending to offer definitive answers to the "Who-Are-You?" question, the book opens up an exciting multidisciplinary dialogue, the contemporary culture-communication dialogue, that poses challenging possibilities for improving interpersonal and cross-cultural communication. A performance-growth model illustrates the theoretical relationships between identity and the communication processes. Identity and its functions in sustaining self in changing circumstances is the central focus; hence, identity is defined as the academic metaphor for self-in-context. In trying to clarify our present state of knowledge about one of the most important unifying concepts in the social sciences, part 1 offers new ways of thinking about identity, culture, and society. Theoretical and humanistic, this section should appeal to an educated general-interest audience.

2

○ Biology, Culture, and Communication

...the powers of survival, of the will to survive, and to survive as a unique inalienable individual, are, absolutely, the strongest in our being; stronger than any impulses, stronger than disease.

—Oliver Sacks, *The Man Who Mistook His Wife for a Hat*

What are the Physical Foundations of the Persona, the Self?

The mind, of course, is logically dependent on the body. It is, therefore, quite reasonable to assume some biological basis of identity (Quinton 1975: 61). In trying to establish mental and bodily criteria of identity, one needs to make some distinctions: first, between mind and brain; second, between consciousness and memory; third, between *a* criterion for judging something and *the* criterion. We shall consider these warnings as we get deeper into the discussion.

Many philosophers have insisted that the basic criteria of personal identity are bodily, involving such sensations as reflection, consciousness, and memory.

John Locke defined a person as "a thinking intelligent being, that has reason and reflection, and can consider itself as itself, the same thinking thing, in different times and places" (quoted in Perry 1975: 12).

Mental as well as bodily considerations are involved in questions of personal identity. Of course, identity is more comprehensive than personal identity; but one can start with the individual person, what each of us calls his or her *self*. The most important single feature is surely memory. Personal identity, being the way in which one knows one's own past, uses the mind's reflective capacity to make the individual aware of past experiences basically through the faculty of memory (Perry 1975: 14). "Memory," wrote Oscar Wilde in *The*

Importance of Being Earnest, "is the diary that we all carry about with us" (Redman 1959: 59). Without memory, there would be no experiencing continuity of personality. Some sort of continuous consciousness is fundamental to personhood and may well be essential for human survival. Perception, however, is an interpretive process not entirely determined by memories. Of course, we depend on memory in our attempts to construct personal narratives of who we are, but our memories are altered by both sensory experiences and by our interpretations of them (Spinelli 1989: 102). Consider Marcel Proust's famous interpretations of his olfactory memories.

Is personal identity bodily identity, memory, or consciousness? This has been a perennial question of philosophers.

Oliver Sacks, in his extraordinarily humane book, *The Man Who Mistook his Wife for a Hat,* would almost seem to argue for bodily identity. He recounts touching stories of individuals afflicted with intellectual and perceptual aberrations that clearly demonstrate an interlocking relation between disease and identity. Sacks even talks of a new discipline that could be called the "neurology of identity," which presumably would focus on how the physiological brain processes intersect with and influence human biography (Sacks 1987: viii). According to Dr. Sacks (1987: 110),

> We have, each of us, a life-story, an inner narrative—whose continuity, whose sense, is our lives. It might be said that each of us constructs a life, a 'narrative,' and that this narrative is us, our identities.

Following this line of reasoning, human beings, through awareness of self (identity), utilize these inner narratives to maintain a sense of personal and social continuity. Indeed the need for "wholeness" in life makes each of us a biography, a story to be understood and told. Put another way, self-consciousness is essential to the unity and continuity of the responsible social person (Eccles 1989: 146). Philosophy, psychology, anthropology, and the communication sciences are all, quintessentially, concerned with questions of identity.

Stories of brain disorder, with their often violent and dramatic effects on personality, are convincing evidence for the biological foundations of the persona, the self. Studies of severe injury to the brain show how delicate is the balance between thought and emotion and how such injuries can profoundly change identification (Sacks 1987; Restak 1984; Poppers & Eccles 1977; Eccles 1989).

As mentioned above, one aspect of the brain most essential for the perception of selfhood is memory (Restak 1984: 220). When memory[1] is lost, there is necessarily some loss of personality. To quote Richard Restak: "In a sense, the richness of memory is a reflection of the richness of personality." Loss of memory is perceived as no less than an "assault on identity" (1984: 220). A related phenomenon is when brain dysfunctions translate into mental illness. In *Solitude: A Return to the Self*, Anthony Storr (1988: 97) reports that severely depressed and psychotic patients often complain of feeling "empty" or "void" a figure of speech but one with no little psychological truth. What they lack is the existential sense of their own value as persons.

The brain is no doubt a physical structure both complex and mysterious. Restak (1984: 295) compares each level of explanation in neuroscience to a multi-layered Chinese box, in which one finds increasingly smaller and more complex boxes. The brain has been similarly compared to a machine, more specifically to a computer. Self-obliteration, it is assumed, occurs in much the same way as accidentally losing data from a personal computer when the lights go out! But, there may be limits to these metaphoric attempts to reduce mind to brain, limits to trying to establish a neurophysiological basis of identity. Such metaphorical models can lead to oversimplifications precisely because a human mind cannot be programmed in the same way that a computer can. Human communication is "awesomely complex," as Thomas Scheff (1990: 27) rightfully instructs us, "with lots of hidden contextual meaning."

Mind and brain, Eccles suggests (1989: 373), are nevertheless functionally interconnected. Self-conscious mind (an active agent) is an integrating force, giving human beings unity of conscious experience from all the diversity of the brain's events. It would seem evident that a primary function of perception, in general, is to allow us to impose some order on the chaos of sensations that constantly bombard us. The biological tendency to organize things into meaningful wholes, to unify our experiences, allows us to make sense out of often conflicting sensations (Spinelli 1989: 38). This evolved human capacity represents the fundamental biological basis for identity.

However, this uniqueness of human beings is due only in part to genetic uniqueness. Equally important is the uniqueness of social and cultural experiences. Mind is always more than brain. The mind, in fact, may be even more daunting, involving a universal biological identity base from which complex cultural constructions constitute only its beginning (Kilborne & Langness 1987).

The Genesis of Selfhood

The question of the origin of selfhood is a case in point. Over forty years ago, the psychologist Gardner Murphy grounded identity in a biosocial matrix and provided us with a general theory of perception that gave us a clearer understanding of the origins of self. I both follow and elaborate on this approach.

The overall thesis of *Metaphors of Identity* is that identity is an evolved human capacity for reflective self-awareness that, through meanings and symbols, guides and transforms human action, ultimately mediating between culture and communication. Naturally people in all cultures have physiological responses that are part of human communication. One has only to consider the effect that physical appearances (clothes, bodily hair, handicaps, and skin color) have had on basic human perceptions (Knapp 1972). Interpretations of our own perceptions are socially influenced.

All cultures, anthropologists tell us, recognize the existence of some entity called "the self." Furthermore, self and personhood obviously develop through communication with others. Identity, therefore, is biologically based but ultimately symbolically transformed by culture. Following Sahlins (1979:65), culture[2] is biology plus our symbolic capacity. This self-organizing and self-reflective characteristic of human systems enables human thought to generate more adaptive alternatives by potentially restructuring the communication system as changes are perceived as necessary for survival. Lower animals do not have identity as here defined.[3] Therefore, one may well conceive of identity as an evolved human capacity that potentially contributes to human adaptability. Questions of identity are necessarily related to other important issues, such as communication, culture, and survival.

Not all forms of communication, however, are equally self-reflective, body language being a case in point. Body language would seem to emphasize the fundamental biological (evolutionary) genesis of identity. For example, most facial expressions on the whole can be universally recognized regardless of culture. Although there are cultural differences in attitudes toward such basic emotions, the dimensions of these gestures appear to be more or less similar across cultures. Certain emotions (fear, anger, surprise, disgust, happiness, and sadness, for example[4]) may well form a "common language of facial expression." In 1971 Ekman and Friesen showed New Guinea tribesmen photos of Caucasians while reading to them stories with a specific emotional content; the natives could indeed pick out the emotion (quoted in Spinelli 1989: 63). Theirs is the only study to examine cultural differences in the interpretation of universal expressions of emotion in a preliterate, non-Western culture (Matsumoto, et al. 1989: 229). It would appear, then, that respondents in all cultures can correctly interpret certain facial expressions, often voice tone as well, more accurately than would be expected by chance (Gudykunst & Ting-Toomey 1988: 171).

Do such studies support the notion that there are universal, culture-free facial expressions of emotion? The conclusion seems to be that, while certain limited emotions may be innate and universal, the rules of emotional display are, nonetheless, culture-specific (1988: 174). "Members of different cultures show the same facial expressions when experiencing the same emotions unless culture-specific display rules interfere" (1988: 172). To illustrate this point, one can cite the example of the Japanese, who are socialized to avoid the expression of emotions like anger; hence, identifying anger is "low" for this cultural group. It has been observed that, more than Americans, the Japanese tend to mask negative emotions with smiles (Matsumoto, et al. 1989: 227).

If facial expressions represent universally recognized basic emotions that are similar across cultures, what about psycho-pathologies? Studies of schizophrenia—a mental affliction confined to human beings—would seem to argue convincingly for the hereditary as against environmental influences for this "thought" disorder. As Restak points out (1984: 282), genetic factors *alone*, however, cannot explain the etiology, development, and course of the disease. The outbreak of any illness is almost always dependent on environmental factors. Even an inherited predisposition to schizophrenia can be modified by introducing environmental changes, such as adding or reducing stress. There is, then, significant interplay between biology and social experiences. Bandura's "reciprocal determinism" between environment and behavior would seem applicable here. According to Spinelli (1989: 147), one can become sick spiritually, emotionally, intellectually, or physically. Another related consideration in this same argument is that rates of mental disease vary enormously from culture to culture.

Understanding the chemical structure of the brain (Restak says schizophrenia appears to be "the behavioral manifestation of an excess of dopaminergic transmission in the brain" [1984: 285]) does not, of course, explain the human experience of mental illness. A more balanced view does not dismiss the biochemical (genetic) factors. One simply need not regard them as sole or direct causes of such disturbances (Spinelli 1989). Although disease is part of our biological heritage, it wears many cultural disguises.

An interesting example of the primacy of culture over biology is found in Dr. Dobkin de Rios's paper "Cultural Persona in Drug-Induced Altered States of Consciousness" (1977). This study clearly demonstrates how, in traditional drug-using societies, even the deepest levels of the unconscious mind cannot be separated from culture. Peruvian Amazonians under the influence of ceremonial drugs tend to experience what their culture has told them they should expect to experience. In other words, what a person thinks about and how s/he feels about life are strongly conditioned by the culture. Hallucinogenic drugs may "bend the mind, but the new shape is still culturally patterned" (Williams 1974: 119).

The Nature/Nurture Argument Revisited

What shapes human experience—genes or culture? Can identity be reduced to an evolved human genome? With much clarity, Sandra Scarr summarizes this argument in "How Genotypes and Environments Combine" (1988: 225). She warns us that it is not a question of genetic determinism versus naive environmentalism.

This dichotomy of nature and nurture, she argues, is a bad one for two reasons: 1) Both genotype and environment are required for development, and 2) False parallels arise when the two constructs are so juxtaposed (1988: 225). What people attend to, as well as what they ignore, are events correlated with individual differences in interests and personality. Hence, people will seek out environments they find compatible and stimulating. The environment, then, becomes equally important in the behavioral equation. Genes and environment are both significant players in the total development of the person, although sometimes with differing roles to play (1988: 235).

Scarr would seem to be suggesting that, while virtually no experiences are uncorrelated with one's genotype, both genes and environments combine to produce development and individuality (1988: 240). Both are *a* criterion to be reckoned with in our understanding of identification. Neither alone, however, is *the* sole causal criterion that explains the identity process. There is still a wide gap between neurobiology and psychology in spite of contemporary attempts to reduce psychological knowledge to that of biology. Human biology is an important key to understanding much about behavior, but there is no reason to think that biology—any more than culture—can explain everything. Psychological understanding of the multi-dimensional construct of identity remains far from adequate.

In *Evolution of the Brain: Creation of the Self*, Eccles attempts to clarify the relationship of the human self to its brain (1989: 219). It is the brain, he argues, that provides the material basis of our eventual evolving personhood, although large parts of the brain may not be essential to this process. The human embryo, he concludes, is naturally a human being but not yet a human "person." Personhood is dependent on the development of self-consciousness in a social context. A person is largely the result of the interaction of self and other(s).

Self-knowledge, then, is fundamentally social in origin. To put it differently, we develop self-consciousness in large part through our communication with other persons. Hegel (quoted in Yaple & Korzenny 1989: 304) recognized this essential relationship of self, mind, and communication in his claim that, in order for there to be a subject, there must be an object:

> . . . in a process of dialogue the human animal must interact with other human animals. Such a process produces society and in this production can be found the origin of self, mind, and communication.

Although "pure" self may be hard to substantiate, the self that develops is the result partly of inborn dispositions, partly of social experiences. There is growing evidence of the effects of culture on the brain itself. Culture, like identity, is an evolved human characteristic that potentially contributes to our survival as a species. Language, as a case in point, may contribute to a reshaping of the very wiring of the brain. Once human beings evolved language and symbolism, communication became possible at a level of complexity far exceeding nonhuman communication systems (Asimov 1963: 330). Ultimately, then, the genetic blueprint of the brain may be affected by our social and cultural surroundings (Popper & Eccles 1977). This line of research, though tentative, is fascinating.

Eccles (1989: 221–22) gives a concrete example of this reciprocal interaction in the case study of Genie, a child isolated from age twenty months to thirteen years. The result for the child's brain was severe damage to the left hemisphere, with corresponding linguistic deprivation. Even though the right hemisphere of the brain to some extent stood in for the much-depleted language performance, Genie was for all practical purposes deprived of person status. The brain,

Eccles explains, is built by genetic instructions (nature), but the development of human personhood is dependent on an enriched social and cultural environment (nurture). With Genie, he reasoned, there was a gap of thirteen years between nature and the onset of nurture.

In an earlier work, Popper and Eccles considered the problem of identity from a biological point of view and concluded that identity and the integrity of self obviously have a physical basis (1977: 115). Following Strawson, they suggested that it is probably a mistake to try to distinguish between body and mind in any strict way. Although both are crucial for personal identity, brain and mind still cannot be equated. Using a computer analogy, one contemporary way of distinguishing mind and brain has been, metaphorically, to consider the latter as "hardware," the former as "software" (Aldridge-Morris 1989).

Thus, Popper and Eccles make the novel claim that the brain is "owned by the self." Adopting Plato's famous metaphor of the mind as pilot of the body, they construct an analogy of the active, psycho-physical self as a "computer programmer." In their book, *The Self and Its Brain*, the brain is seen as the computer (structure) and the mind as the programmer (organizer). Like a "pilot," identity functions both as observer and actor at the same time, homo sapiens having evolved this unique psycho-physical capacity for self-reflection (1977: 120-1). Although there are obvious limits to this human-machine analogy, the metaphorical distinction between "hardware" (brain) and "software" (mind) is especially useful for our discussion of identity in its biological context.

Genes, in actual fact, offer the human animal capabilities, or potentialities, rather than full-blown adult behavior traits.[5] Futhermore, there is not always a clear relation between physical body and the self. In any case, identification of self is not so much a reflection of what truly is there but what we *believe* is there (Spinelli 1989: 87). Something must mediate between the brain structures and the more complicated learning processes (thinking, feeling, memory, for example) before we can speak of an "introspectively aware self" (Eccles 1989: 227). This reflective self-awareness might be called the individual's identity, following this book's more integrative definition of identity as the academic metaphor for self-in-context. In this chapter, biology is of course the context being considered.

While acknowledging the biological basis of personality, hence conceptions of self, we are in danger of sometimes neglecting environmental factors—namely the individuality of each person and each unique situation (Bem 1988: 207). Taking an interactional approach to personality, David Bem sees behavior as a function of both the person and the situation. The organism and the environment are considered together, and the situation becomes a function of the person in this theoretical equation.

Following the Thomases' (1928) well-known dictum, "If persons define situations as real, they are real in their consequences," Bem has argued that persons interact with situations in a reciprocal transaction (1988: 209). Persons perceive the same situations differently, hence are differentially influenced by the same situation. The person acts, the environment reacts, and the person in turn reacts back (1988: 210). This model views the person as an "interacting, intrapsychic ensemble" that changes and develops in interaction with particular kinds of environments (1988: 214). Such an interactional approach to personality can be especially fruitful in conceptualizing the socio-genesis of self-construals and in arriving at a better understanding of the functions of self-conceptions.

In discussing the functions of identity, Robert and Beverly Cairns make this salient point (1988: 184): Ideas of self do not have to be true in order to be functional. Although it is assumed that well-adjusted persons should have a coherent sense of themselves and others, one's view of self may serve different functions from those served by one's view of others. This observation aids in better appreciating problems of communication breakdown that occur between individuals and among groups.

These authors list four "adaptive services" of identity for the individual or society: 1) the promotion of personal integration and well-being, 2) the enhancement of communication with other people, 3) future goal-planning, and 4) the facilitation and adaptation to the physical world. Obviously some of these services (functions) overlap each other. Such a functional analysis of the properties of self demonstrates how the organism's survival, in an evolutionary sense, depends upon accurate recognition of persons and things, especially as some of these might otherwise produce threat or injury to human beings (1988: 185).

Their conclusion is that there is not always a high level of accuracy between self-conceptions and social consensus. In fact, a certain amount of slippage between values, action, and social agreement may not always be a bad thing. The idea of the self as unitary, stable, and fixed over time is, in all probability, an illusion, albeit one that may be functional. Hence, identities can be thought of as "positive illusions," to borrow the title of a recent psychological treatise on identity in modern times (Taylor 1989).

Personhood implies integration, or unity of mind, even though there may well be multiple capacities of the brain (Glover 1988). Although it is probably a mistake to think of identity as a kind of unchanging entity, persistent throughout life, it is the *illusion of unity* that is still quite real with most people. Katherine Ewing (1990: 263) believes that we can explain this apparent contradiction, what she calls "the illusion of wholeness," without reifying a unitary self, an idea which is increasingly being seen as empirically unverifiable. "The experience of a cohesive self must not be dismissed or ignored simply because it is illusory," she explains. It is precisely the illusion of wholeness that is functional rather than the reality of wholeness.

Such seeming contradictions may have positive adaptive value since an individual can always select the appropriate support for behavior—regardless of which way circumstances go (Smith 1974: 82). Plans for the future, although sometimes "convenient myths," or "adaptive fictions," presuppose conceptions of one's self and one's world (Cairn and Cairn 1988: 186). The conclusion is that self-evaluations, public or private, are primarily constructive and adaptive, not simply mirroring objective reality or reflecting social consensus (1988: 191). Although identity may not be an empirically verifiable concept, people nevertheless manage to experience self as a unitary whole. From an evolutionary perspective, one might argue that this cluster of selves is adaptive precisely because it yields a more flexible personality structure.

In short, the self-concept need not be true to be serviceable. Adaptation is not synonymous with accuracy. The "looking glass self," in fact, may not always be functional (1988: 199). Quoting Spicer, Gilbert Kushner (1974: 129) has suggested that identity symbols often function as important sources of prophecy as well as motivation, in effect often becoming "self-fulfilling prophetic images" of great personal power.

An interesting sideline to this thesis is found in Dorothy Spruill Redford's *Somerset Homecoming: Recovering a Lost Heritage* (1988: 188). In explaining why a Negro relative persisted in believing she was a descendant of a freed slavewoman, who in actuality never had any children, she muses: "People believe what they want to—or, when comes to their sense of self, what they have to." The process of self-understanding is, in large part, the continual development of "new life stories" for oneself (Lakoff & Johnson 1980: 233). We shall return to this notion of the fictitious role of identity in later discussions. The illusion of wholeness is crucial to a full understanding of the complexity of identity, especially when trying to explain the fulfillment of compensatory and self-balancing functions. Image-metaphors, too, have helped to illuminate different aspects of the identity spectrum.

Identity and Unity/The "Doctrine of Consistency"

Metaphors are pervasive in language and thought, even in scientific works, and play a central role in describing everyday realities. Metaphors allow us to conceptualize one thing by means of its relation to something else. Basically, we look to metaphors that parallel our own experiences. Rarely, however, do metaphors fit reality in any exact way. They almost always highlight certain features while suppressing others (Lakoff & Johnson 1980). All metaphors, of course, are rooted in particular cultural experiences, hence can play an extensive role in limiting, or facilitating, interpersonal and cross-cultural communication.

There are several metaphors that come to mind in trying to conceptualize the abstract and illusory concept of identity. None are totally without compromise in accuracy. The one that appeals to me, especially when thinking of the functions of identity, is the image of the "juggler" who, in trying to balance the unsteady forces of life, creates an illusion of sorts. Identity seems to me, at least in part, to represent a balance of illusory forces in the individual's existence. This fact in no way diminishes its functional power or its ultimate meaning to persons or groups.

Several psychologists have suggested that the essence of self may be largely unknowable, a kind of personal myth (Kohut 1971; Rosenberg 1979). But, regardless of whether ultimately "real" or not, identity—a unifying element in personality structure—strives toward wholeness and a degree of psychological stability. This capacity has undoubtedly been an evolutionary advantage for human beings, especially in times of stressful change. At the level of brain, the notion of unity may be only a matter of degree. At the social level, such unity—illusory or not—seems essential to human adaptation and to our ultimate survival as a species (Glover 1988).

To return to our argument above, the empirical reduction of mind to brain, through an identity linkage, has serious drawbacks and inevitably leads to some stance of biological determinism. Identity, the tendency to perceive the self as continuous despite life's changes, may help to create the illusion of psychological continuity. It is hard for human beings even to imagine a truly divided mind (split personality). We seem instead to need a sense in which the two can survive as one person. What gives identity its importance, whether real or fictitious, may be this illusion of psychological wholeness. Parfit put it nicely (1975: 207): "[W]e use the language of identity in order to imply such continuity." Murphy reminded us years ago (1947): The self is potentially both homogeneous and stable, heterogeneous and unstable—all at the same time.

The ego (in Murphy's scheme a system of enhancement and defense of self) is, in reality, a "grammatical illusion." There is no *one* self, only a cluster of *many selves*, both culturally and situationally specific. Likewise, identity is temporally appropriate, even though the individual is persuaded, or has a need, to act as if phenomena were a unitary whole. Far from being unitary, it is recognized today that there is more likely to be a series of selves, each of which interacts with its environments according to specific social and cultural circumstances (Spinelli 1989).[6] The "doctrine of consistency" is often incomplete precisely because integration of personality is rarely fully achievable with human beings. Human personality is simply too many-sided and complex.

What about past and future selves? The self is incredibly rich, anchored in time by its disposition both to recall its past and to plan its future. This temporal dimension seems to be inherent in human existence and is a good example of the evolutionary significance of such evolved potentialities. Consider, for example, the unique ability in human speech for language "displacement." Unlike a gibbon, we can talk about things distant in both time and space, an achievement which allows greater linguistic flexibility, yielding better communication potential (Hockett 1960). We live in what Eccles (1989: 229) calls "a time paradigm of past-present-future," the temporal organization that Kant reportedly labeled our "numerical identity." Referring to this diachronic aspect of self, numerical identity asks the question whether, across time, people can still recognize themselves as being the same despite the inevitability of personal changes (Abound and Ruble 1987: 109). It is even fashionable in current literature on personality (with its life-cycle emphases) to make a distinction between "successive selves" (Parfit 1975: 218).

Recent scientific and medical work on multiple personalities further challenges our notions of a continuous identity. The question is do such individuals have two minds or a mind that occasionally splits in two? Nagel has argued that, although the ordinary conception of a single, countable mind cannot be properly applied to such people, the idea of the unity of the person may be one way out of this dialectical dilemma (1975: 237). Persons will still arrive at a unified idea of what is going on around them, some sort of functional integration, in spite of experimentally induced right/left inconsistencies in the brain. The end result is compelling behavioral integration (harmony) at some level or to some degree. Cases of multiple personalities, at the very least, suggest that deeply ingrained Western assumptions concerning the self can confuse rather than clarify our attempts to understand the nature of identity.[7]

Sperry and associates (1979) have studied splitbrain patients and developed testing procedures for this population. Their work, summarized by Eccles (1989: 207–10), demonstrates that each connected hemisphere can behave as if it were not conscious of cognitive events in the other hemisphere. In other words, each side of the brain appears to have its own largely separate cognitive domain with its own private perceptual, learning, and memory experiences. The most remarkable discovery of their experiments is that such patients are still recognizably the same persons as before the operation. Whichever hemisphere is left, there remains a "person." Their conclusion of an approximate equality of the two brain hemispheres in identification, if optimistic, is at least evidence in favor of limited self-consciousness in the right hemisphere of the brain (1989: 210). As Glover (1988) has suggested, coherence is something central to our everyday understanding of people.

Nagel goes even further into futurism with the suggestion of the possibility of brain transplants (1975: 243). With this development, he thinks that it is likely in future that the ordinary, simple idea of a single person will come to seem quite quaint. At the same time, it is also likely that we shall not abandon the idea of one "unitary self" no matter what we discover to be "real." There seems to be a need for wholeness, unity, and configuration that, regardless of whether identity is an illusion or not, will persist (1975: 243).

Identity, then, presupposes an uninterrupted continuance of existence although this fact certainly does not preclude personality change over time. The self can be dissolved through the neurological conditions mentioned earlier, through aging, and of course in the process of deteriorating health. Max Lerner wrote poignantly of the effects of cancer on his own sense of self (1991: 69–74). Illness became a direct threat to the continuity of selfhood as his autonomy and "will to live" were severely challenged by this wasting disease.

We differ from the "lower" animals, argues Eccles (1989: 234), precisely because we have the capacity for unifying our experiences. In addition to successive selves (identity transformations over time), human beings maintain a "core self" that allows our intentions to take on a socially responsible (moral) quality that is not the case with nonhumans. The nature of personhood is ultimately the capacity to take responsibility for our actions in regard to our fellow human beings. Eccles (1989: 236) claims that this valid and central dimension of the human experience, this "miracle forever beyond science," has been largely neglected by philosophers.

A person, according to Reid (1975: 109), is something "perfect" and "whole," not divisible into parts—what Leibnitz called a "monad." Whatever else may threaten change, that self, or I, maintains an illusion of permanence. Our picture of the body itself involves similar illusions. The boundaries of the self-concept, although biologically grounded, are not always defined by bodily limitations. Oliver Sack's (1987) eloquent description of the neurologically impaired reminded us that we may reject parts of our bodies as not belonging to us (with the loss of bodily awareness) or we may persist in claiming parts of the body that in fact no longer exist (where the brain tries to preserve the impression of some missing bodily part). Biology remains an important context for understanding the dimensions of identity in the culture-communication dialogue.

Although the boundaries of self are often indeterminate and fragile, the juggler—powerful image-metaphor for identity—seeks a consistent anchorage of self whether ultimately real or not. Identity's twofold reality lies in its being natural and functionally grounded in both biology and culture. These two factors, of course, have profound implications for human communication (Knapp 1972).

The first reality suggests that one of the primary functions of identity is the enhancement of communication with other people. Communication, although not always something consciously chosen, is nevertheless an inevitable part of the human condition. As Cronen and associates have pointed out, it is natural for human beings to try, however imperfectly, to communicate with one another (1988: 72). Culture, too, is intimately tied to communication. For culture to survive, however, it must be passed down from generation to generation. Although culture and communication are not the same processes, communication is almost always a central component of culture. However, Berger may go too far with his argument that ultimately theories of culture are theories of communication (1990: 139).

Identity and communication, nonetheless, are mutually and causally related. With the advent of mediated communication influences in most parts of the world today, there is now an ongoing relationship between self, public presentations of self, and mass media that must be recognized and analyzed. The communication sciences have made the major contributions to this line of research. However natural, human communication still involves normative dimensions that render the process inherently problematical. Like culture itself, it is difficult to study identity as a scientific subject precisely because of its special ineffable qualities. Culture and identity are subjects about which we humans hold strong value judgments and have innumerable vested interests. Likewise, there is always the possibility that metaphors of identity, which are so prominent in the culture-communication dialogue, may themselves contribute to over-simplifications in scientific discourse.

The second reality involving identity centers around the fact that behavior is always a function of the person's view of self in relation to his or her physical, cultural, and social environments. Personal identity, then, needs to be firmly placed into these multiple contexts. Chapter 3 marshals data from other cultures to show how the images of self (personhood) vary dramatically from one cultural milieu to another.

Principal Points

A major debate in psychology and anthropology—not yet of much concern to the communication sciences—is still James's "One-in-Many Selves" paradox (Knowles & Sibicky 1990), resolved by the illusion of wholeness conception of selfhood: how we rectify the seeming contradiction that, even though we are many different people in different situations and at different times of our lives, we can still maintain—multiple personalities notwithstanding—a sense of self-continuity. The paradox is explained as a "functional illusion." Common metaphorical distinctions have been drawn between the "hardware" (brain) and the "software" (mind) to suggest that the contemporary social sciences are too preoccupied with the former rather than the latter.

Notes

1. Consciousness and memory are different. Consciousness, according to Reid (1975: 115), is immediate knowledge of the present, whereas memory is immediate knowledge of the past.

2. Although Sahlins's approach is perfectly respectable, throughout this book I use the Harris and Moran definition (1989: 107): "Culture is communicable knowledge for human coping within a particular environment that is passed on for the benefit of subsequent generations." Our species develops culture as a means of adaptation to physical and biological surroundings.

3. McGuire and McGuire made the following novel observation (1987: 141): They found that more children defined themselves in relation to their pets than to their mothers, even though all had mothers and only some had pets.

4. Matsumoto and associates suggest that "contempt" may be a possible seventh universal facial expression (1989: 228). They argue that cultures can agree on the most salient expressions but differ in their intensity ratings of the same.

5. Price (1987: 40) reports that the newborn infant can recognize its own self and will cease crying when it hears a tape of its own cry, although not always when it hears another infant's cry. The potential for a cohesive self is biologically inborn in the healthy infant, self-recognition usually emerging in Western cultures some time in the second year (Pines 1987: 20). Most agree that a responsive environment helps to produce a healthy, evolving self (Harwood 1987: 67).

6. My colleague Dr. John Altrocchi (personal communication, May 15, 1991) informs me that he and his associates at the University of Nevada School of Medicine call this phenomenon "self-pluralism." Although I am not implying that they fall into this trap, I am reminded of the warning by Aldridge-Morris (1989) that overly romanticized notions of identity pluralism can encourage the spiraling of diagnoses of "multiple personality." Do we create multiple personalities or adjust to the reality that we have plural potentialities? From an evolutionary perspective, multiple personality may be an adaptive ability "gone amuck."

7. The brain may well have multiple capacities, but we are persons through having the kind of unity that enables us to transcend divided selves (Glover 1988: 53). Aldridge-Morris (1989) says that British therapy stresses getting the MP client to accept two or more *aspects* of *one* personality, thus helping the patient take responsibility for the complexity of personality rather than encouraging multiple selves as a way of daily coping. Kenny (1986: 3), in fact, viewed multiple personality as largely a "culturally specific metaphor" rather than a universally distributed mental disorder.

3

○ History, Culture, and the
Concept of the Person

... *who* I am is answered both for me and for others by the history I
inherit, the social position I occupy, and the "moral career" on which
I am embarked.

—Steven Lukes in *The Category of the Person*

Self and Society/Homo Duplex

Looking at identity from the perspective of history suggests that pure
self is an illusion. The duality that is the dilemma of human existence
always yields some split in identity, the Durkheimian "homo duplex":
on the one hand, the individual rooted in biology; on the other, society
influencing self and role (Lukes 1987: 286). This duality is at the heart
of our inner life and represents an inescapable tension between the
demands of social life and those of our individual, organic natures.
How else are we to understand the relation of the individual to society
except through our understanding of identity? The body, then, is a
necessary condition of personhood, but one which must be completed
by psychological identity (Collins 1987: 73). If the self is an individual's
awareness of a unique identity, the person, according to La Fontaine,
is society's confirmation of that identity, giving it the stamp of social
and cultural legitimacy (1987: 124).

Person is an abstract notion invariably derived through analysis
at several contrasting levels, for example, the familiar distinction
between *personal* and *social* identity. Lienhardt resorted to West
African folklore, with its tortoise metaphor, to symbolically clarify
this dichotomy (1987: 143). The tortoise—sometimes public and
exposed, sometimes withdrawn and hidden—is an illuminating image
of the "person in relations" (social identity) versus the "discrete and

private person" (personal identity). The tortoise metaphor reinforces this duality of imagery between public self and private self so variously represented in cultures around the world—a fitting image-metaphor for the complexities of selfhood.

The social confirmation of identity may be a necessary part of personhood, but no particular social identity is essential. Each culture has its own concept of "the person," determined by the individual's perceived place in the society; and defining personhood is surely not an easy task for individuals or cultural and social groups. The way people perceive and understand the world is, in large part, predicated upon self-knowledge. The wide range of psychological responses, it has been written, reflects different "construals" of self and personhood that are found throughout history.[1]

Historical Perspectives

Person, then, is not as natural, innate, or unchanging as our familiarity with Western culture would suggest. Human thought is a product of history and is culturally specific. Other times and other people did not always share the Western concept of personhood. These are the essential lessons from history, anthropology, and ethnopsychology. We have seen, in chapter 2, how the traditional picture of the unified mind has been challenged by empirical evidence. Similarly, the answer to the straightforward question "Does the concept of 'the person' vary from culture to culture?" is an obvious yes (Shweder & Bourne 1984). In non-Western societies, however, the culturally formulated concept of the person develops according to vastly different principles.

American culture is often said to revolve around the ideal of the autonomous self, as individualism (personal autonomy) has long been a primary focus of American and, to a large extent, Western culture (Nash 1989). Hence, most Americans have difficulty with the idea that the individual is a "social construct," that there may be many selves (as in multiple personalities), or that other groups (Buddhists and Hindus, for example) promote a "nonself" as a spiritual goal (Bock 1988: 203). To further confuse the issue, the words *self, person,* and *soul* are historically similar but not synonymous.[2] How we obtain self-knowledge, then, varies enormously from culture to culture.

Hindu conceptions of self provide an interesting and illuminating example. For Americans, the fulfillment of self is of paramount value. We actively cultivate our individuality. Hindu society is quite different. The Hindu ideal is to transcend individual selfhood and return to some state of "selflessness" (Kotarba & Fontana 1987: 73). In a typical Indian village, as a case in point, identity is ascribed by genealogy and firmly embedded in the caste system (Dumont 1980; 1986). The notion of a "constructed self," i.e., one based on free will (choice), would indeed seem an oddity in this culture.

Dumont feels that, worldwide, modern individualism may be, in actuality, an exceptional phenomenon (1986). The Western image of the clearly bounded self, our "individualistic configuration," in fact, is not found in many societies. Analysis of the Indian material suggests freeing oneself from such individualistic ideals is a way of grasping what Dumont calls "sets or wholes," i.e., societal integration (1986: 9). "Indian society," Dumont (1986: 25) emphasized, "has been characterized by two complementary features: society imposes upon any person a tight interdependence which substitutes constraining relationships for the individual as we know him; on the other hand, there is the institution of world-renunciation which allows for the full independence of the man who chooses it." The individual, argues Dumont (1986: 61), is equivalent to "order" in traditional Indian society or the *dharma* in classical Hindu terms.

Gandhi's thoughts on the self may highlight the contrasts between the two cultural systems. Gandhi pointed out the failure of liberal thought to reconcile *individuality* and *sociality* (Roy 1985: 98). Ideally, there should be no conflict between the personal and the social aspects of individuality. In the Indian conception of self, individuality has no meaning if there are no other individuals. Gandhi, in this particular case, would argue that, without the recognition of personality by others, one cannot arrive at an authentic definition of one's own identity. Sociality and individuality in this conceptualization are supportive rather than antagonistic.

Gandhi conceived of the relation between the individual and society as analogous to drops in the ocean. The drops, even while expressing individuality, cannot survive without the ocean; and the ocean will lose its identity without the drops. Awareness of the existence of others is simply assumed in the Indian way of thinking. The "authentic person," for Gandhi, must be true to both self *and* society (1985: 106). The predicament of modern humans, he argued, is in making personal individuality the beginning and end of the quest for self-knowledge.

Although ideally India epitomizes a communal society marked by group conformity, room is still made for "cultural deviants," those who cannot accept the dominant values of a culture, to use Ruth Benedict's terminology. It is the "renouncer," the religious holy man, who—detached from the world—becomes, in an ironic way, the real individual in Indian society. Seen from this perspective, the renouncer—symbol of austerity and the ascetic ideal—substitutes a cosmic religious identity (the Ultimate Truth) for the more usual social identity shared by the majority in Hindu society.

Where did our Western notions of the self come from? Marcel Mauss has traced the concept of person (*personne*) as it emerged from the Latin *persona*, a "mask" (social role), dating back to the beginnings of Latin civilization (Hollis 1987: 217–19). Gradually, the "person" acquired individuality that existed apart from the mask, or role. Our Western notion of the human person is, basically the Christian one with its attribution of moral character, independence, free will, and responsibility.[3] Finally, the person was attributed with consciousness, thereby establishing the locus of rationality and individual unity in the concept of the self (Fajans 1985: 370). In short, our contemporary notion of selfhood stems almost entirely from Western tradition: from Classical Greece, Judeo-Christian monotheism, from the Renaissance and the Reformation, as well as from the philosophical schools that grew out of these traditions (Lifton 1970). The categories "person" and "individual" are, of course, not exactly the same; but, over time, the latter evolved out of the former, culminating in the modern (Western) concept of the self with its strongly individualistic overtones. Incidently, Slugoski and Ginsburg suggest a date of 1638 for the word *identity* used to refer to "personality and individuality"; the noun *self*, however, is dated (Oxford English Dictionary) even earlier, at about 1595 (1989: 47).

What is increasingly evident is that our modern forms of self are the result of a complex historical heritage. Examining autobiographies, letters, and diaries from Augustine to Goethe, Karl Joachim Weintraub has traced the gradual emergence of the modern Western notion of individuality (1982). This specifically modern form of self-conception (autobiography) came into prominence in the eighteenth century as a byproduct of specific historic occurrences.[4] Individuality is best understood as an historically evolving phenomenon.

People in Classical antiquity, whose lives derived meaning primarily from public affairs and a clannish, kin-based community, were little inclined to assign positive value to an "ineffable self." During the millennium from 800 B.C. until A.D. 200, Weintraub (1982: 137) argued that autobiography was not the basic quest of self and, in fact, tended to reveal little about the inner life of its subjects.

Rather, the Church, Weintraub (1982: 71) believes, was the great culture-creating and unifying force in the Middle Ages. Although cultural forms gave meaning to self (personhood) at this time, self-aware individuality as we think of it was not to be found. The contents of self-consciousness equated more nearly to the consciousness of the society. The notion of an "autonomous, self-defining personality" would have been almost an embarrassment. In the Middle Ages, identity was not personal but communal (Montagu & Matson 1983).

Changing forms of self-conception are useful indicators of changing cultural configurations. The lack of individuality was as much a mark of medieval culture as the emergence of conscious individuality became the ideal for the eighteenth-century Western world. Each age, argued Weintraub (1982: 92), carried the standards for its own happiness. Although the Renaissance was a vital step in the movement toward the conscious cultivation of self, Weintraub (1982: 228) claimed—as have other scholars—that Christianity had a lasting effect on the formation of the Western personality and contributed most to the growth of individualism as we know it today. Generalized individuality seems rooted in the earliest Christian experience.[5]

In such a thumbnail sketch, it is impossible to trace all the subtle permutations of this still-evolving construct. Suffice it to say that conscious individuality, as well as the discovery of the intrinsic worth of diversity underlying it, has led to evil as well as good in the moral struggle over how the individual can value both the self and the world of which it is a part (1982: 333). Like the debates over nature (biology) and nurture (culture) in chapter 2, there is a similar dialectical relation between individual and society in this historical summary.

Weintraub felt that, by the time of Goethe, the self and the world were no longer set against each other. The nineteenth century was dominated by conflicts between individual and society. The individual was now in the world, and individual values ruled without restraint. Autobiography and the personality conception of individuality flourished in the early decades of the nineteenth century. A self was a self, by this time, only in its fruitful interplay with its world, Weintraub argued: "Goethe found strength to live with the world as it was, and with himself as he was." (1982: 371). Goethe's harmonious orchestration of the self is, for Weintraub, a counterbalance to the cult of personality of the nineteenth-century romantic poets, as well as a warning against the excessive self-indulgence more characteristic of modern times.

The question whether we ourselves, or the world we live in, contribute more to what we are is, for Weintraub (1982: 376), a silly one. Goethe certainly would never have thought of separating the two. Wisdom lies not in perpetual self-searching, excessive preoccupations with self, but with active involvement in the world. This is essentially the moral message of *The Value of the Individual: Self and Circumstance in Autobiography.*

The modern, Western meaning of self is, in short, that of conscious individuation: subject as self-defining and self-sufficient. One could argue that Americans have simply carried the notion of individualism to one extreme on a continuum, yet it is unwise to assume that there is no individual identity in social contexts where our theories and methods have assumed none. All individuals and groups must deal with both *public* and *private* displays of self. Cultures simply vary in the amount of emphasis given these expressions.

Alan Roland's *In Search of Self in India and Japan* nicely illustrates this principle (1989: 6). Roland feels that we have to speak of at least three overarching organizations of the self: the individualized self, the familial self, and the spiritual self. Americans are most familiar with the "individualized self" common to Western civilization. Through increasing familiarity with other peoples of the world, we are becoming more aware of the "familial self" ("we-self") of communal groups (e.g., Japan and India); but we in the West are less familiar with the "spiritual self." In fact, we seem to lack adequate terminology to describe the "ineffable inner experiences" of human beings. Roland (1989: 291) further argues that myths and metaphors, parables and other imagery, have inevitably been used by those who have realized a spiritual self to convey some sense of their experiences.

What may be most unique about the current Western version of self (and the journey is not over) is that we can more or less construct our own social identities, "paint" our own "social portraits," in ways unknown to peoples of the past or other cultures (Hollis 1987: 230). In many parts of the world today, life seems to be forever in process of transformation. One need only consider the contemporary building metaphors of self-construction and self-transformation, so commonly employed in contemporary discourses on identity. Indeed the very notion of reconstructing self may be a uniquely modern way of viewing identity. Some concept of the self is doubtlessly found in all cultures, but self must be treated both individually and socially; and there will always be some tension between self and other.

What we learn from such a brief historic sketch is that these categories exist only in the context of particular conceptions of society as a whole. Put another way, a human being's unique identity is determined, in large part, by his or her place in society. Anthropological data will be cited to show how the images of self vary dramatically within different cultural milieus and how identity ultimately becomes a major component in any analysis and understanding of the mechanics of human communication. The way personhood is viewed from culture to culture has profound implications for the culture-communication dialogue. It is important, then, to become aware of these cultural contexts, especially how they relate to communication outcomes.

Identity and Other Cultures/The Metaphor of Moral Career

Ethnographic evidence suggests that many so-called simpler cultures lacked any *expressed* concept of the individual self (Collins 1987: 67). Preindustrial societies rarely considered the self a separate entity as we do in American culture; whereas we, by contrast, are said to hold to a "myth of absolute individualism."

From a comparative, anthropological viewpoint, stress on individuation certainly may be geographically more limited than we have previously thought (Lifton 1970: 46). One can say that different cultures have different identity emphases. It has been shown how the notion of self evolved over time, hence will not be the same in the future, most assuredly not the same even from generation to generation. Seeking contrasts with other cultures can give us a better perspective on our own notions of self and personhood. Brief ethnographic illustrations of self are provided in the following exposition to highlight the plasticity, as well as to elucidate neglected aspects, of these categories in different cultural contexts.

Samoa affords a strikingly opposite portrait of self from our Western cultural assumptions. In *Sala'iliua: A Samoan Mystery*, Brad Shore (1982: 144) points out that Samoan language has no native terms that correspond to the English words *personality, self,* or *character.* A Samoan, he translates, would simply say: "Take care of the relationship" rather than our familiar Western dictum: "Be true to thyself" (1982: 136). Personal qualities, as we think of them, become relative to cultural dictate. Personal identity in Samoa has a stronger social and public nature about it than does American personal identity. Furthermore, it has been argued that an over-emphasis on individualism has been a major obstacle to our understanding nonmodern societies in the past (Dumont 1986).

Personhood may not be an either/or matter. Although the definition of identity used in this book stresses an "evolved human capacity," it is possible to transcend the humanness with persons identifying with dead ancestors, ghosts, and even nonhuman spirits. In Africa, according to La Fontaine (1987: 127), certain sacred crocodiles—manifestations of ancestors—were considered persons for they combined the human spiritual aspect with a living body; but not all crocodiles, he noted, were persons.

Marina Roseman (1990: 228) has studied the Temiar rain forest dwellers of Malaysia who, like other Southeast Asian peoples trying to maintain a balance in the dialectic struggle between community and self-integrity, negotiate the boundaries between self and other quite differently from the Western notion of the bounded, autonomous self. The Temiars separate several components of the self in ways unfamiliar to Westerners. For example, their concept of self is typically both multiple and sociocentric. The Temiars recognize many detachable and permeable selves in both human and nonhuman entities—including, interestingly enough, various detached parts of the body, shadows, and even the presumed "odors" of selves. Temiars maintain the separation of self from others by reciting the word _odor_ as they pass behind another person. This ritual, according to Roseman, helps to guard against the affliction that might result from absorbing another person's odor. This is indeed a very different world than that of the "individuated self" of the West, she argues convincingly (1990: 230). Her major conclusion is that, in order to comprehend the objectives of ritual, we would do well to study the cultural construct of the person, and its accompanying metaphors, since the emotional world is rendered intelligible primarily through the structure of the self (1990: 246).

A more classic example from anthropology of a radically different conception of personhood is Read's account of the Gahuku-Gama of New Guinea, who apparently recognized no general concept of the individual self apart from the one defined by the society.[6] Hence, personal and social identity, for this tribal group, merged into one category (La Fontaine 1987: 130). Personhood, like a status or office, becomes essentially the attainment of prescribed social roles. The Gahuku-Gama view of humanity did not distinguish between the individual's and the society's role expectations. In this case, identity was determined almost exclusively by the individual's _place_ in the society.

Because of this emphasis on the social construction of the person, certain individuals, by virtue of age or sex or their specialized roles, will be excluded from this designation. They remain, culturally and socially, *outside* the society—hence, technically are defined as "nonpersons."[7] Children, by definition, not uncommonly were considered "nonpersons" in such tribal societies. Infants especially were ascribed the status of person only after attaining certain characteristics and behaviors. As naming gives one social existence in many cultures, *late* naming practices often coincided with the attainment of significant stages of development in a society. In Central America, for example, Cuna children were simply called "boy" or "girl" until about ten years of age, at which time they received their "true" names (Alford 1988: 36).

La Fontaine (1987: 130) has reported that, among the Lagbara of Uganda, most women—some men—were considered "not persons." Fortes, who studied the Tallensi of Africa, is quoted as saying that among these people personhood was only validated at the death of the individual. It was the completion of a proper life, the attainment of a "moral career," which qualified an individual for full personhood. Since marriage and procreation were essential for this definition of self, full personhood could be achieved only if the individual fulfilled these cultural prerequisites (1987: 131-2). Hence, changes in self-construals are reflected in changing metaphors that describe such groups and their relations to society. The metaphorical images of this category, it should be noted, change along a moral continuum of acceptance to rejection, thus yielding our contemporary culturally constructed notion of the "social stranger" for certain groups accorded less than full social acceptance. We shall have more to say about this idea of stranger status in subsequent chapters.

To return to our ethnographic evidence, Jane Fajans (1985), using an ethnopsychological approach, suggested that the Baining of New Britain, New Guinea—like most Pacific Islanders—do not normally distinguish themselves as individualized entities, are not preoccupied with the inner or subjective states of personal experience, but instead elaborate upon the public and relational aspects of their existence. This does not mean, of course, that they *cannot* conceive of themselves as unique individuals. The individual, as we know this category, is simply transformed into a socially and culturally defined person. The argument is that one is not automatically born a social self but must learn the roles associated with this category. Person, in this context, is indeed society's confirmation of one's identity.[8]

Ultimately, then, it was the "proper life" (moral career) that qualified an individual for full personhood in so-called simpler societies. Human communication and person status, then, are intimately related. Cultures vary considerably in the ways selfhood and responsibility are organized, but all communication is intrinsically affected by such moral order (what one must do or not do) and in turn becomes a significant aspect of that communication, according to Cronen and associates (1988: 76). Differing conceptions of selfhood (personhood) have profound and differential implications for sociability, hence ultimately for effective interpersonal and cross-cultural communication. Thus, conceptions of selfhood (personhood) are increasingly recognized as having important implications for the communication sciences. Recent research in psychology and anthropology, on the other hand, has focused primarily on "self-construals" and their consequences for cognition, emotion, and motivation (Lutz 1988; Markus & Kitayama 1991).

Although a common-sense idea, some notion of which is present in all cultures, self must always be viewed in its social and cultural contexts. For these tribal societies, personhood was the fulfillment of a kind of moral career, if you will—the validation of prescribed social roles and a more or less lifelong transformation in becoming a part of a continuing social order. This long, drawn-out identity process, however, sharply contrasts with the Western practice of more immediate attainment of individuality, usually upon the conferring of a name. An important question for the culture-communication dialogue is, How does naming help to define personal identity? (Alford 1988).

Naming and Identity/Symbolic Communication

Naming practices are both a part of social perception and also creators of these perceptions. Surrounded with highly potent symbolism, naming is a type of communication that, like many other behaviors, varies from culture to culture. Richard Alford (1988), in his challenging cross-cultural study of naming, states that names symbolize identities. In other words, comparing naming practices across cultures demonstrates how different societies arrive at different conceptualizations of identity.

Naming is an important source of cultural knowledge about the identities of named persons: for example, about family grouping, the sex of the person, as well as clues about the individual's relationships with other people. Primary functions of naming, according to Alford (1988: 54), are to distinguish people, to emphasize family continuity, and ultimately to reflect ethnopsychological conceptions of the self. Although given names are found in every society, there are a couple of instances of virtually nameless individuals. In Korea, as a case in point, women—once married—lack personal names. The transition from a single to a married state is accompanied by a name change ("wife of. . .") that helps to effect an identity change. Adult Korean women become, symbolically, the sum of their various familial roles (1988: 56).

Names may also describe physical traits, character traits, or serve as "derogatory-protective labels." Koreans wait 100 days to name a child to avoid the attention of evil spirits, occasionally bestowing ugly names as a way of warding off such potential dangers (1988: 65). Semantically, naming constitutes powerful cultural messages from the name giver. As Koreans typically value male over female children, a baby girl may be called something like "sorrowful one" (1988: 61). The general thesis is that naming systems both reflect and help to create the conceptions of personal and social identity.

American naming practices contrast sharply with these non-Western examples because of the emphasis given in our culture to self and individuality. American names are more reflective of the flexible and multi-dimensional nature of identity as it is variously experienced in the United States. This flexibility, Alford (1988: 141) argued, allows individuals to present different facets of their identities—fomal or infomal, public or private—in a somewhat more relaxed manner than would be observed in many other cultures. As a form of symbolic communication, naming can tell us a great deal about the multifaceted nature of identity from culture to culture. But, first, let us return to the perennial debates over the individual *in* society.

"Someone, No One"/The Human Dialectic Dilemma

Is individuality culturally specific or a universal in human experience? This is the question Burridge posed in *Someone, No One: An Essay on Individuality* (1979). He argued for the culturally specific, inasmuch as many Eastern cultures often do not have the same notions of the individual that correspond with Western (European) ones. The "I" that is the self's image of itself, Burridge contended, can either reflect "the others" or try to achieve a new individuality. The self's integration of these opposing forces represents its unique identity (1979: 17–18). The term *identity*, in contemporary scientific discourse, is used in two very different ways, according to Fine (1986: 61): one referring to the "true" identity (equivalent to William James's "self of selves") and the other referring to an attribute of self (such as identifying with a group, or "self-in-society"). In this volume, identity is defined as the academic metaphor for self-in-context, the historical context being only one of several dimensions of this complex, multifaceted idea.

Put another way, identity arises from attempts at reconciling these two modes of becoming: the social (person) and the existential (self). One makes him/her a "mirror" of society, the other an "individual" (Burridge 1979: 27). There is, then, always a dynamic dialectic between the existential *self* and the *person* as social or cultural being, just as there is between the present self and the possibilities of becoming something new through self-transformation. If one accepts the contemporary metaphors for this phenomenon, people in Western cultures would seem to be continually "reinventing" themselves. Cultures, however, vary in the degree to which they allow opportunities for expressing such conscious self-awareness and change (1979: 74).

Individuality—even that of autonomous self so familiar in our own culture—may be possible with all people. However, certain cultural conditions clearly encourage or discourage its overt reflection. In contrast to those described above, institutionalized individuality may be distinctive only of Western cultures and has almost always involved some movement between person and individual self—"a thematic fact of culture but one with varying cultural expressions," says Burridge (1979: 116). Rosenberg (1979), in *Conceiving the Self*, suggested that the self in all its complexity is not yet fully understood. This statement applies equally to identity, the academic metaphor for self-in-context, especially as this construct has been debated in the culture-communication dialogue. We might take a look at the field of literature for further insights into the subtle and intimate relationships between identity and communication.

Identity and Communication/A Mind-Machine Problem?

Robert Langbaum claims that twentieth-century writers have all been saying much the same thing (1982: 353): The spiritual problem of our times is essentially a problem of identity, whether the solutions come through art, sex, nature, or salvation as self-realization. There is virtually a crisis of individualism in this "identity society" of ours. For Langbaum, as with other writers, this modern crisis involves a new communication dimension: the advent of media and mass media influences. "The old mind-body problem has now become a mind-machine problem," states Langbaum in *The Mysteries of Identity: A Theme in Modern Literature* (1982: 14). Mediated communication becomes a significant factor in the culture-communication dialogue that cannot be overlooked or denied.

Media, only one type of communication, are nonetheless especially influential and pervasive in today's world. By the year 2000, most information will be transmitted by machines. "Informatics," so argues Thomas McPhail (1989: 55), will increase the world's dependence on communication services, thus forcing abrupt changes in the way we view ourselves as well as our environments. According to Everett Rogers (1989: 85), the computer may be as important a technological advance for infomation societies as was the steam engine for the industrial society.

Perception of self via media adds new dimensions to self-ascriptions. For one thing, the media themselves become significant sources of identification. Media influences, at both the personal and collective levels, create an almost "universal media dependency," says Michael Real (1989: 15). In short, media help to create the environments where identities are formed. The media have a special role to play in the culture-communication dialogue because they can, at the very least, speed up the process of change in both our macroworlds and our microworlds. Therefore, we need to pay careful attention to the media through which communication performances are ultimately realized. As role models for behavior, they influence our personal identities today in much the same way that human interactions (e.g., socialization experiences) did in the past. The reality of globalization and a shrinking world might yet force us to rethink the nature of individuality (Sampson 1989).

Although Real (1988: 13) acknowledges that contemporary life would be inconceivable without our modern means of communication, he poses a challenging question in the book *Super Media*: "How can we learn to direct this information influence in a mediated culture and express our collective identity?" Clearly, there is an important message here. The public, rather than being passive participants, can take responsibility in both creating and expressing culture. After all, the media are only reflections of the cultures in which they exist. Communication and culture reciprocally influence each other. Identities, Real (1989: 40) argues, are created out of the complex interactions of media *and* culture. In short, both the media and the culture help to create individual identities. To quote D. J. Crowley (1982: 14):

> In our communication with one another we mediate, on the one hand, the form and the substance of our consciousness; on the other, the form and the significance of all our social arrangements and social institutions. We create ourselves, and re-create the social/cultural milieu in which we have our lives, in communication...

Crowley's early work on the primacy of communication in human adaptations gave precedence to the human capacity to construct and negotiate everyday experiences through communication channels. Communicative competence, he further suggested, is "one's admission to human and social life" (1982: 30). How we communicate can make a difference socially, culturally and, ultimately, morally. Stated another way, poor communication yields interpersonal and intercultural misunderstanding. However, what is going on in this area of communication, warned Crowley, is only in part associated with the developing academic discipline of communication. The field may be too broad and too important to be left entirely to a single academic discipline. Certainly the transdisciplinary focus of this book suggests a similar conclusion.

Communication today is influenced as much by media as by interpersonal and intercultural encounters (Meyrowitz 1986; McQuail 1989). "Mediated communication" is the modern buzzword in today's interconnected world. Although both types of communication are acknowledged as significant to behavior and identity, the media can be demonstrated to have the potential power to alter relationships, reshape experiences, and even fashion world views (Gumpert 1987). Two significant questions are immediately suggested: What does this type of communication do for human identification, and what is its ultimate outcome in terms of the perennial tensions between individualism and community?

As self is always deeply involved in the social experiences of human beings, we must build theoretical bridges to handle the dualities between existential and social selves. Identity becomes one way of unraveling this dialectic dilemma: the struggle between autonomy for individuals and interconnectedness for social and cultural groups. More significantly, how does identity mediate between culture and communication? Finally, looking at its consequences, has media technology really resulted in an absence of community for contemporary Western societies?

By the late 1970s, commentators on American character and identity were remarking on what seemed to be a new self-centeredness in American life: Tom Wolfe's Me Decade (Wilkinson 1988: 31). The 1980s, however, saw the interpretation of national identity shift toward an emphasis on media influences. The argument is basically that the synthetic reality of the media is invading self, thus impoverishing the individual by blocking out society (1988: 33). The result has been "no sense of place" (Meyrowitz 1986) that presumably results in a lost vision of community (Bellah, et al. 1986). Book titles, such as *The Lonely Crowd, Our Endangered Children, The Status Seekers, Culture of Narcissism,* and *Habits of the Heart,* all more or less picture a shallow American society or, at the very least, individuals existing without deeply rooted and satisfying identities.

There are bound to be changes with Western media influences, but do mass communications necessarily foster the loss of genuine self-direction? Kenneth Gergen's *Saturated Self: Dilemmas of Identity in Contemporary Life* (1991: 49) is just the latest attempt to view the "postmodern self" as a new self-consciousness brought about by what he calls the "technologies of social saturation" causing a "vertigo of unlimited multiplicity." In other words, with technological change comes a multiplicity of different "voices," reasoned Gergen, using the metaphor of voice to symbolize group social aspirations. The relationship between culture and identity becomes complex precisely because of the need to adjust to these discontinuities of modern life. His argument, in short, is that technological change does not favor an enduring community (1991: 211). Rather, the individual is left with only "an array of fragile, symbolic communities, tied together primarily by electronic impulse" (1991: 225).

Although certainly individualism, as we understand that label today, can lead to a lack of commitment, social isolation, and even "psychological narcissism" (Brown 1987: 51), it is still conceivable that technology might produce its own forms of community not yet fully appreciated or understood. Gergen's book may have overlooked important contemporary functions of identity in our modern information society. One cannot automatically assume that "the technologies of social saturation lead us inevitably toward a postmodern consciousness" (Gergen 1991: 230). I would question Gergen's thesis that the Western discourse for understanding self has been so radically transformed. Certainly metaphors of identity have changed: but the functions of identification remain fairly stable over time, only intensifying with the accelerations in the social system(s).

While the demands of society have changed, community has remained an important notion, at least for many Americans in the 1990s. It has been pointed out that both the best and the worst in American life can be attributed to individualism. According to Wilkinson (1988: 71), Americans fear that individualism will make us selfish and destroy our sense of community. Nevertheless, there will always be some "magnetic tension between individuality and community." If the nineteenth century was dominated by a concern with the conflict between individual and society, the twentieth has been preoccupied with the quest for the ideal community (cf. Tinder's [1980] *Community: Reflections on a Tragic Ideal*[10]). Does this shift from group consensus to concern with self-interest reflect a real change in identity structure or merely, as Wilkinson suggests, a change in the sensibilities of the writers about national character? (1988: 41). This provocative question will be addressed in chapter 9.

In the present chapter, I have tried to demonstrate how self is shaped by social pressures and varies with different cultural emphases, ultimately functioning to help insure human survival. The discussion that follows will focus on the relationships among culture, identity, and communication from the perspective of the academic discipline of communication. It will attempt to critique some of the major theoretical approaches to the study of identity in the exciting, contemporary culture-communication dialogue.

Principal Points

Major historic debates over the nature of personhood clearly demonstrate that our familiar, Western concept of the autonomous individual is historically and culturally variable. Self has evolved over time and will not be the same in the future. Person and nonperson status have been represented metaphorically using a moral career analogy. "Homo duplex's" attempt to reconcile individuality with sociality remains the perennial human dialectical dilemma. Furthermore, social communication is ultimately dependent on how cultures define persons. Metaphors of identity appear to have changed without the basic functions of identification altering significantly.

Notes

1. Markus and Kitayama (1991) make the important observation that different cultures have strikingly different "construals" of self, which in many cases determine the very nature of experience in society: namely, whether construing self as independent or interdependent.

2. Fine reminds us that soul has always been closely associated with concepts of mind, spirit, or self (1986: 7). Although the soul played a prominent role in philosophy and psychology before the twentieth century, William James tried to permanently eliminate the "mystical essence" of this construct (1986: 31). Although scientists prefer an empirical approach to identity, there are always normative dimensions to the idea. In this book, it is argued that metaphors become a medium for capturing the more ineffable, as opposed to the strictly empirical, essences of this concept.

3. Dumont warns that the individualism of the first Christians was not exactly the same individualism that we know today and that we should be wary of projecting our familiar idea of the autonomous individual onto the first Christians and their cultural environment (1986: 24). The most notable difference, he (1986: 51) argued, is that the early Christian concept was of an outwardly individual as opposed to our own "inworldly individual." The idea of individuality, then, has undergone profound transformations at different historical stages.

4. Fine sees autobiography as "the narcissism of the common man" and further suggests that the countries which have emphasized individualism the most have also produced the largest numbers of individualistic self-histories (1986: 21).

5. This early democratic and egalitarian movement originally found acceptance among the outcast and the disenfranchised, but eventually organized Christianity itself succumbed to the corruptions of money and power (Dumont 1987: 119).

6. The metaphor for self-in-society among the Gahuku-Gama is the image of skin, which represents the outer covering of the self. Hence, the interesting suggestion by Poole (quoted in Howard 1987: 415) of the "inside-the-skin/outside-the-skin" distinction as related to various cultural notions of personhood.

7. Meyrowitz (1986: 190) reports that rape in Biblical times was not considered an assault against a person, rather a crime against property; a Supreme Court decision in 1894 allowed a state to interpret the word *person* to exclude women!

8.

Self vs. Person Dialectic

```
Personal Dimension          *******  Self: individual's awareness
     *                         *      of a unique identity: "core"
     *                         *      identity, existential self,
     *                         *      biographic self, genetic
     *                         *      (neurological) identity;
     *                         *      "real" self; personal
     *                         *      identity; Id/Ego/; personal
     *                         *      agency; character identity;
     *                         *      "individualized self"
     *                         *
     *     IDENTITY     ****
     *                         *      "spiritual self" and
     *                         *      "cosmic selflessness")
     *                         *
     *                         *      Person: society's
     *                         *      confirmation of identity:
     *                         *      role identities; racial/
     *                         *      ethnic identities; superego;
Social Dimension              *      "situated identities";
                              *      "familial self," and
                              *      social categories: gender
                           *******  identities, master statuses
```

9. Consider the novel case of the adopted person who discovers that s/he is not the person originally thought to be, thus creating self-doubts about the individual's authenticity.

10. Tinder argues that there is a major flaw in any utopian scheme and that our "communal aspirations" may be unrealistic and largely unattainable (1980: 5). This "tragic ideal," however, is not due entirely to mediated communication influences.

4

○ Culture, Identity, and Communication

The problem of the relation between group and individual is so pervading and ubiquitous that it cannot be treated detached from any question of culture and of social or psychological process. A theory which does not present and include at every step the definitions of individual contributions and of their integration into collective action stands condemned.

—Bronislaw Malinowski, *The American Journal of Sociology*

An Introduction

Currently we may be in transition to a new world culture, what Harris and Moran (1989: 101) have referred to as a "cyberculture," fueled by the communication revolution. Understanding the impact of cultural and social factors on behavioral communication, as mediated through identities, is the focus of this book. How is it possible for people in one culture, or social group, to understand those in another? Ultimately, the goal is to help us, as individuals, to become more sensitive to people who do not always share our values, assumptions, and ways of behaving—in short, to become better communicators, more effective participants, in this emerging world culture. What kind of identity is more likely to enhance communication?

Communication is at the heart of both interpersonal and international relations. Humans, it has been said (1989: 32), are potentially versatile communicators, using every medium from smoke signals and drums to television and computers. Most communication is manifested through symbols that differ in meaning according to time, place, culture, and social position. Communication has been defined as "a convergence of meaning achieved by symbolic interaction" (Rogers & Kincaid 1981: 31). When that interaction is between persons who identify themselves as distinct from one another in cultural terms, we are often—but not always—dealing with cross-cultural or intercultural communication (Collier & Thomas 1988: 100). It must be recognized that not all communication involves cultural communication.

The intellectual power of the concept of culture, nevertheless, has long been evident in anthropology (Geertz 1973). Culture is that distinctly human creation consisting of both symbolic knowledge and practical skills. More specifically, culture is "communicable knowledge for human coping in a particular environment that is passed on for the benefit of subsequent generations" (Harris & Moran 1989: 107). Culture often helps to define the "logic of communication"; and, of course, culture and communication reciprocally influence each other (Applegate & Sypher 1988: 59).

Because research is conducted on populations from a different society does not mean, of course, that is it necessarily "intercultural" (Johnson & Tuttle 1989: 469). Not all communication, at all times, has a cultural component. This book examines areas of human behavior that are as much social as cultural in expression. In fact, it is well to remember that all behavior does not even have to communicate. Noncommunication is not equivalent to miscommunication, although the focus of this book is often on the latter, whether culturally or socially derived.

In *Cultural Misunderstandings*, Carroll claims that a culture is a way of seeing the world (1988: 143). "Cultural texts" (such as friendships, love, family, money, seduction, and so forth) express different cultural propositions even when presumed to be identical. Drawing on a wealth of ethnographic interviews, Carroll contrasted the different ways in which French and Americans affirm, or fail to affirm, human bonds.

The French, Carroll (1988: 145) argues, start from the cultural premise that they exist in a social network of great importance. By contrast, Americans often assume that people are "self-made," exist outside such networks and are, therefore, the creators of their own identities. Whereas the American feels it is one's private business to define him or herself as s/he wishes, French culture gives the French person a very different notion of self and identity. One might say that the two cultures use different metaphors to conceptualize identification. For Americans, identity is something personally "constructed," using the building metaphor of identity so pronounced in the contemporary culture-communication dialogue.

It is culture that usually gives people their sense of identity, whether at an individual or group level. It is also cultural knowledge which must be learned in order to effectively communicate within or between cultures. Having said this, the complex relationships between culture and identity are far from fully understood. The reality is apt to be far more complex. As a puzzling case in point, scientists have documented examples of identities without corresponding cultures.

Ideally, we need a theoretical model that brings into focus our thinking about communication as a process and culture as a social construction that is potentially reconstructed.[1] Identity, as academic metaphor for self-in-context, can help to unravel the complex relationships between culture and communication. To begin with, cultural variability does not always directly influence communication. Its impact is more indirect, through the psychological *mediating process of identity* (Gudykunst & Ting-Toomey 1988: 35). A person's self-image (identity) plays a crucial role, then, in how cultural knowledge is interpreted and selectively perceived. Markus and Kitayama (1991) believe that the way people understand the world is rooted in their self-perceptions and self-understandings that have profound consequences for cognition, emotion, and motivation.

Languages, roles, a sense of time and space, thought patterns, social organization—all of these can differ from culture to culture, making cross-cultural communication a complex and daunting challenge. Every person tends to project him or herself into the human communication process and, in so doing, becomes an integral part of that same communication. In this interaction, the self and its social environment are reciprocally determined. In other words, self is not a passive agent but actively selects, potentially constructs, its own realities—hence the metaphorical notion of *constructed identities*.

In spite of its importance, the role that identity plays in the communication process has been somewhat neglected in the culture-communication dialogue. One thesis of this book is that identity, as a significant link between intention and action, can guide human behavior through complex rules that connect culture and communication. Following Collier and Thomas (1988: 113), culture is conceived of as the *context* in which people derive a sense of who they are, how they should behave, possibly where they are pointed in the future. Identity, then, is essentially an adaptive, mediating process that steers human behavior. This approach tries not to confuse culture (structure) with communication (action) or reduce culture to a psychological process. Furthermore, it is *not* assumed that identity and culture are always the same, or even perform identical functions.

Using the metaphorical image of the "conductor," identity orchestrates between culture (rules/codes = the score) and communication (action/end result = the music). According to Fine (1986: 295), it was Kohut who postulated a "superordinate self" that exists from birth onward. In his model, emphasis was on the "regulator" role of identity as psychic organizer in the determination of behavior, fantasy, and feelings. Metaphoric paradigms stressing an "executive self" typically have utilized building metaphors of construction or transformation to dramatically picture a self-in-charge.

In summary, a number of scholars have proposed that *identity* provides a general frame of reference for understanding one's existential experiences. For example, the conductor simile has certainly guided much of communication research in organizational contexts (Pacanowsky & O'Donnell-Trujillo 1983). Except in its psychoanalytic assumptions, Kohut's way of conceptualizing the functions of self is not essentially dissimilar (1971, 1977). This is a metaphorical image of identity, not so much a map for guiding behavior but a compass for steering the directional path, suggesting that identity can affect one's destiny throughout life. As Kohut and others have recognized, however, many problems connected with the self and its structure (for example, the "essence" of self) remain largely unresolved. Moreover, any metaphorical model, it is argued in this volume, remains problematical (Knowles & Sibicky 1990).

Culture and Communication Models

Theories that have tried to explain how individuals or groups in different cultures communicate, according to Kim (1988: 16), have tended to follow basically three traditions: the "positivist" emphasizing prediction; the "humanist" emphasizing understanding; and the "systems" tradition, emphasizing understanding and prediction. It is the humanist tradition that comes closest to the integrative approach chosen for this discussion to explain the relationship between culture and communication. Marcus and Fischer (1986) suggest a similar shift in interpretive anthropology toward the theoretical focus on communication within and between cultures.

Certainly, the most comprehensive cross-cultural research, linking culture and interpersonal communication, has been Geert Hofstede's (1980) study of fifty nations, which concluded that culture is indeed both enduring and resistant to change. His research produced three dimensions of cultural variability: "uncertainty avoidance," "power distance," and a "masculinity-femininity" score.[2] Hofstede pictured cultures with high-power distance as valuing an arrangement of inequality with everyone having his/her rightful place in society. Uncertainty avoidance basically suggests the lack of tolerance in a culture for ambiguity. Cultures high in uncertainty avoidance, then, tend to have high levels of anxiety, a need for formal rules, and a low tolerance for groups believed to be deviant. High masculinity involves an emphasis on money, assertiveness, and unequal sex roles. Cultures characterized by Hofstede as feminine are, by contrast, ones that emphasize people, a nurturant quality of life, and more equal sex roles (Gudykunst 1988: 140). Degree of cultural similarity is the major issue in this model. Focus is on group similarities in general rather than on cultural similarities in particular (Gudykunst & Nishida 1989: 23).

The "individualism-collectivism" typology has been utilized by theorists across many disciplines as the major dimension of cultural variability believed to influence intergroup processes.[3] Through the socialization process, individualism-collectivism is seen as influencing general self-conceptions as well as selected aspects of social and linguistic identity (Gudykunst & Ting-Toomey 1988: 91). Language, a significant medium of communication, is often seen as one of the most powerful unifying factors in culture.

Language is a vital part of the social identity of any group (Gudykunst 1988: 129). Styles of speaking are believed to reflect the overall values of a culture. Collective cultures are said to value more conformity to the group, whereas cultures high on individualism focus on "self" rather than "other." Japan is a case in point. Few people in the world seem to demonstrate such wide contrasts in communication styles than Japanese and Americans (Barnlund 1989). The very qualities that one society nurtures—reserve, formality, and silence— are, according to Barnlund (1989: 57), the ones the other society discourages. Americans value self-assertion, informality, and talkativeness.

Unlike Western countries, Japan does not place much emphasis on the precision of words. Japanese language has been described as "more ambiguous and more evocative" than English (1989: 132). In Japan, language is said to reflect a theme of harmony and group integrity. John Condon quotes a Japanese friend (1984: 11): "English is a perfect language for lawyers...but not for gently getting to know each other." Contrasting differences in conversational styles, he evokes the image of the flag: Japanese conversations, like the curved symbols on their flag, favor indirectness of expression. The American way of talking, by contrast, is more linear and direct in approach. Described as a group having some genuine resistance to verbal skills, the Japanese believe that the success of communication depends less on the quality of the message and more on the sensibilities of the recipients. Failure of communication, reports Smith (1988: 57), is not uncommonly blamed on the receiver.

Japanese language has also been characterized as a "status-oriented" language. English, on the other hand, has been seen as a "person-oriented" language (Gudykunst & Ting-Toomey 1988: 109). Dean Barnlund would say that the group in Japan becomes "the measure of all things" (1989: 154). The Japanese are encouraged to think first of being part of some larger association, whether involving family, school, workplace, or nation. The self and other are simply expressed in more relational terms. The use of imprecise and ambiguous verbal behavior, Barnlund concludes, reflects an "indirect style of communication" that fosters a sense of selfhood emphasizing harmony and group conformity.

It has been said that Caucasians see talk as a means of social control whereas the Japanese are characterized as being more tolerant of silences.[4] It is easy to see how an indirect versus a direct style of communicating can pose problems in diplomatic and business relations between countries. John Pfeiffer (1989) believes that American business executives are totally unprepared to bargain effectively with the Japanese due, in large part, to our ignorance of Japanese culture, specifically native bargaining rituals. Cross-cultural miscommunication can result through lack of shared linguistic backgrounds, including beliefs about talk and silence.

Knowing how to communicate presupposes a great deal more than simply knowing a language. Besides the nonverbal communicative styles (intonation, pitch, emotional tone, and even silences that carry significant meanings from culture to culture), how people arrange their lives (physical settings) can also play a tremendous role in human interaction. The dialectical opposites of individual versus communal identity, claim Gudykunst and Ting-Toomey (1988: 122), are present to some extent in all home environments. The Pueblo Indians, a collectivistic culture, express communal values rather than a concern for personal privacy in their practice of clustering their dwellings. Hecht and associates (1989: 169) offer a simple, but pointed example of the relationship between privacy and space: A sense of privacy may be signaled by closed doors in the United States, double doors in Germany, trees at the property line in England, but—interestingly enough—paper walls in Japan. The ways that human beings use and construct their environments have profound effects on human communication.

Likewise, cultures suggest different identity themes through the various uses of time and personal space. Levine and Wolff employed a Brazilian example to illustrate cultural contrasts in the use of the temporal dimension (1987: 57). They described, in warm and humorous detail, how students in Brazil believed that a person consistently late was probably more "successful" than one who was always on time. A person of status, so they reasoned, was expected to be late!

Proxemics, or the use of personal space, can serve to further illustrate cultural contrasts. In collectivistic cultures, members prefer to stand close and to touch more. North Americans, it has been reported, sometimes find the Arabs' need for close personal space anxiety-provoking. To an Arab, on the other hand, even to smell a friend may be interpreted as an intimate and reassuring experience. Americans, as Gudykunst and Ting-Toomey (1988: 126–27) have written, tend to maintain both more proxemic distance in relationships and to suppress the sense of smell. In short, members of individualistic cultures try to protect their sense of time and space while members of collectivistic cultures assert communal identity by giving the temporal and spacial dimensions more group emphasis.

Hofstede's was indeed a powerful theoretical model for explaining interactional differences and similarities between cultures. Hall's dimensional scheme of "low-context" versus "high-context" was yet another—and similar—attempt to differentiate contrasting clusters of culture traits along a continuum of individual versus group concerns. Communication styles are assumed to be very different in high- versus low-context cultures.

Low-context cultures stress individual values, more linear thinking, direct verbal interactions, and individualized nonverbal behavior. High-context cultures, by contrast, emphasize group values, more circular thinking, indirect verbal interactions, and more contextual nonverbal behavior. Ting-Toomey would say that meanings are "situated" within the larger shared knowledge of the cultural context (1988: 225). While low-context cultures might view an indirect way of handling conflict as "cowardly," she (1988: 229–30) argues, high-context cultures are likely to consider a more direct manner as "lacking in good taste." John Condon (1984: 36–38) is an author who has written extensively about Japanese culture—incidently a high-context culture. He listed some American habits that the Japanese typically grumble about. Included among these: Americans talk too much, interrupt other people often, and generally don't listen enough to suit the Japanese. The two cultures differ primarily in how they handle the I and the we, i.e., the individual as opposed to the group.

Summarizing this research on individualism-collectivism, Ting-Toomey says that the "we" identity systems seek outwardly for social connections and approval whereas the "I" cultures seek privacy and autonomy as their trademarks (1988: 288). In collectivistic cultures the tendency is for people to treat others as "whole persons," while in more individualistic cultures people are treated differently depending on the unique identities that they perform. It has been said that the public self is more important in collective cultures, the private self in individualistic ones. Both Hofstede's model and the Hall paradigm are, it has been concluded, "culturally grounded perspectives" (Hecht, et al. 1989: 166).

The self and its feelings can also become a kind of moral guide for cultural behavior. Ting-Toomey has developed a brilliant "face-negotiation" theory to explain this complex relationship (1988: 213–35). Culture, in this illuminating model, provides the larger interpretive frame in which concepts like "face" (identity) and "conflict style" (communication) can be meaningfully expressed. According to Ting-Toomey, face is a projected image of one's self in a relational situation. "Facework," from this perspective, is viewed as a symbolic front with styles of expression ("affective strategies") varying from culture to culture (1988: 213–35). Self is said to be maintained through the active negotiation of facework in cultures like Japan, China, and Korea. In the United States, self is more often defined as an intrapsychic phenomenon.

John Condon (1984: 33), by way of illustrating Japanese sensitivity to context or situation, has traced the origins of the concept of "saving face." In countries where the idea is common, circumstances count for more than words. "Saving" or "losing" face, although important in both China and Japan, was originally a Chinese notion. The *Kanji*, the Chinese character for "face," was the same as the character for "mask"—incidently, the original image-metaphor for identity. Face is something shown outwardly rather than being the expression of inward feelings. Hence, Japanese culture is said to value outward expression over inner feelings, the assumed case in American culture. In terms of the emphases given to private versus public aspects of self, these two cultures are often viewed as polar opposites.

Paraphrasing Ting-Toomey's model: Individualistic cultures value autonomy and choice (personal attributes), while collectivistic ones value interdependence and reciprocal obligations (role attributes). Each culture attaches its own significance and normative values to different styles of interacting as well as different strategies for negotiating such interactions. Ting-Toomey's theory tries to explain the roots of conflict as well as cross-cultural variations in communication (Gudykunst & Nishida 1989: 30). In short, culture plays a critical role in the facework negotiation process.

How do we critique the effectiveness of such typologies? A major strength of these theories is that they make us more aware of the diversity of cultures. However, a major weakness of any typology which subdivides human beings into such broadly defined characteristic types is the tendency to misrepresent cultural realities. Such models yank individual persons out of their cultural and social settings and, in so doing, tend to assume a universality across time, situation, and cultures (Gudykunst & Nishida 1989: 40). The simple collectivistic-individualistic distinction, it is argued here, has not fully explained the differences that emerge. For one thing, cultures differ significantly in the degree to which they encourage consciousness of individual differences. Ideal types of any kind can become gross over-generalizations wherein homogeneity is often more apparent than real. It is equally important, warns Hecht and associates (1989: 179), to measure individualism at various levels: personal, social, and cultural.

Most nations today are characterized by multi-layers of both social and cultural complexity. At the level of identity, all human activity, to some extent, combines both individuality and sociality. Self is multifaceted and sometimes not always visible in every social presentation (cf. Goffman 1959). Using Cronen's borrowed musical metaphor, cultures are "polyphonic," i.e., made up of different forms of selfhood within single cultures. This polyphonic character of culture, according to Cronen and associates (1988: 79–80), preserves the very heart of identity. This more or less existential position, with its emphasis on the creative aspects of self-definition, suggests that human beings are richly complex, multifaceted, and unique. Life is not just a "script" that people learn and act out. Rather, "interpreted meaning" is fundamental to human beings and their experiences (Kotarba & Fontana 1987: 55).

In terms of identity change, the picture is further complicated by the fact that identity today is something not always conferred ("ascribed"). In the modern, information-based society we live in, identities are more often characterized as "achieved," i.e., based on conscious decision-making or, if you will, "constructed" in this complex polyphonic equation (Marcia 1987: 166). Although we humans operate under some severe cognitive limitations, often from adhering to overly simplified metaphoric views of the universe, we continuously produce meaning about our experiences, somewhat "in the same way," says Crowley (1982: 21), that "a cartographer maps out a territory."

The picture of national groups as "ideal types," therefore, is apt to be multi-leveled and complex. Not all Japanese or Americans, it can easily be demonstrated, act alike. As a broad generalization, cultures like the Japanese may emphasize group identification over individualism. However, we might briefly consider Dorinne Kondo's (1990: 231) powerful and compelling ethnography of identity in a Japanese workplace for a challenge to the monolithic stereotype of the "happy mindless Japanese worker." She cautions us not to over-generalize from images of Japan drawn largely from middle-class managers in large corporations.

The stereotype of a homogeneous Japanese society, with a uniformally docile work force, is seriously called into question. The enacting of identity, she skillfully argues, occurs at many levels and is certainly not the same in all contexts. Power relationships make the real difference—in short, work identities are not the same for all workers! Kondo, herself a Japanese-American, beautifully illustrates the notion of self-in-context, with the conclusion that identities cannot be separated from their performative contexts. There may be some superficial truth in the image of the "automation-like" Japanese worker, but such images need constant refinement.

How, then, can one make sense of labels such as "individualistic"? Surely, this idea—so central to European thought—stands for a free, independent, choosing person. But, as a matter of historic record, in such typologies this individual most typically translates into an adult, white, heterosexual male. Rarely are other subgroups considered; hardly ever is mention made of generational differences when talking about these populations.[5] Kondo's (1991) ethnography is powerful testimony to the conclusion that identities, as metaphors of performance, are possible only in terms of some larger "narrative"—what we used to call culture—made up of specific contexts to be understood and analyzed.

The view of communication as varying systematically as a function of "core values" (dimensions), while theoretically and some-times effectively linking culture and interpersonal communication, assumes an equivalence and uniformity that sometimes makes cultural comparison suspect. What is power, for example, in one culture may not be power in another (Hecht, et al. 1989: 166). The search for universal generalizations is questionable. Problems of translation and "equivalency" may become clearer when we consider a particular cultural case study.[6]

The Principle of Contextualization/The Japan Case

Polar conceptions of personality, such as "egocentric" versus "sociocentric," have shaped a good deal of the discussions about self in the culture-communication dialogue. The Japanese are often characterized by the label "groupism." By contrast, Americans are supposedly all "individualistic." Americans stress attending to self, the appreciation of one's difference from others, and the importance of asserting the self. The Japanese want to fit in with others, affecting instead a harmonious interdependence (Markus & Kitayama 1991). Ostensibly, to be human in Japan is to be inextricably connected to others (Kondo 1987: 246). Ideal self equals ideal society.[7] The primary goal of socialization in Japan is presumably "to produce a gentle, positive, and energetic self sensitive to and connected with others" (1987: 262).[8] The individual is so invariably identified as acting in some kind of human relationship, rather than autonomously, that it has even been written that the Japanese "lack a sense of self" as we understand it (Smith: 1988: 50).

It may not be totally true that the Japanese always deny independent action that transcends the group (Doi 1986). It has been asked, nonetheless: Can the Japanese individual be so submerged in the group that there is not room for a sense of personal identity? (Smith 1988: 67). Rosenberger warns that we may be asking the wrong question when we inquire whether the Japanese are individualistic or group-oriented (1989: 108). The Japanese self participates in both extremes according to oppositions culturally specific to Japan (1989: 85). We are again confronted with the problem of equivalency: Egocentrism in Japan may not be the same as egocentrism in the United States.

More to the point, the Japanese may accept the seeming contradictions of self better than most Americans. With concepts like *omote/ura* (outside/inside) and *tatemae/honne* (conformity to consensus/inner motivations), the Japanese usually do not see any lack of consistency between these polar ideals. Instead, they tend to appreciate the "doublesidedness" of things (Doi 1986: 29). Smith (1988: 70) has argued that the Japanese may be acutely aware of the discrepancies between inner feelings and outward role demands, yet still think of the latter as the real center of the self. Not only do they accept these contradictions of self, the mature individual has a highly developed ability to shift between different modes of self-presentation depending on shifts in social contexts. It has been said that the Japanese are, in fact, fond of delicate nuances in human relations (Smith 1988).

Although the Japanese may indeed possess a clear sense of self, this self may differ significantly from our own (Barnlund 1975; Condon 1984; Kondo 1987; Smith 1988; Creighton 1990).

Another neglected problem is how to explain the next generation when contrasting such core values believed to be held by all members of a culture. Robert Lifton (1970: 26) has written that young Japanese focus upon differentiating the self from traditional groups, while young Americans try to create new groups for "anchoring their chaotic selves." In both cases, there is "simultaneous quest for meaningful self process and community." Although there is little evidence to suggest that Japanese youth totally reject involvement in group life, unquestionably today's young people in Japan are more concerned about individualism, if that word is taken to mean personal growth and self-satisfaction (Smith 1988).

The difficulties with the usual analyses of Japanese self, according to Rosenberger (1989: 92), are threefold: 1) a low priority given to the individualized self when talking about the Japanese, 2) discussions too often couched in Western terms of self that may not be totally equivalent in meaning, and 3) the assumption that the individualized self is always a contradiction to the Japanese system. Smith (1988) has made a provocative suggestion: Perhaps Japan is just a different society with a fundamentally different orientation to self. Certainly some Japanese are likely to feel that Americans have so inflated the importance of the private self that we run the risk of dissolving the bonds that hold any society together (Barnlund, quoted in Smith 1988: 134). The principle of contextualization may be an appropriate one for analyzing and understanding Japan.

Kondo's book, *Crafting Selves: Power, Gender, and Discourses of Identity in a Japanese Workplace*, provides a convincing example of the impact of context on Japanese identity. In this elegantly crafted ethnography, Kondo warns against overly romanticized conclusions about Japanese harmony and connectedness. Barnlund makes a similar point (1989: 155): Human contacts can be superficial in both societies.

Americans might learn to be more interdependent and the Japanese could learn to share the intimate. However, to see "the Japanese" as some sort of utopian model of human connectedness, Kondo cautions (1990: 305), is to fail to see the irony that such belongingness is itself often couched in contradictory power relations.

One must look at both the unintended, as well as the intended, consequences of human actions. As an intriguing case in point, Kondo demonstrated how women workers often subverted their own power by playing roles culturally acceptable for women in Japanese society. For example, when women in the workplace play roles such as "surrogate mother," they may actually help to "seal their fates as being apart from the central story" (1990: 295). This is just one puzzling example of the ironic workings of power within the Japanese workplace.

Place, time, and social grouping are some of the main criteria for defining *context* in Japan; and it is reported that ritual and ceremony are expressions of the most essential values in Japanese society (Smith 1988: 37). Identity, according to Dr. Doi (1986: 80), "is to be aware of one's self as one's self," but its significance lies precisely in the suggestion that such awareness of self will ultimately become the basis for connecting with others. How can we best explain identity, the academic metaphor for self-in-context, and its expressions in terms of the culture-communication dialogue?

Cultural Situatedness/A Performance Model

This book stresses the interrelatedness of culture and communication. Whether defined interculturally or interpersonally, communication involves a "transactional process." When people communicate, they make conscious or unconscious predictions about the outcomes of their behavior (Gudykunst & Ting-Toomey 1988: 18). Different strategies are employed, then, depending on these dispositional and situational factors. Erik Erikson (1950; 1968), the first to use the identity concept in its current psychological sense, defined identity as a universal psychological mechanism for adaptation in face of change. It has little objective reality independent of its sociocultural environment. Even to discuss identity apart from its cultural, social, and situational contexts poses difficulties.[10] Hence, the definition of identity in this volume as academic metaphor for self-in-context. How do we best conceptualize identity-in-culture?

Harris and Moran (1989: 107) use a management approach to the *definition of culture* ("communicable knowledge for human coping within a particular environment") that avoids equating culture and communication. However, Hall—father of nonverbal communication studies—has been accused of seeing the two as the same (Ross 1978). Although culture contains the script, the knowledge that is available for the accomplishment of human goals, culture is not merely communication. Barnlund (1989) makes the obvious, but relevant, point that only individuals communicate, not cultures. Identity becomes especially crucial in this not-so-obvious equation.

Spiro (Kilborne & Langness 1987: 32–58) refers to culture as a collective cognitive system made up of a "set of propositions" (cultural frames) about nature, humans, and society. Collier and Thomas (1988: 122), likewise, suggest that culture forms an "implicit theory" (world view) that individuals, through their identities, can use to guide (however imperfectly) their behaviors and to interpret the behaviors of others. Geertz similarly argued that "societies, like lives, contain their own potential interpretations; one has only to gain access to them" (quoted in Applegate & Sypher 1988: 49). These shared representations, public signs and symbols, can give us a stable sense of identity, hence confidence in dealing with others. More often than not, scholars have utilized metaphorical solutions to the problem of conceptualizing identity-in-culture.

Culture, then, forms the interpretive frame in which people organize and direct their behavior through subjectively, contextually based, identifications. Following Turner (1978: 19), the self-concept is a "relatively lasting, multifaceted cognitive structure that mediates between social environment and social behavior." Certainly, two major components of self-conception are social and personal identity (Gudykunst & Gumbs 1989). Identity, a crucial psychological *mediating process*, is what is really adaptive, not culture per se.

Once seen as a "map *of* behavior," culture is said to be viewed today as a "map *for* behavior," according to Richard Peterson (1979). Culture is no longer considered by scholars as determining behavior, then, but simply helping to prescribe actions. Hence, people use culture—strictly speaking, cultural knowledge—to organize and normalize their daily actions. The relationships among culture, identity, and communication can be represented diagrammatically using the following tripartite scheme, labeled an "integrative, adaptive-growth" model. In terms of communication, this could be called a performance-growth model or simply a performance model:

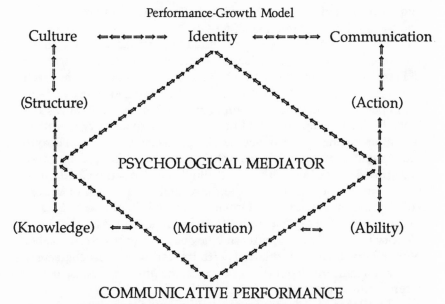

Performance-Growth Model

COMMUNICATIVE PERFORMANCE

Good communication, following Applegate and Sypher (1988: 50), is "appropriate communication," i.e., behavior right for the given social or cultural situations. The interpretive paradigm employed in this book uses field-based data (ethnography) to emphasize the contextual perspective, hopefully without giving deterministic weight to situational factors as such. People typically respond to the *meaning* of the social situations rather than simply to situations themselves (Shaver 1985).

As self-perceptions (identities) are an important link between intentions and communication, I employ the concept of "cultural situatedness" (the contextual principle) to unravel behavioral cues and provide specific cultural or social interpretations. The approach is integrative inasmuch as it attempts to combine interpretations at several levels (macro/micro, group/individual) and to consider multiple functions of identity.[11] There are always layers of meaning when considering identity in the culture-communication dialogue.

Intelligent reflection on experience is said to be the rational ground for human action; hence, social life has been metaphorically viewed, according to Yum (1988: 242–3), as a "game" involving continuous decision-making and strategies. The emphasis, in this perspective, is on people actively pursuing goals. Such an approach is seen as an attractive alternative to the usual communication models in that it is context-based, always including some aspects of the social and cultural environment (Yum 1988). The model employed in this book is similar to Yum's paradigm.

An alternative view of self might be gained through social meanings derived from more "storied experience." The life-story model of identity, as elaborated by Dan McAdams (1985), suggests that even more encompassing than roles may be the idealized *images of self* that appear to function as "main characters" in an individual's life story. In this biographical and literary approach to identity, an *imago* is similar to Jung's 1943 archetype. McAdams believes that a person's most significant relationships are profoundly influenced by these personified scripts (e.g., "the Jock," "Big Daddy," or "the Good Little Girl"). Images of self provide the individual with a plan of action, guiding the processing of information about self. "Imagoes," states McAdams (1985: 126), "are main characters in identity." Furthermore, identity is likened to a life story and the quest of identity the metaphor of that story. Identity formation (with its setting, scenes, characters, plot, and recurrent themes) is, in essence, the process of constructing a self-defining life story.

Similar to McAdams's approach, Elizabeth Stone (1989: 98–100), in her charming and engaging book *Black Sheep and Kissing Cousins: How Our Family Stories Shape Us*, conceives of family stories as "coded metaphor." Like any explanation myth, family stories carry important messages about birth, death, sexuality, injury, and madness that offer possible, if not always plausible, explanations for emotional cataclysms within the family. Such a versatile metaphor serves important stabilizing functions for the family unit.

A person is said to be culturally competent when the individual is able to effectively articulate the symbols and norms (rules, or codes of communication) of the society. Competence equals instrumental *knowledge* to effect smooth and successful interactions or communicative outcomes, what in this text is referred to as "communicative performance." Spiro (Kilborne & Langness 1987) says that culture—as public knowledge—can be learned by anyone, not just a native. Knowledge is naturally important, but it may well be knowledge of what people *believe* to be the cultural norm (Collier & Thomas 1988: 106). The role of "the situation," then, highlights the complexity of intercultural communication, for we need to know how people actually perceive cultural reality in particular contexts. In short, definitions of the situation, "important building blocks of a culture," directly or indirectly influence everyday behavior (Forgas 1984: 191).

As the nucleus around which these phenomena revolve, the role that identity plays in the communication process remains crucial. Intercultural competence, according to Collier and Thomas (1988: 112), becomes the way that social and cultural identities are affirmed, challenged, and validated. Identity is a combination of ideas about "who one is" and "how one acts" in given situations defined differently from culture to culture. Nelson Foote (1951: 20) nicely articulated this salient identity function in the succinct statement: "Without the binding thread of identity, we could not evaluate the succession of situations."

The thesis presented in this book is that identity, as a system of self-reflective awareness, potentially guides human action through perceived rules (symbolic knowledge) that connect culture and communication.[12] Cultural prescriptions, however, are rarely explicitly followed. There is always a good deal of "cultural slippage" in the process of transforming cultural propositions into culturally constituted beliefs, hence the distinction that Spiro makes between "learning a culture" and "becoming enculturated" (Kilborne & Langness 1987: 32–58). He gives the pointed example of a scholar who learns Buddhist doctrines without necessarily making them part of his personal belief system. There is a lot of cultural behavior motivated simply by "cultural clichés": nominal assent to cultural rules not totally internalized as beliefs (1987). It is important, therefore, not to assume that identity and culture are necessarily fashioned out of the same cloth.

As no two persons are likely to perceive the same situation in exactly the same way, human communication is always inherently imperfect. It has been suggested that perhaps the greatest power of human communication lies precisely in this area of ambiguity. One must, we are warned, never lose sight of the "ineffable dimension" of communication for any theoretical model that does, says Cronen and associates (1988: 76), is "uninterested in probing deeply into life's real meaning." Spiro has suggested that cultural symbols have both unconscious and connotative meanings, surface versus deep structure, as expressed most notably in metaphors (Kilborne & Langness 1987).

Music, as a case in point, is at the very heart of culture and obviously plays a powerful role in shaping definitions of self. Our contemporary youth often acquire "self-ascriptions" through music, which introduces them to the major themes of the culture. According to James Lull (1987: 28), music (whether part of the "foreground" or "background" of any communicative situation) is "the metaphorical expression of feelings associated with the way society really is," hence a cultural resource as well as cultural confirmation of identity. As a form of communication, music can provide one of the most explicit expressions of group identity. How important is music today as a source of self-definition for our youth? In trying to answer such a question, one might start by considering Marsh's notion of punk rock as the "music of the unemployed teenager" (quoted in Cashmore 1987: 248).

Intercultural communication, often as not, is contact between persons who identify themselves as distinct from one another in cultural terms. Furthermore, cultural identity, as argued here, is created through "intercultural competence." Social actors learn about these cultural "propositions" and internalize these cultural "frames" through the normal enculturative process, eventually transforming them into personal beliefs. The identification process, then, enhances as well as instigates action and behavior. Both identity formation and identity management occur during the process of communicating.

Relying on the theoretical contributions of Brim (1960), Triandis (1978), Turner (1978) and Pacanowsky and O'Donnell-Trujillo (1983), I see the link between intentions and communication as being affected by three facilitating conditions: *knowledge, motivation,* and *ability* to perform appropriate roles.[13] Communicative performance is simply the end result of this process. Identity is conceptualized as a type of personality adjustment within specific situational contexts.

Being an identity-based theory that attempts to integrate both interpersonal and intergroup levels of communication, this approach has been called an integrative, adaptive-growth perspective or, if you will, a performance model. Whereas earlier analyses often failed to give adequate weight to cognitive and affective dimensions of identity, individual choice becomes a significant factor in this theoretical perspective. People do make conscious decisions about the importance of self and the relevance of their social and cultural backgrounds, even if some people are not always clear about what is cultural, as opposed to social, in their actual experiences.

Brim's original theory of personality held that the proper explanatory variables includes not only motivation (a primary drive to human behavior) but, as well, knowledge of what culture demands and the ability to perform the expected roles of society. Pacanowsky and O'Donnell-Trujillo (1983: 131) have suggested that scholars of culture, specifically "organizational culture," consider communication as cultural "performances." For them, performances are "the very things which bring to completion a sense of reality." In my own theoretical scheme, performances equal communication.

Metaphors of Identity/A Summary Position

Clearly there are a number of contemporary theoretical perspectives to consider in trying to understand identity in the contemporary culture-communication dialogue. Metaphorical resolutions appear to be a favorite means of unraveling the mysteries of identity (Knowles & Sibicky 1990). Certainly one contemporary view is that of self as abstract cognitive structure that guides human behavior, an image-metaphor suggesting an executive role for identity. Whether seen in the context of cultural metaphors, such as "schemata," "scripts," "texts," "imagoes," "world views," "theories," or "cultural frames" of reference for constructing meaning out of human experiences, these "maps for behavior" are both a plan (blueprint) of action as well as being, potentially, the executor of human behavior, interaction, and communication (Kohut 1977; McAdams 1985: 12; Knowles & Sibicky 1990). Such image-metaphors are ubiquitous in the culture-communication dialogue.

Significant progress has been made in understanding interpersonal and cross-cultural communication in recent years; but Gudykunst and Nishida (1989: 18–19) argue that the assumptions scholars make regarding communication and culture, to a large extent, have been a function of particular theoretical paradigms and models—I would add, with their underlying metaphorical imagery. Furthermore, they isolated the "subjectivists" and the "objectivists" theorists as two major contrasting models of the social sciences. The objectivists, employing nomothetic methods of science, tend to be positivists seeing communication as "determined" by the situation (cf. Hofstede and Hall). The subjectivists, using ideographic methods, tend to be antipositivists and see communicators as having "free will," thus trying to understand specific cases rather than generalizing across cultures (cf. Cronen, Chen, & Pearce; Applegate & Sypher; Collier & Thomas).

Although most scholars acknowledge the need for better integration of these theoretical models at interpersonal, intergroup, and cultural levels, the two opposing perspectives may be only partially complimentary. Gudykunst and Nishida (1989: 39) argue, in point of fact, that integration will not be an easy task because ideology, gender biases, and differing styles of interpretation must first be overcome.

Related to this conclusion is the obvious multidisciplinary nature of such research. In addition, there is always the problem of the "normative" quality of most studies dealing with culture, identity, and communication. Scholars with strong value judgments often harden their metaphorical images into too literal interpretations of reality.

It is possible, of course, to combine these two contrasting models somewhat (cf. Ting-Toomey). My own theoretical position is slightly more compatible with the subjectivist perspective. In the tripartite scheme suggested in this chapter, communication and culture are seen as inseparable and situation as essential; but any crude, deterministic "situationalism" is hopefully avoided. Context is what is really the critical variable: relational, situational, surely; but biological, historical, social, and cultural as well. Using a convergent (pluralistic) approach to theories of culture and communication, I view situation as interpreted (mediated) through identities, i.e., through the agency of autonomous human beings, a position not unlike the phenomenological/existential scholars (Turner & Bruner 1986; Kotarba & Fontana; Anderson & Meyer 1988). In short, the attempt is to try to specify complex identity dimensions in terms of the ongoing contemporary culture-communication dialogue.

I believe that the anthropological perspective can offer valuable insights. Metaphor, too, may be an important means of conceptualizing identity in its many dimensions. In the chapters that follow, we shall examine the illusive construct of identity in some depth using ethnography, or field studies, as the basis for comparison. These ethnographic illustrations are drawn from the anthropological literature as well as from many of my own fieldwork projects, involving such diverse groups as Pacific Islanders, sexual minorities in Sweden, and ethnic groups in North America. The academic metaphor of identity—truly a transdisciplinary construct—is employed to generate new ideas about the complicated and intricate relationships between culture and communication for fields as diverse as education, psychology, anthropology, and communication, to name only a few.

Principal Points

Culture and communication models of identity were examined and critiqued in this chapter to demonstrate the importance of the principle of contextualization. A performance-growth model suggests how identity, as crucial psychological mediating process, is situated in cultural and social relationships but ultimately realized in communicative performance. Various metaphorical representations have been used in the culture-communication dialogue to highlight aspects of this many-sided phenomenon.

Notes

1. In this book, the dichotomy between macro- and micro-levels of analysis seems unfruitful since identity always starts with self-in-context; therefore, the microworld and the macroworld eventually merge.

2. Hecht and associates (1989: 177) have extended Hofstede's system to include six dimensions, dropping the term "masculinity" as being too gender-biased and adding "immediacy" and "uncertainty," for example. This extension, however, has not overcome the rather sweeping conclusions of the typology. Such systems, although old ideas methodologically refurbished, have not always provided the analytic bridge between micro- and macro-levels of analysis.

3. Markus and Kitayama (1991: 226) outline two "construals" of self: the independent (egocentric, autonomous, and self-contained) and the interdependent (sociocentric, collective, and relational) as the two major "core conceptions" of salient identities.

4. Silences and the use of indirect forms of communication are widely used in Korea and Japan. *Ma,* or silence, is dominant in Japanese communication where silences between words carry significant linguistic meaning (Gudykunst and TingToomey 1988: 107).

5. Existential sociology has attempted to study familiar but somewhat unorthodox people (not called "deviant"), such as ex-nuns, homosexuals, battered women, wheelchair runners, etc., in order to highlight the situational complexities of identity. Specific groups, in specific geographic regions, vary in the degree of individualism expressed (Kotarba and Fontana 1987).

6. Gonzalez (1989: 495) says that, in dealing with problems of translation and equivalence, the relation must be defined by giving the framework and the conditions for equivalence in any given situation. This makes the slippery concept of context difficult to comprehend in its totality.

7. Millie Creighton (1990: 297) provides a dramatic analogy of this characteristic, using the metaphorical imagery of strings to convey a sense of Japanese cultural connectedness. In order for a massive amount of string to be useful, she narrates, it has to be wound into a desirable shape—a ball. In Japanese culture, the attempt, then, is to shape human beings into such a socially desirable form through their connectedness with others. While

Americans typically place emphasis on independence, the Japanese ordinarily stress interdependence.

8. It has been written that a major fear of adult Japanese is ostracism from the group to which they belong. In Japan, an obstreperous child, Smith suggests, may be punished by being put *outside* the house (1988: 72). In the United States, being kept *in* one's room is more often the form of punishment.

9. To be sure, there are different kinds of American individualism (Bellah, et al. 1986; Wilkinson 1988) as well as a good deal of overstatement in the writings on the subjects of conformity and individualism.

10. The usual dichotomy between personal and social/cultural identity seems unnecessary here. Cultural identity depends on personal identity as all identifications are ultimately experienced through individual selves.

11. This integrative model is not unlike Anderson and Meyer's (1988) "interactive, social action" perspective.

12. This is similar in many ways to Collier and Thomas's (1988) rules theory which focused on cultural identity and intercultural competence as a function of negotiating mutual meanings, rules, and positive outcomes of behavior (Gudykunst & Nishida 1989: 36–41).

13. Collier and Thomas list other interesting dimensions of identity (1988: 113): scope, salience, and intensity. Salience is the degree to which identity is perceived to be important. Rosenberg and Gara (1985: 90) present a theory of identity structure and function that develops the notions of elaboration and contrast. Identities vary to the degree to which they are elaborated, being only fully explicated when a contrast is specified.

II

IDENTITY TOPICS IN SOCIAL AND CULTURAL CONTEXT: COMMUNICATION IMPLICATIONS

Less review-oriented than the previous section, part 2 examines identity in selected ethnographic contexts. The case-study approach highlights important issues in their own right (ethnicity, multiculturalism, gender roles, homophobia, communication, aging, and metaphor) that are of central significance for anthropology, psychology, communication, and literary criticism. This rich descriptive material is meant to help clarify basic concepts and definitions, offer new twists in the interpretation of debates in the culture-communication dialogue, and provide sufficient research data to substantiate the theoretical claims of the book. The use of metaphor as unifying theme brings additional insights into focus, while suggesting novel ways of analyzing age-old questions of identity, culture, and society. The culture-communication dialogue opens up discussions of how we can best attend to critical issues of identity in an increasingly global world made more complicated by mediated communication influences. Although individual chapters might well appeal to specialized audiences (e.g., students in upper-level theory courses in anthropology and communication), in its totality part 2 should have a wide general and professional readership.

5

○ Identity of Place or Mis-placed Identity: Media and Changing Metaphors of Ethnicity and Identity

But now she wants to be Chinese, it is so fashionable. And I know it is too late.... I wanted my children to have the best combination: American circumstances and Chinese character. How could I know these two things do not mix?

—Amy Tan, *The Joy Luck Club*

The Media and Place-defined Identity[1]

Although the media are generally assumed to be powerful shapers of culture and communication, Meyrowitz has argued persuasively that media contribute to social changes today in ways largely overlooked. He sees the media as the "missing link" between culture and personality (1986: 22). In this framework, information combines the study of media environments with the study of face-to-face situations in somewhat the same way identity itself mediates between culture and communication. How do the media unite or separate different people into similar or different informational worlds? What is the relationship between social place and physical place as influenced by the media?

Joshua Meyrowitz (1986) asked these questions and hypothesized that the electronic media—especially TV—have led to radical restructuring of social life and social performance, undermining the traditional relationship between physical setting and social situation. Electronic media are able to do this by merging formerly distinct social spheres, blurring the dividing line between private and public, thereby severing the traditional link between physical and social place

(1986: 71). The result is a diffusion of group identities. Meyrowitz speaks of this result as a "placeless culture."

Using Goffman's metaphor of the drama, which pictured humans playing different roles for different audiences, Meyrowitz borrowed the idea of "back region" versus "front region" to illustrate the shifts from once private (backstage) behaviors to now media-exposed public (onstage) behaviors (1986: 28). Groups whose *place* was formerly shaped by physical isolation (e.g., American Indian "reservation isolates"[2]) are no longer segregated from larger social groupings. Aspects of group identity, then, that were once dependent on particular physical places, as well as the experiences available in them, have been permanently altered by the electronic media (Meyrowitz 1986: 125). The concepts we use to define ourselves, so the argument goes, are influenced today by the media as symbolic place.

The theme of Meyrowitz's powerful book is that electronic media allow people to escape from traditional, place-defined groups (1986: 57). Emphasis is not so much on physical setting as place but on information, or social knowledge, that people have about the behavior of themselves and others (Meyrowitz 1986: 37). "Electronic media affect us," argued Meyrowitz (1986: 6), "not primarily through their content, but by changing the 'situational geography' of social life."

Electronically mediated interactions are no doubt reshaping both social situations and social identities (Meyrowitz 1986: 117). "Geographic identity," or identity of place, has been subtly altered by electronic media, resulting in a homogenizing effect on group identities. No longer identifying as "Samoans" from a specific island in Samoa, islanders migrating to New Zealand, for example, are today more likely to refer to themselves simply as "Pacific Islanders." The fact of migration cannot fully account for this difference. The electronic media, to a large extent, have changed the social rules of behavior. The media, of course, are not the only causes of homogenization or necessarily the ultimate molders of behavioral changes; but Meyrowitz sees the media as an important causal backdrop for such changes. The media have profoundly changed both social relationships and perceptions of self.

Wilson and Gutierrez claim that the communication media formerly kept society together by building a common culture which fed people in different parts of the country a similar diet of news and entertainment (1985: 233). The media, however, have begun to play a different role with the emphasis on marketing to separate audiences. While the communication media once built a mass audience by looking for commonalities, today they may actually reinforce differences between groups (1985: 216). Mass media can no longer afford to exclude minorities. In responding to diversity, the authors see an end to "mass" media influence. Caution is merited in drawing firm conclusions about such a multifaceted process as both cultural homogenization and social diversification seem to be happening simultaneously. The influence of mediated communication is still a reality.

Ethnogenesis/The Metaphor of Identity Construction

Few attempts have been made to look at the complex relationships between ethnicity and the cultural media. Sollors explored this seeming paradox in *Beyond Ethnicity* (1986): Whereas more and more people of different backgrounds share an overlapping culture influenced by the media, there is a strong tendency for certain groups today to insist that they are at least symbolically distinct. The process of emerging ethnicity has been called "ethnogenesis," the development and public presentation of a self-conscious ethnicity. Evidence suggests that, in today's information society, we are dealing less with the revival of ethnicity (language and custom) and more with a resurgence of ethnic consciousness (assertions of identity). John Edwards (1985), who has admirably analyzed such issues, supports the view that "symbolic ethnic markers," more often than not, are harmful to constructive community-building. In the current glorification of "militant multiculturalism," there are abundant rhetorical contradictions in the name of community as romantic metaphor.

Investigating the connections between objective cultural differences and similarities and the ethnic portrayals of such cultural differences, Roosens (1989: 47), in *Creating Ethnicity*, defined *ethnogenesis* as "how people feel themselves to be a people and how they continue to maintain themselves as such," even in the face of contradictory historical evidence. What happens to "objective culture" in ethnic interactions, and how is the media influencing human perception?

Evidence strongly suggests that people are becoming more culturally uniform. Nevertheless, some ethnic groups try at the same time to differentiate themselves by deliberate appeals to traditions (the "survival of cultural baggage" metaphor) and reinterpretations of history.[3] Many aspects of what is really going on are obscured by the use of concepts, such as "culture," "cultural uniqueness," and "past" and are often perceived by outsiders as "fake ethnic" claims. One thing is for certain, such cultural revivals are never truly a return to the past. The past is usually reconstituted to serve the group as they try to go forward (Roosens 1989: 125). The children of immigrants, for example, cannot return to a former culture that they never had. Any second- or third-generation culture is truly a "cultural mutation," to use Roosens's terminological appraisal.

Although certainly profoundly modified by media reality, the peculiarly modern tendency for certain groups to try to keep their cultural traditions (clinging to an ethnic identity) has created a huge gap between the rhetoric about culture and the everyday realities of social change and adaptation. Carroll maintains that social and cultural changes are not identical and that we may be committing a serious error when we confuse the two (1988: 136).

People today may create identities from very few cultural relics. Roosens (1989: 20) suggests, as a dramatic case in point, that naive Canadians are being forced by Indian arm-twisting to recognize a "nonexistent" Indian people. The example given is that of the Hurons, a people who recently have sought to recapture their ethnicity after being nearly culturally obliterated (1989: 32). The Hurons are described by Roosens (1989: 57) as an example of a "counterfeit culture," a deliberate attempt to construct a stereotypically "Indian counter-culture." They are described as no longer knowing their own language, and probably today would not even be identified by an outsider as phenotypically Indian.

Polyethnic countries are everywhere evident in the modern world, yet *ethnic group* is still a term often confused with *culture* in daily usage as well as in scholarly discourse. Werner Sollors has shed considerable light on this confusion (1986: 25). Arguing that the attempt to maintain ethnic distinctiveness, despite a good deal of cultural assimilation, is ultimately a source of cultural vitality, he supports the view that such "defiant ethnic revivalism" calls for a rethinking of theories of ethnicity and a clarification of the terms that describe this process of self-definition.

Ethnicity, according to Sollors (1986: 25), is a fairly new word coined by W. Lloyd Warner as early as 1941. In many parts of the world, ethnicity became fashionable in the 1960s, in vogue by the 1970s. For most people, however, the term retains connotations of minority, lower class, or else migrant status (1986: 39). Unfortunately, the metaphors used to describe ethnic groups have often reinforced this negative imagery.

Derived from the Greek word *ethnikos*, the label originally meant "heathen," not people in general but outsiders or "cultural strangers." This contrastive feature is central to the notion of ethnicity, thus generally excluding dominant groups—hence, the common-sense question, "Are Yankees ethnic, too?" Defining people contrastively gave way in the midnineteenth century to the more familiar meaning of ethnic as "peculiar to a race or nation." Nonetheless, we still retain the idea of "nonmainstream culture," as well as the religious connotation of "heathen" (Sollors 1986: 25). Writers themselves have sometimes employed conflicting metaphorical images in trying to represent the changes that have occurred in interethnic communications.

Sollors (1986: 84), for example, suggests that the "melting pot" metaphor, which has dominated the ethnic rhetoric for decades, represents an ethnic extension of the religious drama of redemption and rebirth, portraying ethnicity in the imagery of melting in contrast to the stubborn hardness of boundaries.[4] This metaphor of regeneration has gradually been replaced by a more instrumental, building metaphor suggesting that identity is something self-constructed ("achieved" identity) and morally "good." The popularity of such a generative metaphor is, according to Sollors (1986: 221), that it provides a kind of "moral map" of what people take to be "wholesome change." Metaphors help to create identities and identities often feed on metaphors, but this fact cannot assure agreement on the meaning of identity in the culture-communication dialogue.

Ethnicity has been transformed from a social liability to a desirable identity. There is, in fact, an almost voluntary ("multiple-choice") aspect of identity as a modern ethnic, claims Sollors (1986: 33), who gives the splendid example of two American-born brothers: one identifying as German-American, the other opting for a Franco-American identity. This perspective sees ethnicity as a dynamic metaphor emerging through potential negotiations of identities, by groups or individuals, in specific social contexts.

The New Ethnicity/"Defiant Cultural Revivalism"

What is the real substance of this ethnicity is the question that continues to challenge scholars of identity. When considering the "new ethnicity" (as political pressure groups), distinctions can be drawn between motivation, knowledge, and performative ability as three different aspects of role behavior. It is easier to say that one favors participating in a certain ethnic lifestyle than actually doing so.

Modern ethnic identifications work more by external symbols (symbolic identities) than any actual cultural ability, knowledge, or performance (Sollors 1986: 35). Although emphasis today is on perceived rather than real cultural differences, recognizing this distinction is not meant to downgrade the emotional significance of such attachments, which can be demonstrated to persist long after actual cultural content has dramatically changed. It is precisely the psychological, or emotional, significance of ethnic identities that remains functional. Hence, more attention today is given to the attitudinal level of identity (subjective aspects) than to overt behaviors (objective aspects), to private versus public areas of behavioral change, and ultimately to situational contexts for understanding changing identifications.

Ethnic status, in our contemporary mediated environment, can be conspicuously devoid of solid cultural content. Consider Sollors's provocative question concerning ethnicity in the United States (1986: 35–36): "Are ethnics merely Americans who are separated from each other by the same culture?" Consensus is that the term *ethnic* should be used sparingly and with caution since not all scholars can agree on the cultural basis of ethnic identities. A moral polarization is more common today, supported by our simplistic metaphorical images of culture, ethnicity, and identity. In this "idealized antithesis," ethnocentrism becomes "bad" and ethnic "good." Americans now value ethnicity regardless of what it is, concluded Sollors (1986: 179).

Sollors argues further that scholars themselves may participate in the ethnicizing process with their dualistic tendencies (1986). The media, too, offer previously isolated out-groups new forms of recognition, participation, and control (Meyrowitz 1986: 181). Although ethnic feelings and concerns are more documented and commented on by today's media, there is also increasing reaction against the rhetoric of current ethnic debates. Certainly media play a central role in reshaping relationships, hence social and cultural identities as well.

Meyrowitz (1986: 135) perceived the real sign of the times to be our sense of rootlessness caused by a media-influenced "placeless culture." "Contrary to general belief," he expounded, "the recently popular search for 'roots' and 'ethnic identity' may not be a sign of rising group identity in the traditional sense, but an indication of its decay." There is still an enormous gap between everyday *social* realities and unsupported discourse about *culture*. Confusing the culture construct with that of society is surely part of the problem, rendering sometimes overly simplistic solutions. Identity does not necessarily involve the maintenance of a separate culture, and social changes may not detract from ethnic self-awareness. In fact, such changes often enhance self-conscious identifications.

Ethnicity/Color, Class, and Culture

There are, then, definite limits to ethnicity. In *Beyond Ethnicity,* Sollors outlined how race in ethnic studies has been largely ignored since the National Socialists' campaigns of "genocide" in the name of "race," which gave the word a bad name and supported the substitution of ethnic for race (1986: 38). Race, therefore, virtually disappeared from scholarly discourse following extended criticisms of its scientific basis in the 1940s and 1950s (more recently as a result of the Pop Culture movement, which consistently lumps society with culture, labeling any group with socially perceived differences a "culture"[5]). Keefe and associates claim that "the role played by physical attributes in establishing markers of and variation in ethnicity would appear to deserve greater attention" (1989: 6). In what ways, for example, are ethnic identity and group formation dependent upon physical differences?

It has been predicted that by 2080, whites in the United States will no longer be a majority (Wilson & Gutierrez 1985: 18). At the same time, blacks are economically and socially a diverse group. A large percentage, unfortunately, risk becoming polarized into an "underclass" (1985: 25).[6] With the United States more racially integrated than at any other time in history, the media and other institutions seem positively responsive to racial diversity. In fact, today it has been argued that the "successful" image of blacks in the American media may be as far removed from reality as negative portrayals in the recent past (Wilson & Gutierrez 1985: 112).

Nevertheless, van Dijk (1987), using the method of discourse analysis, tried hard to make a case for racism in his analysis of out-of-context statements about ethnic interactions in the United States and Holland. In considering the research conclusion of a major American study (Schuman, et al. 1985) that "attitudes about general principles of racial equality and integration have steadily improved," van Dijk invoked the nebulous notion of "symbolic racism" when he found insufficient support for actual racism (1987: 224).

His study, like a lot of research on so-called cultures today, is a not-so-subtle academic polemic about racism without much concrete evidence. Granted that racism—substitute the word "ethnicism"—can be subtly combined with other forms of ethnocentrism, it seems unsatisfactory to lump them together under the umbrella term *racism*. When van Dijk recognizes that ethnic attitudes are embedded in present socioeconomic contexts, the result of perceived competition for scarce resources, he is on firmer grounds (1987: 228). To further erode his argument, van Dijk uses "ethnic prejudice" ("the mental program of racism") rather loosely (1987: 222). Recognizing differences does not automatically translate as implied "inferiority." It would be equally interesting to look at the possible prejudices of minorities toward the majority.

In my own study (Fitzgerald 1986), which involved contrasting attitudes of Polynesians and New Zealand whites, I found that each group held certain stereotypes about the other. Sometimes these were fairly serious misunderstandings, more often simply amusing. Thus, when each was asked about the other group's presumed food habits, both said essentially the same thing. "Bloody beer and fish and chips!" was the inaccurate and cryptic response. A certain amount of mutual out-group stereotyping may be inevitable when ethnically different groups live side by side, but these perceptions often serve different functions (such as, strengthening in-group ties at the expense of an out-group) without necessarily implying "racism." It really boils down to which group makes the major adjustments and in what situations. "Symbolic racism" is invoked when one can no longer find *real* racism?

Race, however, does not so easily go away. Race may be only one aspect of ethnicity, but such an important aspect cannot be swept under the carpet of a broadly conceived ethnicity. The categorical separation of race and ethnicity leads to false generalizations. As Sollors (1986: 38) has argued, we may end up with hypocrisy about our past as a result. Ethnicity often involves *color, class,* and *culture.* Today we tend to give most of the weight to culture.

We accept cultural differences but play down their racial and especially their socioeconomic consequences.[7] A wealth of evidence exists to indicate some relationship between socioeconomic status and communication styles, yet American scholars in the communication sciences remain excessively timid about addressing issues of class—not to mention race—in the culture-communication dialogue. As information about ethnic minorities is formulated and transmitted through mass media—TV is the prime example—Marcus and Fischer believe that the tendency to minimize the "socially negative" is reinforced by the widespread diffusion of communication technologies (1986: 38). Certainly class, or economic positioning, remains a controversial case in point.

Roosens (1989: 13) has argued convincingly that self-affirmation (creating ethnicity), although not a uniform process in all parts of the world, is related to the defense of social or economic interests. In short, people change ethnic identities only if they can profit by doing so. All people seek material survival, improved living conditions, and enhanced personal status.

"Not all people act this way all of the time," claimed Roosens (1989: 156), "but most do most of the time." Economics, then, play a crucial role in present ethnic aspirations; and the media—operating under economic motives—often give sympathetic support to ethnic causes, even sometimes to misleading charges of "ethnocide." "In all case studies," wrote Roosens,

> ethnicity has to do with material goods, whether in a positive or negative way. . . . .The longing for material goods does not by itself procure ethnic identity and ethnicity. Ethnicity, however, is directly concerned with group formation, and this with power relations. [1989: 158]

Ethnic groups, through media dialogues, then, become "pressure groups with a noble face" (1986: 14). Ethnic identity, it can be demonstrated, is a powerful psychological reality whether based on authentic culture or not.

An interesting paradox is that the most vocal champions of cultural revivals are almost always the educated elitès among such minorities. This is paradoxical because the slogans of ethnogenesis are formulated by the very people farthest removed from the traditional culture. Roosens argued that a certain level of economic prosperity must first be obtained before the cultural struggle of ethnic groups can achieve any lasting effect (1989: 153). This economic theory suggests that claims for revivals based on reputed tradition must rely on a substantial degree of economic security.

My earlier study of the New Zealand Maori university graduate suggested a similar conclusion (Fitzgerald 1977). The most traditional, physically isolated of the group were often the ones least concerned with self-conscious identity and self-defined ethnicity. The same theory applies to the children of immigrant parents as later generations are usually economically more secure and thus retain more political clout. As such, their demands are more likely to be accepted by members of the larger society.[8]

Sollors (1986: 29–30) has argued strongly that among ethnic groups in the United States, there is little cultural distinctiveness that can be historically authenticated. Rather, labels, slogans, and self-naming have become the important contemporary goals. "Romantic racialism" (championed by what has been called the "Aren't-Negroes-Wonderful School") has replaced real racism, and symbolically the ethnic has taken the place of the "truly chosen one."[9] "In America," continued Sollors (1986: 31), "casting oneself as an outsider may in fact be considered a dominant cultural trait."

"Vulgarized Cultural Relativism"

Certain general principles, if not totally understood, would seem to be almost universally agreed upon today: 1) People should have a right to their own "culture" without being at all sure what that culture is, and 2) People have a right to maintain their own cultural identity whether involving a separate culture or not. In short, regardless of historical circumstances, ethnic groups are claiming the "right" to both a separate identity and a matching culture of their own choosing. This presumption rests on the dubious assumption that cultures, in fact, can be discarded or created as a matter of human will. Social realities may be more complex than the cultural metaphors we use to describe them.

This philosophical shift in perspective has been traced to a "vulgarized cultural relativism" for its ideological support (Roosens 1989: 152). In its heyday, cultural relativism, a powerful doctrine of intellectual critique, was a strong liberal challenge to the neglect of human diversity (Marcus & Fischer 1986). A form of egalitarian humanism, the original position simply stated that other cultures (societies) should be viewed from their own perspectives, trying not to impose on them an outsider's values. Cultural relativism has come to be interpreted as "the equal validity of all value systems," making moral judgments virtually impossible (1986: 32). Unfortunately, an unwholesome polarization can surface when anti-relativism is offered to balance the excesses of cultural relativity. Although we may wish that people determine the content of their own cultures in an unrestrained manner, it is an error to confuse culture with society or, by extension, cultural change with social changes.

Related to the elastic use of the culture concept—more central to the concerns of this chapter—is the widespread tendency to treat culture and identity as essentially the same entity, assuming that where you find one (identity), you necessarily find a supporting other (culture). This book questions such an assumption. It is suggested that identity, due in large part to media influences, loses its place-defined quality and, in both form and function, begins to act independently of culture per se. "Ethnic group" and "culture" were concepts more or less interchangeable in scientific discourse until the early 1970s. The terms *culture* and *identity* are still blurred in popular discourse. Confusion of the constructs involving color, class, and culture remains a thorny problem for social scientists.[10]

People often gain a sense of alikeness by being isolated together, sometimes only then becoming conscious of minority status because of feelings of exclusion. Meyrowitz claimed that sharing special experiences creates a paradox as far as minority consciousness is concerned (1986: 132–33). While many such minorities loudly proclaim special identities, often based on putative cultures, unconsciously they hope to shed at least part of their "specialness" in becoming a part of a larger grouping. Protesting too much ("defiant ethnic revivalism," to use Sollors's label), in reality, may suggest a widespread degree of cultural assimilation.[11]

Meyrowitz warned that this paradoxical call for both recognition of differences and blindness to them should not be interpreted to mean that minorities espousing separate identities actually want to be in a separate culture isolated from fellow human beings. Group identity can be both positive (inclusive) and negative (exclusive), hence the familiar modern-day dialogue between social reality and cultural rhetoric, defined as "unsupported or inflated" discourse.

People can be different, then, in various social ways while still sharing the same culture. The rhetoric of distinctiveness, as Carroll (1988: 145) has reminded us, may change without the culture itself altering very much. In other words, when an individual changes socially, the cultural premises (the logic which gives order to the world) do not necessarily change. What is changed, Carroll argued, is the way of expressing the basic truths, not the truths themselves. Hence, she acknowledges the attempts of black Americans to try and create an African-American "culture," i.e., accentuate belonging to a different social group, but strongly suggests that black Americans traveling in Spain, Africa, or France will still be seen as Americans first (1988: 142). To confuse social change with cultural change is an error with serious implications for intergroup communication.

The notion of cultural authenticity is surely grounded in the idea that ethnic identity requires validation in concrete cultural or lifestyle differences; but, as Roosens (1989: 152) has informed us, cultural identity need not presume the existence of an "objective cultural continuity." Though seemingly a paradox, it is possible today to find examples of *cultural identity without a corresponding culture*. Cultural absence, however, does not preclude identity persistence. In fact, in many cases change actually accelerates identity formation.

The Lumbee of eastern North Carolina, a racially mixed group (black, white, and Indian), whose struggle to gain acceptance as "Indians" was studied in 1980, and the current movement by American blacks to have the term "African-American" adopted by the larger culture, are both social facts described by Keefe and associates as reflections of a contemporary concern with ethnic identity as political force rather than cultural authenticity (1989: 2). The new labels, for both groups, may be a way to avoid the more negative connotations of previous racial terminology. By defining oneself, ethnically or otherwise, a group escapes classification by others. Ethnic identity, as one among many possible identities in a hierarchy of identities, remains a psychological reality to be reckoned with, whether or not it is based on authentic culture.[12]

Keefe and associates (1989: 33) studied Appalachian and non-Appalachian students using three dimensions of ethnicity—structural, cultural, and symbolic—concluding that, although cultural ethnicity did not emerge in the study as very significant, symbolic and structural Appalachian ethnicity were still apparent. Parenthetically, they further suggested that, if such cultural differences do not exist from the past, it is expected that the group may well create new ones in the future in order to support the idea of difference.

The thesis is fairly clear. While cultural differences are minimal in distinguishing mountain people from newcomers, structural (class?) and symbolic ethnicity are used to construct (employing the typically American instrumental metaphor of construction) what it means to be Appalachian: "They 'know' they exist but they cannot articulate many distinctive cultural traits beyond recalling stereotypes" (1989: 34).

The Metaphor of "Cultural Property"

Richard Handler (1989: 20) offered the metaphor of "cultural property" to vividly suggest how scholars have attempted to validate ethnic identities in the face of cultural erosion. Culture becomes the property that proves the existence of a group. This possessive metaphor marks the group's existence in a concrete way and, as well, provides it with a sense of worthiness. Questions of ethnicity are often fueled by established metaphors of identity.

Citing "Ethnicity in the Museum" as an example of the metaphor of cultural property, Handler examined the issue of slavery in Colonial Williamsburg and its presentation in contemporary museum contexts (1989: 23–24). Blacks, always a significant component of the Colonial workforce, have been variously portrayed in museums over the years. In the 1950s, slavery was something not talked about; by the 1980s it was insisted that slaves had a "culture," which, argued Handler, presumably "allowed them to lead lives worth living. . .even under cultural domination." This insistence on an identity based on a distinctive culture presents African-American "culture" to the public as unproblematic; the autonomous slave culture is thereby mystified and romanticized so that the real horrors of slavery are minimized by the representation of resourceful slaves using successful cultural resources (Handler 1989: 25).

Although Handler would certainly applaud the contemporary movement to include ethnic minorities in mainstream museums, he raised an intriguing hypothesis that deserves more attention: The display of ethnic culture in museums, Handler (1989: 19) suggested, "reproduces an ideology of culture that homogenizes and domesticates rather than enhances cultural diversity." In a sense, Handler argues, all such groups are being more or less identical (doing the same thing) in such self-conscious claims for uniqueness based on so-called authentic culture. The metaphor of cultural property may function to prove minority existence but, more importantly, gives these same groups social recognition.

This conclusion supports a similar position held by the Spindlers (1990: 11), who argue that the current controversy in American education (What culture is to be maintained and passed on to the next generation?) is, in reality, a problem of how to interpret the heated rhetoric surrounding the so-called cultural debates. They believe— this author concurs—that the reality is one of psychological needs and social participation rather than seeking "cultural distinctiveness." What is relevant in today's information society may not be culture per se, but identification. Socioeconomic status[13] of minorities, another important variable, is often conveniently left out of the equation altogether "for sake of simplicity" (1990: 13).

Due to media homogenization and support, ethnics are becoming more alike even while many such groups continue to identify as "different" in certain expressive domains of their lives (a need for diversity in face of homogenizing media unity). A paramount concern for formerly underclassed groups is surely self-esteem, or the attempts to gain recognition and respect as values in and of themselves.

Royce (1982) has hypothesized that people identify as ethnics today because such groups offer extended-family functions in a time when family has diminished as a major force in people's lives. Ethnogenesis seems to be one path to this end. The influence of the media on achieving such reconstructed ideologies is enormous.

An intriguing example of how the press has helped to create sympathies for a group's identity symbols has been illustrated in the case of the recent attempted sale (in London) of a preserved and tattooed head of a Maori warrior. The case squarely raised the thorny issue of human remains as cultural property, whether belonging to the Maori of New Zealand or to archaeological science. The Maori warrior incident drew international media attention; and, because of a sympathetic press, the head was eventually returned to New Zealand (Keefe 1989: 4).

Besides seeking material goods, ethnic groups are clearly seeking recognition, respect, and self-esteem. Roosens (1989: 159), however, has reminded us that claims for material goods and resources are often intimately related to the process of gaining recognition and respect since our culture largely equates the two. Thus, some form of "positive discrimination," he argued, may be a necessary way of recognizing certain groups as worthy members of society (e.g., African-Americans). It would appear that the upsurge of ethnic consciousness (ethnogenesis) is only related to the perceived socioeconomic gains it allows individuals whose identities have been submerged or whose status has been denigrated in the past. In such a case, identity functions as a political assertion of pride in what the minority regards as its rightful heritage, in spite of any considerations of cultural authenticity. The picture, in actuality, is apt to be a great deal more complex.

Metaphors, Media, and Social Change/Second-generation Cook Islanders in New Zealand

Ethnic identity, however, can be more than merely economic advantage-seeking. This was certainly the case in my study of second-generation Cook Islanders in New Zealand (Fitzgerald 1988, 1989).

In 1985–1986, on a Fulbright travel grant, I returned to New Zealand on my third research trip to investigate aspirations of second-generation Cook Islanders born, or else reared, in New Zealand. Ethnic pluralism is a familiar characteristic of modern societies, and New Zealand is no exception. Under conditions of rapid social change, there is often intensification of ethnic identity at the same time that culture per se is diminishing. The present study was an attempt to raise some theoretical questions about identity as it relates to migration, generational position, and media influence.

Scholars, such as Bonnemaison (1985: 30), make a strong argument for cultural identity in the Pacific as essentially a geographical identity, one that "flows from memories and values attached to places." Place, or geographic residence, has been a dominant metaphor for the definition of self in the Pacific.[14] Certainly, an abiding anchor for many Pacific Island people, including migrants, has been this profound sense of land and place. Bonnemaison's image-metaphor for this phenomenon is that of a tree rooted in the earth. Furthermore, he argued, there may not be authentic identity beyond places of memory. This line of reasoning raises questions about the maintenance of identity over time, especially as migration brings about shifts in place and subsequent shifts in the loci of identity. The critical issue for second-generation, New Zealand-born Cook Islanders is how to maintain identity over the generations.

Although identity for most Pacific Islanders is still forged in the relationship between person and place (island home), what about individuals who have only dim memories of the traditions their parents associate with the true homeland? As 50 percent of those ethnically classified as Polynesians are today born in New Zealand, what are the implications for such children born or reared in one place (New Zealand) but who still identify with another (in this case, the Cook Islands, 1600 miles from New Zealand)?

Other related questions: What happens when individuals have neither the skills nor the understanding to uphold the traditions of the parent generation? For the New Zealand-born Cook Islanders, what is the *place* to which they feel the greatest attachment? What is the primary locus of their identity? Finally, what has been the effect, if any, of the electronic media on identity for this generation? In this case, should one speak of "identity of place" or "mis-placed" identity?

This study, then, looked systematically at aspirations and strivings of second-generation, New Zealand-born Cook Islanders who lived in Wellington, New Zealand.[15] Methodology included the usual anthropological participant observation as well as an extensive psychologically oriented interview schedule that probed for aspirations regarding such things as language, marriage, church attendance, work habits, visits to the Cook Islands, community participation, and even aspirations for their children's futures. Major emphasis, then, was on "hopes and fears" for the future of Cook Islanders in New Zealand.

As the theoretical perspective conceptualized identity as personality adjustment within specific social contexts, individual choice became a significant factor. Earlier analyses, by contrast, tended to slight cognitive and affective dimensions of identity. People do make conscious decisions about the importance of ethnic origins and the relevance of their cultural heritage. Thus, following primarily Brim (1960), Turner (1978), Pacanowsky and O'Donnell-Trujillo (1983), who have viewed personality differences as primarily characteristics expressed in social roles, major explanatory variables were, not only motivation—the much over-used explanation for personality—but, as well, knowledge of role demands and the ability to perform these roles. Aspirations of second-generation Cook Islanders were examined, then, considering these three factors: *motivation, knowledge*, and *ability* to perform appropriate social roles.[16]

The data suggested that identity, for the New Zealand-born, was often situational, more often symbolic than real (based on authentic culture); certainly, at minimum, bicultural if not multicultural. Choice was dependent on more than mere sentiment about place. Despite its limitations, I too used the contemporary building metaphor of self, identity being seen as something potentially negotiated, or created, within specific social contexts. It is possible, however, that such an instrumental metaphor is a peculiarly American way of looking at this complex reality.

Place was obviously complicated by the migration process itself. In New Zealand, though, there were attempts made by Cook Islanders to recreate substitute places—mini-Cook Island environments that symbolically bolstered and reinforced identity and affiliation with "things Cook Island" (for example, *tere* [dance] parties, *uapou* [religious] celebrations, or hair-cutting ceremonies at the Cook Island community hall). Thus, one did not completely lose memory of place due to several overlapping factors: a strong parental socialization, which included images of a nostalgic island paradise; the Island Church's continuous reinforcement of symbolic links between New Zealand and the homeland; possible periodic visits to the Cook Islands; and finally renewed aspects of the expressive culture, including language, music, and dance still alive in the New Zealand context.

Research results suggest that identity, for this sample, takes on an optional, almost voluntary (multiple-choice) quality, often more symbolic than real if one considers ethnicity solely in terms of authentic cultural tradition. Reiterated here is the debate discussed earlier over cultural content in ethnic identity. Interview questions, however, were aimed at measuring actual cultural participation, or cultural performance. In communication parlance, good communication equals appropriate performance, which involves more than mere motivation if identity is to have validation from outside the group (person validation or media validation). The essential question was whether performance is compromised by generational status, migration, or media.

Identity becomes an individual's strategic choice in a multicultural context, a kind of "situational selection." Within certain obvious limits, a Cook Islander may choose identification in a more or less self-conscious way. This model is in line with Roosens's (1989) notion of ethnogenesis, or the development and public presentation of a self-conscious ethnicity—perhaps a worldwide phenomenon due to media influences. Although ethnic identity can stand for almost anything, covering an entire range of entities from symbolic identity to radical cultural revivals, Cook Islanders in this sample did not manifest radical cultural revivalism as described by Roosens for the Canadian Indians (1989).

To return to the theoretical variables outlined above: The data suggested strong motivation to identify as some form of Cook Islander. This motivation, however, was not primarily culturally inspired. The present research documents a case where ethnic identity is still alive in a modern, urban setting although identity, in this case, did not necessarily involve the maintenance of a separate culture. Ethnic identity can be distinguished from objective culture even though today there are often acute discrepancies between social realities and everyday discourse about culture.

To the extent that identity was grounded in place (Cook Islands), the migrant was by circumstance displaced, and the New Zealand-born generation found its memories of the original place shifting and rapidly growing dimmer with time. Eventually the identity became mis-placed when most day-by-day experiences were firmly New Zealand-based with symbolic identity focused on a largely imaginary island culture. Evidence strongly suggests that New Zealand-born Cook Islanders are becoming assimilated into their country of birth, with some primary commitment to New Zealand, yet without totally repudiating all things Cook Island. When asked, "What is Cook Island culture?" few were very articulate about its essence. Most, nonetheless, had strong and positive feelings about this "culture." Cook Island culture, it was felt, places a high regard on all human beings and human relationships, despite differences in social class, age, or wealth. This was, at least, the cultural ideal.

For almost everyone, the essence of this "Cook Island way" was the family, or kinship ethic: "With the Cook Island family," explained one young man, "you never feel alone." Coupled with this generous spirit was the notion of a people who are basically happy, friendly, and outgoing (perhaps less intense than the Samoans, more casual than the Europeans), often characterized by a marked sense of humor. Being fundamentally a religious people, it was felt that they could teach Europeans a bit about "caring, friendliness, and showing one's emotions"—in short, about "being happy." There are often contradictions between public and private conceptions of what culture should be like. This was certainly true in the present study.

At the core of identity, then, lay the issue of self-esteem, self-affirmation, which provides feelings of pride in the group.[17] The sense of self-esteem is often spoken of, in everyday discourse, as if it were itself a cultural element. There was observed, then, a strong sentiment (motivation) for affiliation with "things Cook Island," this being the closest "emic" (insider's) equivalent of the concept of culture among these respondents. But, in the Cook Island scheme of things, culture was primarily identified with the extended family. Note that this observation is essentially Royce's discovery. People identify today as ethnics because such groups offer stable extended-family functions in an age of the declining family.

Identity surely is related to strivings for acceptance and belongingness. This factor may account for the strong sentiment (motivation) for affiliation with "things Cook Island." The essence of the Cook Island way in the 1980s was first and foremost family, respect for the elders, a sense of community (albeit restricted), and a continuing link with an idealized island paradise.

Although the motivation to identity with "things Cook Island" was not absent with this generation, knowledge of Cook Island culture, or actual participation in Cook Island activities in New Zealand (i.e., cultural domains such as langauge, food, dress, naming, ceremonies), was much less obvious; in fact, in this sample, it was statistically weak. There was passing mention of the need to maintain or revive aspects of "our culture and traditions," especially Cook Island Maori language; but there appeared to be little concrete knowledge of what these customs were and how they would be revived. Cultural erosion, then, was well documented by this study. Roosens's claim that the second generation, being a "true cultural mutation," cannot return to a traditional culture that it never had in the first place would not be challenged by this research.

Motivation to identify with a particular group or even a fair knowledge about this "culture" did not assure the ability to perform appropriate role behaviors in a New Zealand context. The second generation of Cook Islanders has had to choose new ways of life, linked not necessarily to the Cook Island culture, but to their own "semiology of place."

Performance of role behaviors was complicated by place being primarily, if not exclusively, New Zealand-based. Even with knowledge of the Cook Island heritage, there were relatively few places in New Zealand to act out this knowledge (i.e., the more restricted contexts for cultural elaboration somewhat analogous to those of American Indians isolated on reservations). Certainly, for this generation, economic rewards were more often New Zealand-inspired. This fact would seem to lend full support to Roosens's (1989) hypothesis that ethnicity may be gotten only though sacrificing what the group calls its culture.

Economy surely has a lot to do with cultural choice. Economics, then, were fundamentally important in the New Zealand equation; but psychological (existential) factors were of equal significance. Ethnic identity, at all times, is a powerful psychological reality, whether based on authentic culture or not. Identity is something that lies on a continuum marked by both negative and positive poles. This group seemed to recognize both the negative, as well as the positive, aspects of cultural retention and identity maintenance.

On the positive side, a major function of any ethnic identification is surely the anchoring of personality in smaller, more personal units as culture change renders role expectations more impersonal or problematic. Social changes, rather than detracting from ethnic self-awareness, often enhance identities. This was essentially the scenario for the first generation, thrust into a strange and unfamiliar environment as migrants. To some extent, the same may be true for these children of immigrants: not fully integrated into New Zealand society, yet sometimes too shy to venture out of the more restricted places of cultural security. This conclusion adds confirmation to Meyrowitz's (1986) brilliant observation that minorities espousing separate identities do not actually want to be in a separate culture. Identity, in this framework, functions as a kind of "face saving" device until the group is psychologically ready to proceed along the path to integration or accommodation.[18]

It is well to remember that identity often combines self-interest (the economics of identity maintenance) with strong affective ties (the psychological components of the identity structure). It is this affective component that is so often persistent, even when obvious changes in both culture and role behavior have already occurred. Identity can touch the very core of self, an existential quality metaphorically described by one scholar as "the taproot to the unconscious." For many Cook Islanders, the foundation of identification is less "culture with a large C," or even "status politics" (the new ethnicity's emphasis on economic and political gains). Rather, identity is more a fundamental sense of belongingness based squarely on kin relationships (family). Functionally speaking, identity for this group is a type of psychic shelter in times of stress and rapid change.

Too much concern with culture, cultural revivalism, and exclusive identity may have negative implications for these locally born children of immigrants in New Zealand. To insist on a cultural identity that "only partly fits," as Lowenthal (1985: 318) has stated the case, can be "a kind of patronizing colonialism dressed up as liberal social science," or even a kind of psychological compensation for economic inequalities. Such revivalism, rather than helping this generation solve its problems of identity, may intensify identity conflicts. At least a certain portion of the sample studied chose to abandon ethnic attachments altogether as a rational choice of action.

Research that over-concentrates on the replication of island culture in New Zealand will, by design, tend to exclude individuals who have become assimilated into the larger New Zealand culture and who no longer identify with the Cook Islands. One of the fascinating discoveries of the present study was the numerous examples of individuals who had already made such cultural shifts. About 16 percent of the sample had no interest in maintaining cultural affinities. They did not participate in ethnic associations, politics, or cultural events. A study of these "lost" islanders may be as crucial as studying only those who have remained within the cultural fold.

Although some groups no doubt find it more interesting to appear as cultures rather than be regarded as an underclass or a race, it may be insulting to suggest that they cannot, or should not, participate in the present world arena which has become so instantly accessible through the electronic media. The natives of Melanesia and South Africa, in fact, have accused anthropologists of adhering to a zoo theory. They claim that scholars want to keep an area and its people underdeveloped so as to have "pure" cultures to study!

This generation of Cook Islanders was certainly marked by the disappearance of many island symbols of distinctiveness, and many had only dim memories of the traditions that their parents associated with the "true" homeland. Any over-emphasis on cultural identity (based on authentic culture) may, in fact, be counter-productive. A good example would be language loyalties. What was the "first" language for this generation? Language used in the home was predominantly (79 percent) English; the "mother tongue" for the majority of these Cook Island New Zealanders was clearly English. In New Zealand there were, in fact, special difficulties involving different dialects and a high rate of intermarriage. If the language (Cook Island Maori) were to be taught in the schools, which version of the language would be chosen?

Two media outlets for Cook Island news in Wellington (at least, at the time of this study) were the "Pacific Island News" on radio and "Tangata atu motu," a television program. The young people in this sample were asked if they listened to either program regularly. The distinction between ability to perform roles and knowledge or motivation to do so became even clearer: Only 10 percent mentioned listening to either news event and then only "occasionally." The vast majority (90 percent) did not. A typical reply was: "No, can't understand it when in Maori language." Ethnic consciousness, based on language loyalty, then, is a short-sighted strategy unless it is certain that the next generation will be motivated to follow.

In a rapidly changing world, Pacific Islanders are concerned about who they are and where they are going. What did this research have to say about the future of identity for second-generation Cook Islanders in New Zealand? The majority of the New Zealand-born still preferred to identify as some type of Cook Islander. To reiterate a central theme of this book: *Identity may have important functions that transcend culture as such.* It seems possible that Cook Islanders may not need any inflated Pacific Island culture to establish their identity. With or without culture, identity has persisted.

Increasingly, however, this generation of Cook Islanders has been combining places, island and New Zealand, in dynamic ways; in so doing many have become "hyphenated New Zealanders": Cook Island New Zealanders or New Zealand Cook Islanders, depending on the emphasis. Certainly, many individuals in this sample have considered both the costs and benefits of cultural exclusiveness. One cannot afford to ignore the sinister implications of ethnic revivals. A substantial number of Cook Islanders have chosen between ethnic identification and national identity and have decided on the latter.

One neglected aspect of the ethnic equation has been the response of the dominant society. Identity persistence can be explained, to some extent, by a weak opposition from the largely European majority in New Zealand. The climate today is definitely more accepting of minority aspirations, and this acceptance is nowhere more apparent then in media coverage. However, in spite of the present goodwill of the dominant society toward ethnic aspirations, it is questionable whether, in all cases, assertions of ethnic identity best serve the needs of the entire community.

The communication media bear a special responsibility because they are potentially able to educate the general public about ethnic issues. Although they often treat the smaller ethnic minorities as fringe audiences, the media in New Zealand seem to be responding positively to racial and ethnic diversity. It is now the goal and policy of the New Zealand news media that, ideally, there should be integrated news coverage. The lack of opposition to cultural aspirations, then, has been fundamental to the legitimization of ethnicity in New Zealand. Furthermore, access to media and technology prevents any real turning back for this generation. There is slim chance that the second or third generations can ever return permanently to the Cook Islands, homeland of their parents or grandparents. No matter how this generation may feel about its socioeconomic position in New Zealand society, there is effectively no going home again.

For one thing, the media have changed the locus of former identities of place. Merging social spheres and severing the traditional links between physical and social space, the media result has been, as Meyrowitz predicted, a diffusion of group identity yielding a more or less "placeless culture." Even individuals in the first generation are no longer likely to identify themselves in New Zealand as Rarotangans, or Aitutakians (two of the fifteen islands within the Cooks), but simply as Pacific Islanders. Those in the second generation carry the diffusion even further, identifying as New Zealand Cook Islanders or Cook Island New Zealanders. The electronic media have changed the social rules of behavior. Neither generational position nor the fact of migration fully accounts for these differences.

Roosens has argued that it is exceptional for people to lock themselves voluntarily into traditional cultures when there are economic incentives to participate in a larger technology (1989). Economic factors were indeed important with second-generation Cook Islanders in New Zealand. Television, Roosens writes, has made the mass influence of material products significant in ways unheard of a few years ago. It is generally recognized that the young universally are attracted to Western material goods advertised through the media, for these products symbolize personal freedoms over restricted parental controls (1989). In addition, no generation today can totally ignore the work demands of a modern economy and remain successful within it. According to Roosens (1989: 135), there are limits, despite the present academic emphasis on "romantic racialism," to how far a power majority can be asked to adapt to the needs of an underclass minority.

My study of second-generation Cook Islanders (Fitzgerald 1988, 1989) demonstrated that self-affirmation is related to social, economic, *and* psychological interests. Although there are surely complexities in trying to organize bicultural—in this case multicultural—education for children of immigrants, this research strongly suggests that a vibrant and peaceful ethnic identity is possible in a truly multicultural society. Ethnic identity would seem to have important psychological functions, hence should be nurtured, without falling into the trap of assuming there must be a corresponding separate culture. The challenge is to encourage a strong national identity, while still recognizing a variety of different interest groups, ethnic styles, and the persistent need for separate minority identities which carry with them a degree of self-esteem, dignity, and pride. This pattern of recognizing "cultural" identities without separate cultures, fits the official, though at present unrealized, goal of an emerging multi-culturalism in New Zealand.

We shall have more to say about this thorny issue of multiculturalism in chapter 9. At this point, suffice it to say that over-enthusiastic approaches to multiculturalism can have negative as well as positive effects. Edwards (1985: 131) believes that all education worthy of the name is fundamentally multicultural—of course, societies should promote tolerance and understanding—but he also recognizes a darker side of this debate. Militant multiculturalism can actually be used to force people into positions of less, rather than more, awareness of cultural and social diversities (1985: 136). Ultimately we need some middle ground between current academic debates and public discourse. Before we grapple with this complex controversy, let us turn our attention to another important context for identity enactment, namely the gender puzzle. Gender identities can challenge our most sacrosanct assumptions about identity as it is presently being discussed in the culture-communication dialogue.

Principal Points

Fundamentally the culture-society debate revisited, this research represents a case where identity is alive and well in a modern urban setting, but this identity does not necessarily involve the maintenance of a separate culture. There is often an enormous gap between everyday social realities and rhetoric about culture. Social changes and cultural change are not identical, and to confuse the two often leads to serious misinterpretations about communication. Identity, due in part to mediated communication effects, loses its place-defined quality and, in both form and function, begins to act independently of culture per se. The conclusion is that identity can have significant functions that transcend culture as such. This argument raised the question of how best to nurture a strong national identity, while still recognizing the psychological need for various minorities for separate and symbolic "cultural" identities. An ethnographic example from the South Pacific illustrated how the media contribute to changes in both culture and identification, thus challenging positive implications of so-called cultural revivals.

Notes

1. A condensed version of this chapter appeared in *Media, Culture & Society* (SAGE: London), 13: 193–214, 1991, and in P. Scannell, P. Schlesinger and C. Sparks, eds. *Culture and Power* 112–133 (SAGE: London), 1992.

2. Compare the "geography of Indianness," when the reservation itself becomes a significant place for self-definition.

3. Consider the predictions of unity *and* diversity in *Megatrends 2000* (Naisbitt and Aburdene 1990).

4. Echoing this position is the amusing Ford Motor Company's English School Melting-Pot ceremony for foreign-born employees (1916), who would undergo a ritualistic rebirth especially designed by their employers. During the graduation exercise, they were led down into a symbolic melting pot, eventually emerging fully dressed in American clothes and carrying an American flag! (Sollors 1986: 89–90).

5. In defiance of all anthropological common sense, today we speak of "cultures" of men and women; youths and elderly; gays; the deaf; organizations or corporations; media; the workplace; blacks and whites; "cognitive," "symbolic," and even "subjective" cultures. Many anthropological studies perpetuate the trend started by Montegu (1972), i.e., substituting

the term *ethnic group* for the more emotionally loaded label *race*. Others have followed with the substitution of *ethnic group* with the very elastic term *culture*, eventually resulting in confusion of the constructs of race, ethnicity, and culture.

6. Fox and associates made a particularly strong case for ethnogenesis being a replacement for formerly class-based forms of social protest (1978: 130). This insightful observation suggests that ethnicity may be a more salient strategy than socioeconomic *class* for the mobilization of a political following. Arguments can be advanced against such a position.

7. Ron Miller has described attempts of the American Civil Rights Movement to rethink its course (1989: 6). If *race* remains at the center of the movement, so he reasoned, it is bound to fail. About 70 percent of America's underclass is black. In practical terms, this necessitates a strategy of downplaying exclusive minority-interest programs in favor of those benefiting all members of the growing lower classes—a political coalition that could stress similarities rather than differences. A brilliant observation even if one unlikely to succeed in our present climate of denial.

8. Some have argued that Hansen's law ("What the son wishes to forget, the grandson wishes to remember") proves that assimilation does not occur in a consistent way, but Herbert Gans says that Hansen's law applies only to academics and intellectuals; in fact, he argues strongly that the whole ethnic revivalism of the 1970s was mainly a revival limited to intellectuals (quoted in Sollors 1986: 216). He concludes that there is little empirical evidence for such a "law."

9. Communication scholars who misuse the constructs of cognitive or subjective culture to justify black-white differences in social behavior demonstrate the subjective, cognitive power of "romantic racism." While differences in communication patterns between blacks and whites are consistently observable, there is the real possibility that these are more attributable to social status than to either ethnicity or culture. Research that controls for social class differences (rather than labeling such differences "cultural," "ethnic," or "cognitive cultural styles") is needed to validate the numerous ethnographically based communication studies that posit a black culture versus a white culture as reality. Compare Hanna's (1986) suggestion that "body in motion" behavior for black Americans has its roots in Africa and the experiences of slavery; Ting-Toomey's (1986) contention that Blacks retain a distinctive subjective culture of values and norms of interaction in the context of the white culture's influence; and Kockman's (1986) more serious claim that many communication problems between blacks and whites result from differences in their "cultural frames of reference." All such studies cry for empirical challenge, especially when the examples given in the literature are so patently noncultural!

10. Consider Wallerstein's provocative counter response about culture (1990: 64–65): "Why then is Roy Boyne, and many others, so agitated about, so defensive about, the *chasse gardée* of culture? I suspect that he sees in 'culture' the expression of human freedom and free will against the evil mechanical oppressive demons that govern us (the 'political economy'?). If so, he is truly barking up the wrong tree. If anything, culture is a word that describes what constrains us (in the most effective way possible), by shaping our 'will' that seeks to assert its 'freedom'), and is not a word that describes our ability to escape these constraints."

11. "[A]n Afro-American and the grandson of a Polish immigrant will be able to take more for granted between themselves than the former could with a Nigerian or the latter with a Warsaw worker" (Sollors 1986: 14).

12. Dr. Elizabeth Natalle, a communication colleague, made the valid point that, regardless of whether social, racial, sexual, or cultural differences are at issue, we still need to deal with these differences. Precisely, but my personal caveat remains that, if we are not clear about the kinds of differences we are talking about, the solutions chosen to address such diversity may be inappropriate.

13. Cultural issues are hotly debated in the communication sciences. Consensus, however, is not always forthcoming. Whereas some European and British scholars get hung up on critical cultural analyses of a somewhat questionable Marxist ideology, American communication scholars are apt to be turned off by this approach, so much so that they deny socioeconomic (class) realities altogether, emphasizing instead some version of the romantic, but nebulous, notion of cultural revivalism.

14. "Spatial identity" is similar to "identity of place." A North American example might be the "geography of Indianness," where the reservation itself becomes a significant place for self-definition: "Despite the persistence of native traits, theirs is not the aboriginal culture, but a 'reservation culture,' a distinct and novel form, adapted to their peculiar mode of existence. It is the groups with these 'reservation cultures' that constitute what is referred to as the 'Indian problem'. . ." (Wax, et al. 1989: 2).

15. The Cook Islands are now independent, although migrant Cook Islanders in New Zealand hold dual citizenship somewhat in the way that Puerto Ricans do in the United States. The second generation, caught between two countries, makes for an interesting social and political subject for anthropological investigation.

16. The fact that my model treats ethnic groups as categories of interaction examined in a framework of social role behavior in no way precludes analyses based on broader, structural variables, which obviously can set limits to personality. The present theoretical frame is extended

by the addition of questions about media influence, à la Meyrowitz (1986).

17. According to Markus and Kitayama (1991: 230), the concept of self-esteem should be replaced by the term "self-satisfaction" when dealing with cross-cultural data because "esteeming self" may be primarily a Western phenomenon. Their argument for recognizing diversity in individual versus interdependent cultures (Cook Islanders can be associated with the latter) is a valuable one in pointing out some of the complexities of the situation.

18. Similarly, Stone (1989: 6) has made the point that family stories, though not always factual, are central to our individual identities, often "nudging and pushing" immigrants (or children of immigrants) "in the direction of assimilation." She does not, however, see this process as "bad." Like identity itself, family stories are, metaphorically speaking, blueprints of reality guiding the individual in times of stressful change, or social and personal dislocations.

6

○ Males in Transition: An Identity Challenge

An adequate theory must account simultaneously for the considerable behavioral similarity between women and men on the one hand and for the implication of membership in exclusive social gender categories, which through their social constructions, define contrasting expectations for women and men on the other.

—Suzanne Skevington and Deborah Baker, *The Social Identity of Women*

Constructions of Masculinity and Oppositional Identity

The male sex role in many Western societies has become damaging to the health of men. The number of book titles, both scholarly and popular, stressing the negative side of traditional male behaviors is growing rapidly: *The Hazards of Being Male, Beyond the Male Myth, What You (Still) Don't Know About Male Sexuality, The Phallic Mystique, Sexual Solutions, Men From the Boys, Changing Men, The Flying Boy: Healing the Wounded Man,* and *Recovery Plain and Simple,* to name only a few.

Statistics in contemporary America come to the same conclusion. It is men who are primarily dying of heart attacks, hypertension, ulcers, suicides, AIDs, and early death. Herb Goldberg's *The New Male: From Self-Destruction to Self-Care* symbolizes this genre of books on males and masculinity with its strong suggestion that the American male is indeed in crisis (1980: 30–31). He predicted that, being more susceptible to degenerative diseases, men will be living ten years less than women by the next century. The paradox, he stressed, is that the most health-nurturing behaviors are associated with "feminine" values whereas "male" attitudes are more often associated with physical self-destruction. The relationship between the social and cultural construction of male gender and these alarming health warnings is reasonably clear. Inspired by the women's movement, men, it is fairly certain, can do something about the situation.

Don Johnson argues that men have no choice (1989: 59). They must change their traditional gender roles; yet, in doing so, they will seek an identity that is comfortably and truly masculine. Nearly twenty-five years have elapsed since the initial challenges of feminism in the mid-1960s; and men have responded in a variety of ways depending on factors such as class, race, and age. Seidler feels that men have reacted to feminism with a high degree of sympathetic detachment rather than commitment to fundamental changes in themselves (1989).

Certainly we see more media attention to the so-called "male mystique" ("What Do Men Really Want?" asks Sam Allis of *Newsweek*, June 24, 1991). If change has occurred with American males, what is this new male identity? How has culture influenced its construction? What is the relationship between the media and the process of transforming gender identity?

I would like to approach the subject of personal definitions of masculinity and changing male roles from an identity point of view. What have been the functions of the traditional male role? Is the masculine ideology really universal? Have the societal pressures for being a man really changed in our own culture? How can we better understand the dynamics of gender identity?

One rather interesting line of research (Herek 1987: 68–82) has examined the notion of "being a man" in contemporary American society and its relationship to the still widespread "fear of homosexuals." In other words, is there a connection between the social construction of male gender and the reaction of homophobia—the extreme psychological hostility felt and acted out toward gay men in particular?[1] Is this association true of other cultures? The empirical evidence for such an observation, Greg Herek suggests, is threefold: 1) Experiments show that, by and large, men hold more homophobic attitudes toward homosexuals than do females. 2) Males, at least in American culture, retain more traditional views of gender and family roles than females. 3) Negative attitudes toward lesbians and gay males have consistently correlated with traditional views of gender and family roles. It may also be true, as Helen Hacker (quoted in Kimmel 1987a: 17) has argued, that "masculinity is more important to men than femininity is to women because men have so much more at stake. . . ." But, surely homophobia is only a symptom, not the cause of this emphasis?

Caution is merited in drawing firm conclusions about such a complex process; but the explanation may lie, in part, in the socialization experiences of males and females, which surely transcend American cultural boundaries. Sexual identity is not the result of human physiology alone. Sexual aims and sexual identities are structured during early childhood experiences. The meanings we give to sexuality are socially, culturally, and psychologically conferred (Almaguer 1989: 81). Within limits, then, there is the argument that children of different sexes are treated differently by adults, consistently reinforced for sex-appropriate behaviors, and thereby taught specific sex-linked communication styles (problem-solving strategies, conversational patterns, conflict-resolution techniques, and so forth). Miscommunication between the sexes as adults, at least in part, is seen to be related to these differentially learned and reinforced childhood behaviors (Maltz & Borker: 1982). As different cultures place different emphases on what is considered appropriate male or female behaviors, communication styles not unexpectedly vary from one cultural group to another.

We need to distinguish between the biological existence of the sexes and the social construction of gender roles. Some researchers believe that the discontinuity in male socialization creates special identity problems for boys. As a case in point, boys and girls, it has been suggested, develop different relational capacities. This fundamental difference in male versus female gender formation carries crucial implications for adult role behavior. In many cultures, not just our own, there is early female indulgence of male babies, with close identification with mother. At the appropriate age, boys are suddenly yanked out of that security, often with violent and dramatic initiations to accomplish this feat ritually and symbolically, and expected to "be men." Compare Raphael's *The Men from the Boys*, which explains how male initiation ceremonies accomplish this symbolic break. Many scholars concur that there are special liabilities for boys who try to overcome this previous sense of psychological unity with mother in order to achieve an independent identity defined by the culture as masculine.

Almaguer has argued that women generally develop more permeable ego-boundaries than men due to their greater bonding with their mothers (1989). They develop expressive or nurturing qualities, becoming more empathetic and interested in "relational" issues. Consequently, they are not as likely as men to seek connectedness through their sexuality. Young boys, on the other hand, typically do not develop such affective qualities. "Their gender identity crystallizes around becoming fiercely independent, rational, competitive, tenacious, manipulative and, above all, dominant" (1989: 81). Furthermore, these characteristics are often defined "in opposition" to feminine qualities. "Thus, male identity emphasizes difference over sameness, separation over connectedness, boundaries over continuity, and independence over interdependence." (1989: 82) The message is clear. Although biological sex is, of course, rooted in nature, gender and sexual identities are not.

Another complicating factor in gender socialization for boys is "father absence." It has been estimated (Family Research Council statistic) that an American father spends, on average, less than ten minutes a day in direct conversation with his children! Robert Bly (1990) has called the result "father hunger." Since boys in many societies have to imitate a father rarely observed, anthropologist Nancy Chodorow (quoted Meyrowitz 1986: 204) has argued that little boys have not always experienced the masculine world first-hand; therefore they have tended to approach identity tentatively and largely in terms of abstract rights and duties.[2] Boys have had more experience with what they are *not* supposed to be like than with what they are to become. In such circumstances, boys find their identities necessarily difficult to achieve.

Lorraine Tamsin confirms Chodorow's conclusions about the negative effects of fathers' absence on male identity (1991: 88). In effect, boys must often identify with a "fantasized masculine role." In *Gender, Identity and the Production of Meaning*, Tamsin restates a recurrent theme in the gender-theory literature (1991: 186): The masculine "self-strategy" is still one based primarily on opposition in many cultural contexts.

Men learn as children that identity is not an easy task. They must distance themselves from women and anyone they perceive to be "like women." To reiterate the thesis presented here: Men who feel that they have to be different from both women and homosexual men construct an *oppositional identity*, an identity based on negative (opposite) poles, rather than positive ones. This is only a hypothesis but may explain a good deal about the male psyche in many cultures, or among certain classes within a single culture. The question is, How widespread is this phenomenon of oppositional identity? What are the broader, structural factors influencing its etiology, persistence, or change?

"Manhood in the Making"/The Metaphor of the Voyage

Anthropologist David Gilmore has examined male ideology in light of a broader theory of economic adaptation (1990: 230). Couched in ethnographic context, manliness is viewed as a symbolic script, a cultural construct, that is both variable from culture to culture but, interestingly enough, not always necessary in all cultures. The thesis of this valuable book is that there may well be something in complex competitive environments that demands from males the more traditional role responses inherent in the stereotypic manhood ethic.

Manhood ideologies, in short, are adaptations to social environments. Gilmore regards manhood as an inducement for high performance in the struggle over scarce resources (1990: 224). Gender ideologies are seen as pressuring people into acting in certain ways that have indirect adaptive structural consequences.[3] This theoretical approach links masculinity (manhood imagery) to its broader social and psychological ramifications. The harsher the environment and the scarcer the resources, argues Gilmore, the more traditional definitions of manhood will be stressed.

Although the causal connections are admittedly more tenuous, Gilmore feels that there is a systemic relationship between gender ideology and the material conditions of life. Culture is, after all, a human device for adaptation. Gender identity merely serves this cultural end. One may recall earlier discussions of identity functions in the culture-communication dialogue.

Like the problem of assuming a sameness between culture and identity (chapter 5), there has been a tendency in analyses of gender identity to equate sex and gender and both with an idealized and polarized identity. A gendered, or sexed self, is not always unitary at the level of personal identity (Skevington & Baker: 1989). Likewise, there is always the possibility of multiple identifications not fixed to male or female positions, such as sexual preferences (Butler 1990: 75). Gender is historically and culturally specific. Furthermore, it is most often *beliefs* about gender rather than gender differences themselves that are at issue. Ethnographic accounts attest to this observation. A male sex, for example, need not assume a corresponding male gender identity although in most cases cultural conditioning assures its happening.

Cultures vary tremendously in their assignment of sex roles. Although certainly influential, biology alone does not determine human behavior. Gender becomes largely a symbolic category, an overlapping continuum of possibilities. Many, if not most, cultures exaggerate the biological ends of this spectrum by defining as culturally proper "opposite" behaviors for men and women. Gilmore feels that the answer to the manhood puzzle lies primarily with culture (1990: 23). Why does culture use these biological potentials in often specific ways that we associate with a "male ideology" or "masculine ethic"?

"Are men everywhere alike in their concern for being 'manly'?" asks Gilmore (1990: 9). Examining the ethnographic evidence for sex-appropriate roles, he concludes that there are indeed some striking regularities across cultures. Although not all cultures can be characterized as "macho," manhood in most known cultures of the world is seen as something psychologically problematic, a critical threshold through which all boys must pass. Tests of masculinity (such as circumcision rites, whipping, hazing, and other forms of masculine endurance) become crucially important in the development of a masculine identity. Female gender identity, it should be noted, is rarely questioned in the same dramatic and public way (1990: 11). In many cultures, there is a strict demarcation between the cultural domains of men and women as well as scornful prohibitions against those who dare to invade the "cultural space" of the opposite sex.[4]

Some males learn, at an early age, to assume a culturally approved masculine pose often built on the negation of anything believed to be "womanly." One must recognize, within any single culture, the existence of differing responses to this "masculine imperative." Thus, rather than viewing men as a homogeneous gender, it is more helpful to see men as a heterogeneous social grouping. Not only do responses differ from culture to culture, but also from region to region and, as well, by class, race, age, and ethnic background. At least in modern societies, there are always many "masculinities."

However, in cultures that place an excessive emphasis on male imagery, masculinity has often involved a negative identity learned through defining self oppositionally, i.e., through negation of self— what one is *not* rather than what one *is*. Seidler (1989) has pointed out that male identity in many contemporary societies is an identity learned through defining itself as opposed to "emotionality and connectedness." In cultures that stress such "compulsory masculinity," boys are mostly concerned with proving that they are not like girls. Theirs, then, is an "oppositional identity." In considering the relationship of identity, culture, and communication to gender issues, it is easy to see how the human potential has sometimes been aborted by too rigid social or cultural conditioning.

Communication distortions may occur when the masculine self-image is excessively oppositional, defensively filtering out potentially positive responses that might threaten one's view of self (Goldberg 1980: 127). To let go of a destructive self-image has been interpreted as a kind of "identity annihilation" for many men (1980: 162). The question for the contemporary male, liberated from the economic and social-conditioning constraints of a masculine imperative, is how to move away from the more destructive aspects of an oppositional identity (without abandoning a sense of maleness) toward societal reintegration and psychological growth. We need some theoretical bridges to accomplish this goal.

Identity "Elaboration" and Identity "Contrast"/Theoretical Bridges

The constructs "elaboration" and "contrast" are two critical properties of identity-in-culture that may help theoretically to explain identity change. Since positive self-images tend to be more elaborated than negative ones, Rosenberg and Gara have suggested that the notion of *elaboration* plays a central role in identity function or dysfunction and that identities vary considerably in the degree to which they are elaborated (1985: 94). Therefore, as we shall discuss presently, metaphor analysis may be one way to help individuals further their options and choices. Rather than restricting themselves to identities that limit personal growth, the goal is to adopt a degree of elaboration, or personality flexibility in role behavior. Men allow themselves more gender elasticity, as it were.

The American men's movement may illustrate how this process works. In today's information world, men are increasingly forming support groups and discovering that they, too, can be sensitive and caring, expressive as well as strong and assertive. Unfortunately, creators of the media perpetuate the belief that the beginning of the men's movement in the United States started with Bill Moyers's PBS special "A Gathering of Men," a 1990 documentary on the poet Robert Bly, author of *Iron John*. In actuality, it is probably a good deal more historically accurate to see the men's movement (men's movements[5]) as a reaction to the women's movement. Allis claims that the women's movement made men examine their own feelings but did not substantially alter what society expected of them (1990: 81).

The viewpoint currently held is that the American men's movement has tended to focus on psychological modes of expression rather than grappling with serious political and social issues, as has

been the case with the women's struggle. Interpersonal communication has been of central focus. The goal is to help men overcome
cultural restrictions against revealing feeling and emotion. American
males seem to want to be in touch with their emotional selves; at
least this may the case with middle-class men who have tended to
make up the bulk of these associations.

Another important property of identity structure and function
is *contrast*. Not the negative contrast of oppositional identity, but a
positive assessment of similarities and differences. This is especially
the case with sexual identities. An identity can be said to be fully
explicated only when its contrast is also specified. Hence, the point
made earlier that understanding masculinity calls for a parallel
understanding of its perceived opposites (femininity and homosexuality).[6] One learns to appreciate difference rather than trying to
reject it when found in one's self.

The properties of elaboration and contrast give us theoretical
perspective on why identities are judged as satisfying or unsatisfying
by individuals and groups within a given cultural context. They can
guide us in better understanding the nature of individual change. In
short, such theoretical constructs afford us a fresh perspective on
identity-in-culture.

Anthropology has made important contributions to the debates
over the meaning of masculinity cross-culturally. The quest for
manhood, most pronounced in societies where men must fight for
contestable scarce resources, is pictured as both culturally precious
and psychologically elusive (Friedl 1984; Raphael 1988; Seidler 1989;
Lattas 1990; Gilmore 1990). Real men do not emerge "naturally" but
must be shaped by culture, "nurtured" and "prodded into manhood,"
according to Gilmore (1990: 106). Using the imagery of the voyage,
Gilmore sees a metaphoric connection between masculine rites of
passage and the difficult stages of male psycho-social development
(1990: 123). Speaking of the traditional "macho" cultures and their
voyage to manhood: "[T]hey all navigate a pathway to manliness that
is without clear signposts." Thus, one finds in the ethnographic record
numerous examples of "virility anxiety," the obsessive worries about
male validation manifested differently in different cultural contexts.[7]

This "voyager to manhood" often encounters what Ray Raphael
(1988) has labeled the "crisis of masculinity." Raphael felt that the basic
plight of the contemporary American male is how to establish an adult
masculine identity in a unisex environment that lacks clear-cut rites
of passage for men. Initiation serves as a bridge from one natural stage
of life to another, similar to Garfinkel's (1986:9) "road to manhood,"

the "voyage" being a metaphor for male growth. Raphael (1988: 184–5), however, argues that we lack the structural supports for this difficult transition.

Initiations in any culture should help to "separate the men from the boys," but at least in America these rituals have become largely dysfunctional. The result is a separation of men from men, and ultimately from women as well. Since men still need to validate and affirm their masculinity, so the argument goes, the frustrations of an unfulfilled manhood create "makeshift males" instead. It is difficult to break the cultural pressure to make our lives as males fit the metaphors that give the imagery of power to our existence.

Manhood may indeed have to be validated in most cultures of the world. Male risk-taking, if Gilmore (1990: 99) is correct, ultimately can be related to economic productivity; but the presence of androgynous cultures raises challenging questions about the universal need for masculinity in male development. How universal is the stereotypic male experience? Can we find examples of masculinity without opposition?

Masculinity Without Opposition/Androgyny and Other Cultures

Although Margaret Mead (1935) had already pointed out the variability of sex roles in *Sex and Temperament in Three Primitive Societies*, Gilmore chose to cite Levy's (1973) study of Tahiti and Dentan's (1979) ethnography of the Semai of Central Malaysia as "androgynous cultures" that do not seem to care about manhood as we define that concept. I shall briefly summarize these colorful accounts (Gilmore 1990: 201–9; 211–19).

Tahiti

Levy's study of Tahiti, formerly part of French Polynesia, showed a clear lack of sexual differentiation and sexual role playing. As Paul Gauguin is said to have observed much earlier: "[T]here is something virile in the women and something feminine in the men" (quoted Gilmore, p. 203). By cultural dictate, there were no jobs or skills reserved exclusively for either sex. Men apparently had no fear of acting in ways Westerners considered "effeminate."

Theirs, then, was not an identity based on oppositions, but rather one characterized by role "cross-overs." Men showed no discomfort (no evidence of anxiety) in assuming a female gender identity. There

were no observed differences between males and females in character
or moral characteristics. Effeminacy, according to Levy, was a general
and ordinary kind of male personality. Furthermore, Tahitian language,
it was observed, does not express gender grammatically. Few
environmental demands were made on Tahitian men. The economy
fostered an unusual degree of cooperation as families helped each other
out both in fishing activities and in the harvesting of vanilla and taro.
The ethnographer described Tahitian temperaments as mild, gentle,
and unaffected. There was, however, a modest rite of passage for boys,
with superincision of the penis involved.

Another interesting feature of Tahitian culture was the
institution of the *mahu*, the village transsexual who elected to be an
honorary "woman" and sometimes (although sometimes not)
homosexually entertained men and boys by offering sodomy and
fellatio to "her" clients. She was an accepted part of this androgynous
cultural scene.[8] Levy says that men showed no interest in proving their
masculinity in relation to the *mahu* or in the culture more generally.

The evidence here suggests strongly that masculinity is not a
matter of much concern for Tahitians. Manliness is not "separate and
opposed" to femininity; apparently it is not an important symbolic
and behavioral category in this island paradise.

The Semai of Central Malysia

Another example cited of an androgynous culture is the Semai,
described as among the most retiring people in the world (Gilmore
1990). Aggressiveness is *punan*, or taboo, among these Malaysian
people. Not wanting to hurt another person's feelings, they express
no sexual jealousy; hence, adultery is rampant. Passive and
noncompetitive, the Semai personality is founded on a strictly
nonviolent self-image. There are no sporting competitions, no contests
in this culture. Children are rarely disciplined, and the Semai do not
distinguish between a male-public and a female-private realm so
commonly observed in other societies.

In the economy, there is little stress on personal property. Land
is relatively plentiful. There is, among these gentle people, no private
ownership. Semai place little importance on sex differences either in
assigning social roles or in assessing temperament. Women, less
frequently community leaders, nonetheless participate in political
affairs. Few traits, then, can be associated by them as distinctly
masculine or feminine. The only strong symbol of virility that persists
is the men's blowpipes, which are still highly coveted by most men.

The Tahitians and the Semai, in Gilmore's summary, represent cultures that do not seem to care much about manhood as we usually understand this notion. Neither has an identity based on oppositions. Gilmore surmises that they both lack economic incentives to strive or compete as men do in many male-dominated cultures. When the economy is cooperative, ambition is devalued. "In short, there is little basis for an ideology of manhood that motivates men to perform under pressure or to defend boundaries." (Gilmore 1990: 218)

Although not proven, his is a materialist stance, hypothesizing a causal relationship between ideology and environment which, in turn, influences psychological identification. His conclusion that there is little or no social pressure to "act like men" would seem to support the feminist position that cultural variables outweigh nature in the gender puzzle (1990: 219). The Semai and the Tahitians, for whatever historical reasons, have elected a strategy of avoiding stereotypically male confrontations. Gilmore felt this was the probable explanation for their lack of a strong manhood ideology based on an oppositional identity (1990: 219). We can profit from greater familiarity with ethnographies which compare differences and similarities between men and women in identity construction as well as those that consider the reactions of others to these identities.

Androgyny/A Problematic Metaphor?

Will the "androgyne" (not all male or all female) become the future flexible gender type—"rational and emotional, strong and nurturent, assertive and compassionate, depending on the demands of the situation"? (Meyrowitz 1986: 194). Empirical evidence has suggested that the so-called androgynous person may be a more "successful" psychological type than the more traditionally identified masculine or feminine personality (Bem 1974). It is equally clear that a number of contemporary scholars have sought to eradicate the sexual divisions on which many societies are presently based—ultimately doing away, not only with male privilege, but with the sex distinction itself (Butler 1990). How useful is "androgyny" as a concept in providing a theory of human personality development? (Singer 1976).

Androgyny, from the Greek word *andros* (man) and *gyne* (woman), is the classical metaphoric image of the "part-woman/part-man" personality with traits of both genders. As an ideal type, the androgynous style seeks to break the historical (but no less arbitrary) connections between sex and gender. As a scientific metaphor, however, the concept has been viewed as utopian, provisional, and often misleading. Warren (1980: 184) has warned us of the problematic nature of such an ideal. First, there is the difficulty arising from its metaphorical status. Recall that metaphor tends to highlight one aspect of reality while obscuring another. Secondly, Warren argued, if taken too literally, the concept can have implications inconsistent with its real purpose, which is to eradicate sexual stereotypes.

Psychological androgyny, Warren (1980: 183) pointed out, is only a metaphor as the traits being combined are not naturally or inevitably the monopoly of either sex. There are dangers in interpreting this metaphor. With metaphors, there is always something you are trying to understand in terms of something else (Dr. Mark Turner, personal communication, 1991). Use of such analogies helps us to grapple with context. But therein lies its major weakness as a scientific tool, especially in the analysis of a normative ideal? The use of metaphor to understand complex socio-cultural changes in gender relations raises an important question: To what extent does the "androgynous metaphor" broaden or restrict our understanding of gender identity?

Androgyny can be even more problematic if the imagery is unclear. Is androgyny to be understood as hermaphroditism? Would it imply shared roles, the healthy person always having traits of both genders in equal proportions? Would it allow for a variety of options, acceptable gender alternatives and thus greater gender freedom? Or, might androgyny become itself a new normative stereotype? Warren (1980) asked these questions and concluded that androgyny, a provisional concept at best, can be a dangerous goal if the imagery is illusive, thereby perpetuating myth rather than personal freedom.

A truly reciprocal relationship between the sexes, admits Lorraine Tamsin (1991: 182), would require the abandonment of the rigid, mutually exclusive, two-gendered system—something approaching androgyny. However, she refrains from using the term because "[i]t is not differences between human individuals that should be eradicated—but restrictions on differences in self-strategies arising from gender categories." In short, her argument is that we need to get past the gender categories that restrict us. Androgyny, as a metaphor for mixed gender, can too easily be read as effeminate masculinity. This interpretation no doubt explains why many American men resist such a label.

In the American men's movement, there is certainly less than total agreement over masculine image-metaphors. The question of how to personally define masculinity is, in fact, up for grabs in many postmodern societies. American males appear leery of the "soft male," preferring instead the combination "tempered macho"—what Sam Allis (1990: 80) has amusingly called "the devoted family man with terrific triceps." Certainly, in the media the "sensitive male" would seem to be giving way to a more hardened "warrior" image, even if this animal has been much "declawed" from his primeval origins. It is often difficult in today's world to tell which of these images is most appropriate. The new man-talk (such as "wild man" and "warrior" males), as presently debated in American circles, may suggest the wrong image-metaphors for a liberated male rhetoric. Sam Keen (1991) argues against such terminology, and its supporting metaphors, as confusing and potentially destructive. Male affirmation through such imagery as drumming and warrior rituals certainly does not sit well with all organizers of this multi-leveled movement.

If the ethnographic evidence is correct (that sexual stereotypes serve larger economic ends of a society), then—in the name of androgyny—we are likely to end up valuing the masculine ethic, whether in women or men while continuing to devalue the more nurturing qualities ("feminine") as being economically unsound. This is at least a hypothesis to be considered. Warren (1980), of course, would agree that all individuals ought to be encouraged—not forced—to develop their full range of human potentialities (what she calls virtues) without arbitrary sexual categorization. Androgyny is a metaphor that must not be taken too literally as it is itself culturally determined and context-specific. What concrete evidence do we have that men are really changing role behaviors?

"Changing Men"/"The New Male"

What are the costs and benefits of defending a "view of sexual self" that is so negatively formulated? When men finally realize that an oppositional identity can have negative consequences for themselves (health statistics should be a constant and dramatic reminder), they can stop being "martyrs for the male role"; only then will personal changes become possible (Kimmel 1987a: 79).

After looking at research on the reformulation of the gender roles of the American male, the following questions arise: What have been some contemporary changes? Have American men been appreciably influenced by the gains made by women? Is the male identity becoming less oppositional? Is the male sex role becoming less hazardous to men's health? Finally, how has the media participated in these gender transformations?

A recent American Health/Gallup survey (quoted in Johnson 1989: 60) revealed that men and women were in close agreement on the characteristics that make up an ideal man (good husband and father, sense of humor, ambitious, and intelligent) but suggests that men are lonely, confining themselves in large part to talk about work and sports ("shop talk/jock talk"). As a group, men appeared to be more isolated from their families, apparently still could not share their feelings with other men, and, sadly, a significant number of men felt "stripped of their identities."

Other studies—limited mostly to white, college-educated, young male samples—do suggest that real changes have taken place in the traditional male role. Thompson and Pleck found that students recognized three major dimensions of the traditional male role (1987: 23–36): 1) status, 2) toughness, and 3) anti-feminine norms. What was most interesting, however, was that, as a group, the men in this sample did not fully endorse these traditional male role norms. "Toughness" was supported only slightly, "status norms" were neither supported nor rejected, and the "anti-feminine norm" was even slightly rejected. Whereas they recognized the presence of the traditional norms, they did not concur with or totally reject them. In fact, some individuals endorsed the traditional attitudes toward men, at the same time endorsing contemporary views about women! Changes in the direction of liberal attitudes toward women may not always predict similar attitude changes in men, concluded Thompson and Pleck (1987).

What such studies say to me is that changes in gender perceptions, at least among American middle-class males, are taking place, albeit gradually and selectively. It is also increasingly recognized that we need more information on the areas of most or least change and more adequate samples that include minorities. Finally, we need to develop more effective communication strategies for bringing about personal changes. Metaphor analysis is suggested as one such strategy.

Another area of research on masculinity has been that of physical appearance, or body image, as the physical "embodiment of masculinity." Although traditionally we have thought of women as being more concerned with appearance, Mishkin and associates (1987: 37–52) have asked: What is the role of body image in men's lives? How do men feel about their bodies? They showed line drawings (seven body types) to college-aged men and discovered that 95 percent expressed dissatisfaction with some aspect of their bodies, greatest dissatisfaction centering on chest, weight, and waist. They also found the ideal body type to be a "muscular mesomorph." Men felt dissatisfaction, they argued, to the degree that they deviated from this ideal.

Furthermore, they hypothesized that body image, figuratively speaking, can be a kind of polarization of opposite body types, male and female. This conclusion is squarely in line with my hypothesis of an oppositional identity. Thinness, they questioned, may be the last bastion of the feminine and muscularity a reaction against sexual equality. One way men can express and preserve traditional male characteristics is by literally embodying them, thus giving physical concreteness to an oppositional identity.

As a lot of adult identity problems have been traced to father absence, another fascinating research focus is that of men in domestic settings. Joseph H. Pleck has looked at American fathering in historical perspective (1987: 83–97). The images of fatherhood have changed dramatically throughout history. In the eighteenth and early nineteenth centuries, the father was moral overseer; he profoundly influenced children's educational and matrimonial choices. In case of child custody, it was the father who had the legal rights at this time. Interestingly, though, educators in the nineteenth century came to view children as needing a "feminine" influence. Women's "purity," according to Pleck (1987: 87), ostensibly gave them a more "suitable" advantage over men for "rearing of children." At the same time, the new discipline of psychology was still male-dominated. European theorists gave primary attention to male influences and were highly suspect of the "feminizing effects" of women on children. Hence, father's absence and passivity became linked in the public mind with perceived juvenile delinquency of the 1950s (cf. the film *Rebel Without a Cause*).

Studying one sex calls for some reference to the other. Women's expectations of men pose perplexing questions in the culture-communication dialogue. Kathleen Gerson (1987: 115–30) asked: What do women want from men? What are the influences on women's work roles and family choices? Her study had some interesting conclusions. First, she found divisions among women: primarily, those committed to a career, nondomestic types, and those wanting to be full-time homemakers, the domestic types. One cannot easily generalize about all women was her conclusion. She noted that over 60 percent of her sample entered adulthood with nondomestic aspirations, only to become traditional over time. In short, structural situations were found to differ between domestic and nondomestic women who were influenced in different ways by men, and who developed different expectations of men.

In a similar vein, Gary Fine looked at women in male-dominated settings (1987: 131–47). His thesis was that certain women are better able to be accepted by male colleagues than others because they are able to decode male behavior patterns. Using an ethnographic approach, he looked at how women adjust in predominantly male settings. He argued that to be accepted, women have to choose to "be one of the boys." That is to say, they might become more relaxed about off-color humor and obscene language patterns, eventually accepting a certain amount of sexual teasing. His point was that women have the potential to disrupt established patterns of male interaction. As these are cultural (rather than gender) traditions per se, he argued that women can learn to use the cultural codes for more effective communication. However, he does not question the ultimate implications of this thesis, which would seem to condone rather than question the values of male-dominated settings. Not everyone would be content with these conclusions.

Notions of gender often support masculine hegemony and heterosexual power, Butler argues cogently (1990: 34). In fact, "to make gender trouble," in her opinion, is to keep gender in its place by "posturing as the foundational illusion of identity." This more radical thesis would ultimately like to see the contemporary discourse on sex itself overthrown! Whether or not we are willing to go to this extreme, we might entertain the possibility that women may be more capable of adapting to the behavioral styles of men than men are at adapting to the behavioral styles of women. With an oppositional identity as a solid line of defense for many men, this might be a reasonable hypothesis.

In conclusion, although the women's question cannot be answered without addressing men's issues as well, one of the goals of a men's perspective (different from the traditional focus) is to try to demystify masculinity and put it back into the hands of men. Rather than being "martyrs to their socially defined role of man," men can learn to work out effective communication strategies for transforming components of masculinity. Ultimately, then, men must find positive alternatives to an oppositional identity (Goldberg 1980; Kimmel 1987b; Gillette & Moore 1990).

At the individual level, some promise may lie in the technique referred to earlier as metaphor analysis, which will be summarized presently. Before that exercise, however, let us turn to media images of masculinity in contemporary Western contexts.

Media and Male Images/"Masculinity Declawed"

There is no single identity theory to explain males and masculinity, but so far we have considered gender-identity theories which suggest that sexual division of labor, and its attendant sexual stereotyping, are related to the economic structures of societies, or else to socialization experiences which may be encouraging an androgynous personality style. Also, we introduced the notion of possible transformations of gender identity. An equally important factor in this complex gender equation is the advent of telecommunications and media influences on male-female identities and interactions.

Masculinity, as reflected in the media, is certainly often a perpetuation of a romantic obsession with the male-female ideal. Media (especially movies, television, and radio) still systematically distort reality in favor of entertaining fictions about sexuality. In a society such as ours, where men do not always relate well to other men, images of manhood come increasingly from male figures in the media. Garfinkel calls these media heroes "our modern-day archetypes of manhood" (1986: 109).

Goldberg (1980: 120), too, feels that already complicated male-female communication is made even more complex in today's age of liberation and changing gender expectations by the often inconsistent messages from the media.[10] It is not difficult to find contradictory media images today: the competitive aggressor side by side with the more sympathetic androgynous male, for example.

Consider the movie *Q & A*, in which the traditional masculine roles are held in almost comic relief while the largely androgynous lawyer-hero emerges morally victorious, even if frustrated by the System. An even more typical example of contemporary changes in gender roles can be found in Blake Edwards's charming film *Switch*. In this spoof on male-female roles in modern society, a macho male, after being killed by three avenging women, is allowed to return to earth as a "woman" and, in the process, painfully learns to appreciate both styles of interpersonal communication, male and female, without sacrificing either.

Although not discounting socio-economic factors as important, Meyrowitz has suggested that the current merging of masculine and feminine behaviors is related to the merging of information systems (1986: 185). It is no accident, he argued, that the drive toward sexual equality was begun in the mid-1960s by the first generation in the United States raised on television! Furthermore, he concluded that women have been traditionally isolated in the domestic sphere (both physically and informationally) resulting in a private/public split between the sexes. Television, he suggested, brought the same information, the same "outside" world to both men and women. It was television, then, that "liberated women informationally" (1986: 211). Although Meyrowitz would agree that content of programs is still often geared toward traditional romantic and cultural ideals, he believes that more information today is shared, regardless of content. This sharing has brought about a new consciousness, a trend toward an androgynous style of behavior that combines aspects of the traditional and nontraditional behaviors of both sexes (1986: 225).[11]

The media operate largely in the public sphere but influence the private—ultimately how we view ourselves, including our gender identities. McQuail (1989: 252) points out that "the media are not really one thing but a nexus of complex mediating messages, images, and ideas." There may well be a more modest role for the media as "molders of behavior" than once thought. After all, media operate in pre-existing social and cultural contexts. Individuals select significant messages from communication content, often with unintended consequences. It is also increasingly recognized that there are circumstances where interpersonal influences outweigh those of the media (1989: 272). Media effects, after all, are multiple, complex, and always a part of the cultures in which they operate. This interpretation tries to avoid reifying media, or culture, in the analysis of so-called media effects.

Associated with changes in self-image is the issue of work roles performed by men and women in modern post-industrial societies. In the Western world we live increasingly in an information society where a large proportion of people, men and women, are engaged in service and information tasks. Work roles are becoming more similar, then, for both sexes. There is less need, therefore, for a special division of labor based on physical strength when knowledge (access to information systems) is more significant for cultural performance. Enhanced awareness of performance, regardless of gender categories, may translate into improved efficiency.

Normative changes relating to sexuality, however, carry great significance for most cultures. Daniel Yankelovich says that a virtual "cultural revolution" has already transformed the social and sexual rules of American life (1981: 71–78). This change translates as wider freedom of choice in the sexual area and more options to exercise in interpersonal communication. New work styles (such as dual-earning families) in today's service, information, and high-tech economy are fundamentally altering our definitions of masculinity and femininity. Although many people feel ambivalent about changes in gender roles, few apparently want to return to the traditional standards of sexual relations. Americans may long for the warmth and closeness they associate with family life of earlier times, but Yankelovich (1981: 74) claims that this "longing" does not mean "going back to the old rules." The revolutionary *potential* of the media, then, resides not so much in content of the message, but in the means of handling the messages, which ultimately affects the nature of work itself, power relations between the sexes, as well as the values, attitudes, and identities most adaptable in society (McQuail 1989: 77).

The sexes are becoming demystified as both cultural knowledge and social roles are increasingly shared. Meyrowitz (1986: 193), however, raises an intriguing question about the *rate of change* for men as opposed to women. Research summaries have suggested that men often endorse changes for women but turn their backs on the consequences of such change for themselves. As Margaret Mead once pointed out, it may be easier for women to move into the more highly valued work traditionally performed by males than for the reverse to happen. One could say that there is little encouragement from society, through the media, for men to want to participate in what traditionally have been viewed as feminine activities. Men may be experiencing a kind of "culture lag" in the area of changing gender roles. The women's movement may have made men more aware of their own feelings, but this new awareness has not substantially altered societal expectations for men in many cultures (Allis 1990).

The assumption that male and female are merely mirror images of each other has been seriously reevaluated in recent times. Research suggests that violations of male/female gender roles are differentially sanctioned for men and women, with different consequences for each group. Page and Yee (1985: 109–127), in an empirically based comparative study, reported that gender nonconformity is viewed more seriously for males than for females, giving some support to the "male as norm" findings. Being male appeared to be seen as the norm, hence males were judged more harshly when they were thought to deviate from the norm. This conclusion supports my supposition that changes in gender conceptualization in American society, due to the primacy of the economic imperative, are likely to give heavy emphasis to the "male ethic" for both males *and* females, while at the same time paying lip service to a liberation rhetoric for both sexes. We might take a look at a non-Western example for further clarification.

Maori Male-Female Identity/A Case Study

A few years ago, while studying an educated group of Maoris in New Zealand, I asked the following question: How does identity for Maori males and Maori females differ and why? (Fitzgerald 1979). Using the theoretical scheme outlined in chapter 4 (performance-growth model), I discovered that, by and large, Maori women were culturally less conservative than Maori men, especially in terms of adapting to the larger New Zealand society. Maori men, on the other hand, typically derived more status from their affiliation with the Maori subculture.

I used the concept of *cultural centrality* to explain people's attitudes and behavior that ultimately help to shape their identities. With Maori males having greater access to traditional knowledge (the Maori subculture being more "central" for identification), Maori men develop a traditional reference orientation, derive more *mana* in the Maori setting, and gain primary psychological satisfactions from this same cultural context. My tripartite theoretical model (employing the psychological constructs of motivation, knowledge, and ability) was used to show how performance of role behaviors was related to differential rewards in a bicultural society. Women—often forbidden to participate in traditional Maori religious and political activities—as a result, were more receptive to European-inspired roles as New Zealand society became increasingly integrated. On several indices, Maori women were revealed to be more progressive, more open to cultural changes, and less traditional in attitudes and behavior than their male counterparts.

Although both men and women were motivated to identify as Maoris, access to Maori cultural knowledge and the ability to perform Maori roles have been historically different for the two genders, the rewards for performance being heavily skewed for males in the direction of the traditional subculture. The primary function of Maori identity, after all, has been the need for belonging to a cultural group that is still emotionally gratifying. Traditional Maori culture, according to Sinclair (1985), has always emphasized the importance of men over women; and Maori men have retained this cultural pre-eminence in many areas of Maori life in New Zealand. For one thing, men are considered to be ritually "purer" than women. The notion of female "pollution" to this day has kept the sexes divided into male and female domains (Fitzgerald 1979; Sinclair 1985).

Karen Sinclair (1985: 27–46) has documented how traditional gender rules do not always act as cultural constraints, at least for older Maori women. Especially in terms of the larger society, but also in certain public Maori affairs, older women have begun to take more active roles. When age and gender intersect, the social universe of old men becomes more circumscribed while that of older women becomes more expanded. These women, Sinclair argued (1985: 27), perform in public arenas previously inhabited only by men. "In the Maori case," she stated, "it is not merely that gender distinctions diminish; there does, in fact, appear to be a genuine reversal." The aging experience of Maori men and Maori women may follow different paths. For men, whose cultural focus has been the traditionally defined Maori community, their roles are less transformed.

Her thesis is that age accounts for the expansion of the social universe for women and contraction for men. My own, earlier analysis, suggested that the reward structure of the larger New Zealand society (of which Maori culture is but a micro-unit) largely affects personality development and identity salience. The notion of *cultural centrality* is one theoretical way of explaining gender differences as responses to both situational factors and differential rewards.

I do not see any major contradiction in the two approaches. Certainly, both Maori men and Maori women undergo marked changes in their behavior because of expectations from the Maori and New Zealand societies, whether these changes are viewed from a model of bicultural conflict or from a gender-age perspective. The ethnographic observation remains the same. Men and women have different group loyalties, and "identity saliences" vary by gender. Turning to the individual as focus of analysis, we might consider a promising new avenue for bringing about personality change through changing metaphors of identity. What is the efficacy of metaphoric analysis for generating new insights into self-change?

Metaphor Analysis/Promises of Change through New Imagery

Anthropology has been long familiar with metaphors (Sapir & Crocker 1977). Educators, too, have effectively employed metaphors in pedagogical contexts (Penfield & Duru 1988); but it is primarily to psychology that we must turn for a consideration of how metaphor—guide to past as well as future behavior—relates to self-concept. Emphasis here is on the creation of new image-metaphors for understanding and improving one's life.

The assumption is that metaphors, as they closely approximate the physiological properties of feelings more than semantic words, can become a crucial therapeutic medium for sharing emotions, relationships, and experience (Grove 1989: 19). In shedding outmoded metaphors learned in one's past, the individual begins to take control of negative feelings about self. It is as though the individual's mental schemata are stripped away and brought to the point where rebuilding is then made possible.

Metaphors carry both positive and negative implications for individuals and societies.[12] As far as gender assumptions are concerned, there are sometimes profound and unacknowledged influences at play. The ethnographic literature is full of examples of "metaphors of masculinity" that have functioned negatively to perpetuate social divisions. By evoking emotions associated with a defensive "compulsive masculinity," men in such societies have justified the social domination of women and other groups felt to be "socially inferior" (Brandes 1988: 207). The argument, then, is that the contemporary male needs to learn to analyze old, harmful metaphors of masculinity in order to recreate new ones that will be more positive and adaptive in a changing, mediated communication society.

If metaphor can shape cultural meanings, to the extent that we learn to control metaphors affecting our lives, the better able will we be in taking charge of our own lives. We can shape the meanings that work for us as responsible individuals in society. David Deshler argues convincingly that metaphors assist us in reflecting on our personal lives, our culture, and our socialization (1990: 296): "Through metaphors, we can examine and exorcise the 'ghosts' of our socialization so that we can freely choose meanings out of which we want to live our lives and experience them through metaphor." Although not limited to gender images, this approach is a positive attempt at self-transformation.

Deshler (1990: 301) says that this process of recognition, reflection, comparison, and creation evoked by metaphor analysis can help individuals to become aware of distorted societal expectations. Image-metaphors from the popular culture, disseminated through the mass media, communicate cultural messages that are both subtle and pervasive. If we do not critically reflect and analyze such metaphors, we become vulnerable to manipulation from sources as wide-ranging as advertising, entertainment, and other mediated communication channels (1990: 302). Deshler advocates *metaphor analysis* as a positive way to better understand our cultural values, hence ultimately aiding us in making sensible cultural choices (1990: 305). It is imperative, then, that men begin to seriously reflect upon the dominant metaphors of maculinity that coninue to shape male gender behaviors or else fall prey to subtle manipulations from media and other cultural sources.

Overcoming Communication Distortions

Certainly identity remains an issue in the question of changing role relations between the sexes. Men, in most cultures, have held on to a strong sense of identity with the public realm of experience, so much so that Seidler (1989: 107) believes that the personal sense of self may have suffered by comparison. Seidler's argument in a nutshell (1989: 108): Men have a weakened sense of individual identity compared to women. Whereas women are sometimes rendered culturally invisible within the public realm, men are too often left "invisible to themselves."

Can men adjust to women's roles as easily as the reverse? The answer is complicated. Certainly the oppositional identity, to the extent that it persists in men, can only make it more difficult for them to accept traditional women's roles.[13] In addition, in a consumer-driven society such as ours, the encouragement may be of behavioral patterns that fit the economic goals of the society—the more hard-driven masculine ethic—even if today this ethic is often shared by both women and men. The danger is that an androgynous pose will give way to a less flexible masculine ethic held in common between the sexes.

In summary, as Goldberg (1980: 127) has so eloquently phrased it, a "caring culture" will place emphasis, not on "compulsive masculinity," but on psychological growth for men and women. It is increasingly clear, he points out, that both sexes will have to make significant social and psychological adjustments to overcome the major communication distortions between the sexes. One can end this discussion of gender in the culture-communication dialogue on a note of optimism. If the American male can overcome the vestiges of an oppositional identity, based on negation of feminine virtues and homosexuality, there are exciting choices available for the "new male" in our changing, media-driven, information society.[14]

Principal Points

Looking at a variety of cultures, this chapter has considered the meaning of traditional oppositional masculinity and, using the metaphor of voyage as "pathways to manhood," traced some historic as well as contemporary transformations of this gender identity, including a consideration of androgyny in other cultures. The evidence for identity change was found in male images in the media in a Western context, as well as in the case study of Maori male-female identity in a non-Western one. Metaphor analysis, at the individual level, was offered as having great promise for identity transformation.

Notes

1. Responses to the gay liberation movement, which cannot be separated from the male identity crisis, have often been marked by denial or frustration. However, there seems to be a glimmer of hope: At the first International Men's Conference (Austin, Texas: Oct. 18–20, 1991), three out of the forty-six presentations explicitly addressed gay male issues in the context of the evolving "new male" in contemporary culture.

2. Psychologists William and Claire McGuire (1987: 139) report that boys are more likely to spontaneously describe themselves in terms of their maleness as the number of females increases, and self-consciousness about one's maleness was found to be exaggerated in fatherless homes.

3. Empirical evidence from psychology indicates that women and men are today more similar than different on most psychological indices (Skevington and Baker 1989). Gilmore (1990) would certainly agree; in fact, he would argue that both may need social incentives to be assertive!

4. Lattas (1990: 83) has argued that, in the Kaliai region of New Guinea, male power assumes a visual, perceptible form through procreative imagery, "through sexual metaphors that simultaneously eroticize space and power." Since the men's house is the supreme spacial symbol of male power, the solution when a local woman became a cargo cult leader (hence, appropriated male political power) was to rape her in the men's house! (1990: 84). Sex is a way of objectifying power. The above-below spatial metaphors common in architectural features of the men's house became the imagery for all relationships when a "superiority" was asserted over an "inferiority."

5. There are several types of men's groups in the United States: the "profeminist" men (usually including gay men); the fathers' rights/men's rights groups that, sometimes, can be hostile to the women's movement; the "mytho-poetic, Bly-type" groups—incidently, the ones the media most often offer as "the" movement—that use folk tales and quasi-anthropological motifs to discover the mysteries of manhood; as well as the "toxic masculinity" groups that explore ways to relieve the more destructive traits of the old masculinity, thus trying to improve the health of men in our society

(New York Daily News 1991: 2E). This chapter utilizes at least three out of four of these approaches.

6. Dorinne Kondo makes an intriguing, if speculative, argument about gendered identities in Japan (1990: 298): Masculinity is defined in opposition to women, yet at the same time performed for women. Each sex, she argues, needs the other as "audience" for its own performance of gender identities. This brilliant observation calls for fuller exploration.

7. An intriguing example of such anxiety in the anthropological literature is the exotic condition known throughout Southeast Asia as *koro*, a kind of male hysteria that rests on the psychosomatic belief that the penis can retract into the belly, eventually killing the individual. Gilmore considers this the ultimate separation metaphor that reflects the underlying pressures for "achieving masculinity" in Southeast Asian cultures (1990: 173).

8. David Greenberg recounts Gilbert Herdt's story that more recently the Tahitian *mahus* have begun to take jobs as female impersonators in nightclubs for tourists (1988: 59).

9. One promising therapeutic use is *metaphor analysis*, which can generate new perspectives on our lives. Basically, the argument is that metaphor can be employed as a type of problem-solving, a kind of reframing of conflicts in terms of analogies, ultimately for bringing about changes in personal identities.

10. Recent newspaper articles suggest a new genre of female writers who are portraying men as the "fictional bad guys" (Nancy Shulins 1991: F14). Goldberg claims that a lot of media rhetoric today perpetuates stereotypes that all men are "exploitative, insensitive and destructive abusers of women" (1980: 106). He feels that men may well be the last subgroup in our society that can still be so negatively stereotyped without public outcry (1980: 103).

11. The super-macho pose in contemporary American films may be explained as a reaction to the "sissy image" that many men still associate with an androgynous male. In the media, the "sensitive" male seems to have given way to the "gentleman warrior," even if this image-metaphor is only a modified version of "masculinity declawed," to use Garfinkel's colorful expression of this type.

12. Pearl Katz (1990: 457) has studied drill sergeants' "emotional metaphors" and how these relate to role performance, with the hypothesis that learning to interpret emotional metaphors can have positive adaptive value in particular kinds of specialized roles in society.

13. Meyrowitz has considered the negative implications of women invading traditional male spaces (1986: 183). Men may need secure places where they can rehearse male roles. One can compare Raphael's lament that

the demise of significant male initiations is resulting in "makeshift males" (1988).

14. Garfkinkel considers homosexuality "the dark pool of masculinity" (1986: 162–63). His thesis is that fear of homosexuality is a major barrier inhibiting closer relations between men; hence, the taboos surrounding homosexuality cannot be divorced from the problems that heterosexual men face in homophobic societies.

7

○ Homophobia and the Cultural Construction
of the Social Stranger

I am straight, correct, normal and good. You are abnormal, wrong, deviant and bad. Your demeanor nauseates me. Your behavior is immoral, sacrilegious. I don't want you teaching my children, in my armies, leading my congregation in church, joining our clubs.

—Perry Garfinkel, *In A Man's World*

The focus of this book has often been on groups that are more or less culturally distinct. It is possible, however, to ask how culture affects the self-concept of minorities that are not culturally distinctive, yet, through discriminatory treatment by the society, take on the characteristics of a "subculture" with a separate identity that reinforces feelings of being different. Sexual minorities, I believe, fall into this unique category and, through their presumed contrast, illustrate important relationships among the concepts considered in this book (namely, culture, identity, and communication).

To the extent that homosexuals (gay males and lesbians) constitute exceptions to our cultural assumptions about sex and gender, they may give us important clues to how meanings about social relationships come about. Metaphor—with its concreteness of imagery—often helps to organize a debate; thus, we need to examine some of the image-metaphors that surround the debates about homosexuality in the culture-communication dialogue.

Labels and Reality/"The Myth of the Composite Portrait"[1]

First, let us try an exercise of startling contrasts. Suppose you opened your morning paper to discover the following headlines: "Explosion of Battleship Iowa: Heterosexual Implicated," or further along: "Heterosexuality, Doctor Claims, Caused by Hormone Imbalance." In the next column, you read unsuspectingly: "Practicing Straights Flaunt their Lifestyle," or further down the page: "Rare Form of Cancer Linked to Normals." One could go on. The majority does not usually label itself a problem group. Nor does it worry about how its sexuality was formed ("caused"). Certainly it does not assume that all "straights," or heterosexuals, can be pictured as a single category, forming a "composite portrait."

On the other hand, the label "homosexual" has become, in many cultures, a wastepaper-basket concept in which are dumped all manner of characteristics supposedly inherent in a same-sex orientation. In reality, homosexuality is no more unitary than heterosexuality. Following Alfred Kinsey's original view of sexuality along a continuum, one could even argue that there is no such thing as being totally heterosexual *or* homosexual! In discussing this many-sided issue, one must try to curb the tendency to oversimplify complexities.

Modern researchers, rather than denying homosexuality, stress the plurality of types. Bell and Weinberg entitled their book *Homosexualities* (1978), a choice of plural title that recognizes that homosexual adults are a remarkably diverse group. They warned us that, before we draw any conclusions about all gay people, we must consider factors such as race, age, sex, education, and occupation.[2] Furthermore, it is suggested that lesbians and gay men are best understood when seen as whole individuals, not simply in terms of sexual preferences. Barbara Gittings (personal communication, 1987) calls this approach "putting love back into the scientific equations."

Where sexual preference is forced to take on a power of its own, there is always the danger of making gay identity so central that this "master status" can overshadow all other identities. The notion of *master status*, one that frames all others in importance of self-definition, can be based on many factors other than gender; but such a view of self is often negative rather than positive precisely because the category tends to inhibit the individual's creative capacity to fashion other identities (Johnson & Ferraro 1987: 125).

In the past, psychologists and sociologists studied "sick" populations or else homosexuals in prisons. Evelyn Hooker (1956), in her classic study of a nonpatient population, called this misrepresentation the "iceberg phenomenon," recognizing that the majority of homosexuals are always, because of social circumstances, hidden beneath the surface. If we only concentrate on dysfunctional types, it is hardly surprising that we conclude that all homosexuals are guilt-ridden, psychological misfits. The book *Homosexualities* presents a range of types that amply demonstrates that relatively few gays conform to the stereotypes that many Americans still hold about them. Presently we shall consider how these value-laden myths and stereotypes are derived from culture and transmitted through the media. There is certainly today increased media coverage of gay issues in the United States; but two important questions remain: How accurate is this coverage? Has it really contributed to more positive self-images of gay citizens?

Modern research increasingly suggests that most homosexuals are indistinguishable from the heterosexual majority, certainly in respect to non-sexual aspects of their lives (Marmor, 1980; Woodman & Lenna, 1980; Bell, Weinberg & Hammersmith 1981). Despite the popular misconception that gays are easy to identify, Kinsey said that only one in seven males and one in twenty females were recognizable. Using a somewhat narrow psychobiological approach, Masters and Johnson even found little fundamental difference in sexual physiology and sexual response between homosexuals and heterosexuals (1979). Furthermore, the conclusion of much of this research is that gay men are mostly like other men, lesbians mostly like other women despite the difference of sexual orientation (Hotvedt 1982: 288). Sharp divisions between so-called gay and straight individuals have not been found.

The Kinsey Institute publication *Sexual Preference: Its Development in Men and Women* (1981) tested the most common social science theories about origins of homosexuality and concluded that "[n]o particular phenomenon of family life can be singled out, on the basis of our findings, as especially consequential for either homosexual or heterosexual development" (Bell, Weinberg & Hammersmith 1981: 191). They point toward a biological explanation without, however, specifying how this mechanism might work. Modern science clearly, then, does not relate homosexuality per se to pathology (Masters & Johnson 1979; Marmor 1980; Ortner & Whitehead 1981; Weinberg 1984; Greenberg 1988). Rather, particular social and psychological adaptations largely depend on the types of adjustments possible within socially prescribed contexts. Social definitions, not just biology or psychology, determine the status individuals occupy in a society.

As the title of this chapter suggests, the way that homosexuals are treated in a society results in the cultural construction of the social stranger. Although there are undoubtedly similarities as well as differences among many such identified groups, in this case social oppression appears to be the key factor that leads to a "non-shared humanity" for homosexuals (Pillard 1982: 103). Looked at from the point of view of the culture-communication dialogue, this discussion will consider how myths and stereotypes are derived from culture and transmitted through the media, with specific assessment of their implications for self-definition.

Personhood is culturally and socially constructed. In most cultures, sexuality is *presumed* to be heterosexual; therefore, Butler argues that a "culturally mandated heterosexuality" constitutes a form of "cultural prejudice" against homosexuals (1990: 108). "Presumptive heterosexuality," according to Butler, functions with discourse to communicate a threat to gays and lesbians: You are culturally correct (straight) or else you are culturally incorrect (gay). Thus, through a process of cultural and social exclusion, society creates the category of social stranger, although Butler prefers to use the metaphorical image of the "cultural outlaw." (I presume that cultural outlaw refers to a person excluded from normal legal protection and normal human rights guaranteed by the culture.)[3]

There is obvious need, then, to reexamine our assumptions about sexual minorities, as well as the scientific metaphors (models) that are employed to explain something as diverse and multifaceted as homosexuality.

Cultural Legitimacy and the Concept of the Stranger

Much of what people associate with the term *homosexual* may be no more than stereotypes maintained in order to justify behavior that discriminates against gays and lesbians. These extreme, often pathological reactions against homosexuals, called "homophobia," have taken dramatic forms throughout history. In Hitler's Germany, for example, perhaps as many as 200,000 homosexual men perished in Nazi concentration camps for no reason other than having had a sexual orientation defined as "deviant" (Heger 1980: 14).

In the United States, especially since the AIDs epidemic, homosexuals are still frequent victims of hate-motivated violence (Kirk & Madsen 1989).[4] "G.A.Y.?" = "Got AIDs Yet?" reads a graffiti that visually expresses the extreme distaste that many nongays have for homosexuals. The Gay and Lesbian Task Force says that gays are seven times more likely to be crime victims than the average

American citizen. Occasional media attention tends to focus on violence as almost an "understandable response to homosexuals" (Paul 1982a: 359). Homophobia is supported by anti-gay myths (beliefs that help to explain and justify behavior) which, being emotionally based prejudice, are often unassailable to change by intellect alone, argue Kirk and Madsen (1989: 112). Trying to talk people out of homophobia, according to these authors, is difficult if not impossible.[5]

Part of the discovery of self for persons in a sexual minority is the realization that one is considered a "devalued person." Sociologist Barry Adam (1978), in *The Survival of Domination*, suggests that acknowledging this fact is a significant psychological rite of passage for any stigmatized individual. Homosexuals must deal, not only with coming to understand their sexual orientation, but also with society's stigmatization of that orientation. Certainly a majority of Americans feel that homosexuals suffer the greatest amount of discrimination of any group in this country (quoted in Paul 1982a: 353). Gays are not different primarily because they are homosexual. They differ, in large part, because they are stigmatized and thereby treated differently.

Let me make clear that not all societies have punished or even feared homosexual behaviors. Anthropologists long ago documented that, in over 64 percent of a sample of world societies, homosexuality in one form or another was considered normal and socially accepted for certain members or at certain periods of life (Ford & Beach 1951). Those interested in the cultural construction of gender can profit from greater familiarity with ethnographies that document homosexual practices in other cultures (Fitzgerald 1977a; Whitehead 1981).

In some cultures, male homosexuality was expected of all young men in connection with initiation ceremonies. Shamans (medicine men) were frequently homosexual, and both male and female homosexuals have had their unions recognized as legal marriages in certain Caribbean and African cultures (Fitzgerald 1977a). In the Transfly region of New Guinea, as recently as 1977, ethnographers discovered tribes where homosexual behavior, rather than heterosexual, was the *cultural preference*! (Kelly 1977; van Baal 1966). The authors relate this preference to an unconscious need to regulate population growth. Among the most exciting recent ethnographies are Gilbert Herdt's (1981, 1984, 1989, 1990) valuable works on the meaning of homoeroticism in Melanesian culture. Herdt rightfully claims that the cultural meanings and folk psychology of homosexuality require more careful documentation of sexuality and gender socialization than has been the case in the past (1989: 364).

The Closet Metaphor and Externally Imposed Identity

To love someone of the same sex is, after all, hardly so extraordinary. Same-sex behaviors would be remarkably inconsequential if society did not make them so portentous. When defined in this way, however, the implied inferior group is disqualified from full participation in society (Adam 1978). Its members are subjected to categorical treatment through an externally imposed identity. The powerful metaphor of closet, as "symbolic annihilator," socially isolates and controls gays and lesbians.

Language and discourse are vital to an understanding of self-construction—how a group manages its identity. Names become insults in themselves: "dike," "fag," "fairy," "queer." Such labels express the subordination of gays or lesbians and reinforce the stranger status in society. Prejudice becomes socially reproduced through discourse. (Incidently, in the United States alone, this stranger metaphor applies potentially to no less than twenty-four million American citizens!) Thus, van Dijk (1987: 389) mentions the interesting concept of "name taboo" where pronouns are overused in reference to minorities ("they," "those people") instead of addressing persons by name. A form of linguistic distancing, name denial is one of the ways prejudiced people deny individuality and social membership to minorities. Language becomes symptomatic of social oppression.

It is undeniable that many gays in our society are still social strangers. The *metaphor of closet* is an apt image of the constant insider-outsider dilemmas that face homosexuals in many societies. Probably no gay person is fully in harmony with the values and standards of a predominantly heterosexual society. Butler (1990: 87) argues convincingly (using the metaphor of cultural outlaw) that *homophobia*, the fear of homosexuality, is ultimately the fear of losing cultural legitimacy, thus being socially excluded. The challenge will be to remove barriers to full involvement for sexual minorities in all social institutions.

Oppression against sexual minorities, Barry Adam (1978: 43) suggests, is maintained by the "myth of the composite portrait," which embodies three related axioms: 1) Presumably, gays and lesbians are always a "problem"; 2) they are all alike; and 3) they are supposedly recognizable. These axioms are played out in an all-too-familiar script: "They," it is assumed, are animal-like (but, oddly enough, not "natural"[6]). Subhuman categorization is often reinforced by pseudoscientific labels, such as "regressive," "fixated," or "immature."

They are, of course, all hypersexual (Adam 1978). Related to this distaste of a presumed sexual lifestyle, a 1987 Gallup Poll showed that 52 percent of the respondents preferred not to work with gays, 25 percent strongly objecting. Two-thirds thought that gays should never be hired to teach in elementary schools (Kirk & Madsen 1989: 70; 85).[7] "They" are often viewed as all too visible, meaning that failure to be totally invisible provokes resentment from the larger society. Yet, trying to make oneself invisible—the ultimate existential insult of a closet status—denies one's own sense of self and well-being and leads to personal fears and anxiety. The result is a psychological double-bind. The cultural message is clear, according to psychologist Garfinkel (1986: 167): "Our laws, our attitudes, our one-line jokes and innuendos blatantly victimize homosexuals." Through the metaphor of closet, we ultimately exclude gays and lesbians from full social participation. Can we doubt that, as a group, homosexuals are still social strangers?

Internationally, it has been estimated that there may be upward of three hundred million lesbians and gay men (twenty-four to twenty-five million in the United States alone), making homosexuals the largest and most far-flung minority on earth. The group, worldwide, is also one the most oppressed (Gitech 1980: 15; Harry & Das 1980). In a number of countries today, homosexual acts remain illegal. Gays have been executed (Iraq, Iran, Uganda), sent to "rehabilitation" camps (Cuba, Mozambique), sentenced to long-term hard labor (Pakistan and the Soviet Union), and committed to mental institutions or prisons (China, United States). A large number of refugees from Cuba have been gays fleeing the oppressive conditions on that island (Gitech 1980: 15).

Although a majority of Americans now hold to a general principle of equality for all people regardless of race, sex, or age, many do not want to accept an equality based on sexual preference (Kirk & Madsen 1989). Private homosexual acts between consenting adults (similar to the famous Napoleonic Code that freed much of Europe from institutionalized homophobia) have been decriminalized in twenty-six states, but there are intimidating laws on the books prohibiting "unnatural and perverted sexual practices" (1989). North Carolina and Tennessee still have the infamous "crimes against nature" statute used to harass gays into submission (Miller 1989: 279). Even in the U.S. military, we have made little progress eradicating double standards for gay citizens. The United States is said to have some of the most severe anti-homosexual laws in the Western world (Garfinkel 1985). The AIDs epidemic, even with the present "sympathetic" media backlash, has surely made the bid for social acceptance more difficult in America, where homophobia is not just personal but institutionalized.

For individuals, there are a number of results of such oppression (Adam 1978). One is psychological insecurity and fragmentation of identity, what sociologists call "ambiguity of identity." Having fewer psychological or social supports than majority group members, homosexual men sometimes cope with stigmatization through promiscuity. Garfinkel suspects that promiscuity largely reflects a male approach to sexuality (1986: 175). Gay males are simply being males first. The only difference between gay and straight men is that homosexual relations have had fewer checks and balances that typically surround male-female relationships, e.g., bonds sanctioned by marriage. The existence of unsupervised gay ghettos (out-of-sight, out-of-mind) may have perpetuated some of the more negative aspects of this stigmatized minority. This fact makes controlling the spread of AIDs so difficult. It is not accidental, then, that anonymous sex (Humphrey's *Tearoom Trade*, 1970) has a high correlation with low self-esteem and ambiguous identity. The important point is not that some gays are promiscuous, but that promiscuity is one among several strategies for coping with being treated as inferior.

Another coping device is denial of self or "flight from identity." In *Gay Men, Gay Selves*, Thomas Weinberg (1983) details how some men construct a gay identity, involving usually three separate stages: from initially acting on sexual impulse, to self-suspicions about one's identity, and finally to self-labeling. Weinberg makes the important distinction between behavior and identity, between the "act" and the "actor." A man may engage in same-sex activity (aware of what he is doing) without self-definition as a homosexual.

It has long been observed that there is often as much as a six-year gap between one's first homosexual experiences and self-identification as a gay person (Dank 1971: 182). Although research is sketchy in the area of gay women's "coming-out" experiences, it has been suggested that (perhaps due to the more lenient attitudes of society toward displays of affection among women) the "coming-out" process for lesbians takes longer than for men. It has been said that lesbians typically emphasize the importance of emotional attachments over sexual ones. Thus, sexual activity plays a different role in the coming-out process for gay men and lesbians. According to De Monteflores and Schultz (1978: 67), gay men tend to act on their homosexual feelings at least two years before any intellectual understanding of the label "homosexual," while for lesbians, homosexual behavior occurs about four years *after* such self-understanding.

This conflict over "being" and "doing" can result in the paradoxical distinctions between *homosexual/homosocial* and *heterosexual/heterosocial* behaviors wherein identity, sexual behavior, and social behavior do not always coincide, making the stereotypes about homosexuals even more baffling and contradictory.[8] Consider the example of the woman who lives heterosexually for many years before establishing a same-sex relationship, which even then may not coincide with her self-image (Manderson 1980: 71). I would argue that homophobic cultures encourage such complex, often contradictory responses.

Other ways of dealing with oppression include various forms of social or psychological withdrawal, often from potentially positive supports from the homosexual community itself. Hence, the gay individual who adopts a low-profile conservatism believed to be approved by the dominant group, in an attempt to be more respectable than the respectable, even if this sometimes means punishing other gay people for being "different." In-group hostilities become a reflection of the stranger status imposed from the outside. Homophobia is not limited to straights!

People can and do move from one category to another as self-definitions change over time, but I believe that the development and maintenance of personal identity cannot be divorced from the background of a largely repressive heterosexual world with its mostly negative portrayals of lesbians and gay men. I shall further argue that society, in a strange twist of events, helps to create a quasi-"culture" where there would be no need for such if gay people were given social equality. At the very least, we need to rethink our stereotypes and what they do to homosexual identity and self-concept. The media, too, have some moral responsibility in this confusion between cultural status and social status. Identity centrality (the cultural construction of the gay master status) and a sense of common fate (the social positions accorded homosexuals in society) have both influenced gay and lesbian self-constructions.

Sexual minorities, it should be noted, have always employed *positive* challenges to subordination, often quite creative ways of surviving in repressive societies. Probably the first step toward self-liberation is an internal rage reaction, a resentment of one's lack of place in society (Adam 1978: 116). As a comment on gay identity within the contemporary American political context, the adoption of a gay or lesbian identity is usually seen as a positive psychological stance. Liberation implies the psychological need to assert self. Unfortunately, the dominant group is apt to interpret such assertiveness as an affront to its authority. Violence from the majority is often associated with fears that gays are going to flaunt their lifestyle. The power of labels is real.

When gay men and lesbians have been pushed back into their "closets," gay humor can become one symbolic means of using language and gesture to destroy some of the worst types of societal oppression. Unfortunately, "camp wit" is often mistaken for the deliberate desire to act out the gestures and dress of the opposite sex (*La-Cage-Aux-Folles* style). Cross-dressing and homosexuality remain persistent associations in the minds of most Americans. Although true transvestism occurs among some homosexuals, cross-dressing may be more prevalent in the general population, both in the United States and cross-culturally (Fitzgerald 1977a; Kirk & Madsen 1989). Belief and reality rarely coincide in this deeply entrenched misapprehension.

Liberation surely starts with liberation from self-oppression, but eventually individuals must work toward building a sense of community which helps reaffirm positive identities and protects them from some of the most hurtful restrictions imposed by a homophobic environment. Indicators of these communities are gay and lesbian residential areas, community centers, gay business groups, religious organizations for homosexuals, and so on. Many personal and social gains have been achieved through the self-help movement. We shall look at the way the gay self-help movement developed in Sweden, considered to be one of the most liberal societies in the world with respect to sexual identity and behavior (Fitzgerald 1981: 56–68).

Gay Self-help Groups in Sweden/A Case Study

Self-help groups in general have been defined as "voluntary small group structures for mutual aid and the accomplishment of a special purpose" (Katz & Bender 1976: 9). Major attributes include a relatively small size, and formation is by peers rather than from without the organization. Hence, referrals to professional agencies are minimized. Instead there is stress on personal responsibility of members in face-to-face interactions. Assistance is not perceived as being met by existing social institutions.

In addition, self-help groups provide, for many, a reference group for bringing about desired personal and social changes. Identity formation is a crucial function. Such groups offer various emotional supports. Occasionally they are cause-oriented, enhancing for some a sense of personal and political identity (Borman 1976). Gay self-help groups, however, are only special examples within the more widespread self-help movement. In the United States alone, there may be close to a million self-help groups, such as sensitivity groups, consciousness-raising, consumer groups, and medically oriented associations. These groups tend to coincide with the breakdown of traditional social supports and, to a degree, always reflect some inadequacy in care-giving institutions to meet the needs of certain classes of persons in society.

Lesbians and gay men have joined the ranks of those who have discovered strengths in working together in small, personalized groups where they can be themselves (Fitzgerald 1981). Self-help, in this context, is a special type of support system, *by* gays and *for* gays. It is interesting that the self-help movement is virtually unknown in Scandinavia. This is not accidental as their concept of social welfare is much more firmly established than in the United States (De Cocq 1976: 203). Most people are adequately cared for. The self-help idea in Sweden, then, exists primarily for people toward whom society has remained somewhat indifferent, i.e., neglected minorities such as gays.

The first gay group in Sweden officially started in 1950 as a local chapter of a Danish gay organization and was formed in response to persistent scandals and persecutions in Sweden. Twelve individuals banded together to form a group that, in this particular case, took the form of a protest movement. The initial aim of the Association for Sexual Liberation (RFSL) was to provide a safe meeting place for lesbians and gay males. From the beginning there were separate associations for men and women but operating under the same umbrella structure.

Today total membership amounts to about ten thousand, with twenty-five chapters throughout Sweden (The Swedish Information Service 1990). As the original group quickly became too large to act as a true self-help group, the working committees within RFSL have taken on the primary self-help functions. The parent organization coordinates such mutual-aid groups as the gay Christians, gay AIDs counseling groups, the gay socialists, and even a gay Alcoholics Anonymous.

The gay Christian group will serve as an example (Fitzgerald 1981). Formed in 1977 by a gay man studying for the priesthood, this group attracts individuals seeking to resolve conflicts between religion and sexuality. Many members still feel rejected by society. The self-help association offers them a sense of community, certain psychological supports, as well as more acceptable alternatives to the commercial gay outlets, some of which we now know may have contributed to the spread of AIDs (e.g., gay saunas). This group, however, never intended to be a separate church for lesbians and gay men. Individual members continue to worship in their individual churches, joining together only for the purpose of exploring the relationship between homosexuality and religion. In one sense, such mutual-aid associations act as "broker institutions" helping to interpret the gay situation to the larger society and vice versa. Such a function is the opposite of a ghetto mentality, or separatism based on sexual preference.

Other important services provided by such groups include social activities. RFSL operates its own gay club, run by and for gay clients. Consciousness-raising, or identity functions, are ever present. Certainly "the befriending service" (gay outreach) is another significant feature of such associations, including a gay switchboard, peer counseling, and a gay radio station in Stockholm. As well, there are many associated educational functions.

Some major advances achieved since the 1950s include the following: 1) the removal of the laws against homosexual activity between consenting adults, age of consent being fifteen in Sweden; 2) the placement of same-sex unions on the same footing as common-law heterosexual unions through a custom known as *sammanboende*, a kind of quasi-legal marriage (Denmark recently passed a similar law); 3) the achievement of a completely modern program of sex education, wherein homosexuality is treated—undramatically—as another way of expressing potentially meaningful relationships, emphasis being on the relationships rather than sexual behaviors; and 4) in 1979, the removal of the "sickness" label—after a large number of Stockholm men and women, mostly in RFSL-affiliated groups, phoned their employers to say that they were "too sick with homosexuality to come to work." This event was in keeping with the 1973–1974 decision of the American Psychiatric Association to remove its sickness label.

An even more daunting challenge to the gay community came with the AIDs epidemic, the first case in Sweden being reported in 1982. The Swedish response to this health crisis illustrates its traditional humanitarian regard for sexual minorities (Finer 1989: 1–10). Long characterized by a tradition of "popular movements," the Swedish approach to the epidemic was to elicit the help of voluntary organizations in its attempts to educate the public about the disease.

A major strategy for combatting AIDs in Sweden has been based on direct financial subsidies from the central government to the voluntary organizations themselves (1989: 4). Traditionally open to matters of sexuality, authorities provided AIDs prevention information promptly, trying to avoid public panic and the emergence of anti-sexual attitudes toward particular groups. Support systems (for information, training, visitors' programs, and a telephone advisory service) were well coordinated at the grassroots level. Gay and lesbian organizations responded immediately without the kind of social resistance initially encountered in the United States.

Although no one in Sweden can be tested involuntarily, Sweden is the only country in the world to have compulsory reporting of all individuals found to be HIV-positive. At the same time, there is strong political opposition to discrimination in the workplace against people found to be HIV-positive. Today Sweden has perhaps the most extensive testing program in the world (1989: 5). Although the rate of actual AIDs cases in this country is now doubling about every fourteen months, the Swedish situation compares favorably with many other parts of Europe. Its successes can be traced to quick action, the country's open attitudes on sexuality, and the initial priority support for its voluntary organizations, gay and non-gay alike.

Certainly these voluntary associations have been beneficial to homosexuals in Sweden (Fitzgerald 1981). Through local self-help groups, lesbians and gay men are allowed more social alternatives and more humane choices. Opportunities for socializing are no longer limited to the exploitative commercial channels. Not only in terms of personal growth and change (providing social outlets, a sense of community, and positive identity), self-help groups become themselves vehicles for such changes. Ultimately one can argue that such grassroots activity is what "participatory democracy" is all about: "people in action on their own behalf" (Katz & Bender 1976: 241). These mutual-aid associations offer purpose and social supports to individual members and, as well, act as a collective response to the sometimes conservative societies in which they occur. In essence, they are an important part of the communication process, helping individuals to reduce their sense of being social strangers. Hopefully, such organizations can contribute to the adoption of more enlightened and humane attitudes toward sexual minorities.

In many cultural situations, the crucial matter for homosexuals is image, the cultivation of a viable self-image as well as a public image. Myths and stereotypes about gays are derived from culture but often transmitted through the media; therefore, it is to media presentations that we now turn for an understanding of the functions of prejudice.

The Limits of Media Influence and the Concept of Handicapping

The media are playing a major role in reshaping societies. Meyrowitz has argued convincingly that the merging of information worlds is encouraging more egalitarian forms of interaction (1986). Since the telecommunication explosion, culture is something more or less shared by all people, including social strangers. Potentially, then, media offer previously isolated (closeted) groups new forms of social participation and control (1986: 181).[9]

Through increased access to new information sources, some groups are learning not to accept their prescribed places in society, their restricted "cultural" domains. Despite the rhetoric to the contrary, many minorities today—gays and lesbians included—do not really want to separate themselves from the rest of humanity but prefer to communicate in the larger cultural arenas made possible by the communication revolution.[10] If "strangers" in society ever gain equal access to the larger culture, to retreat into the false security of a ghettoized separate "culture" would be a form of psychological regression. To what extent is this notion of a shared humanity only a utopian dream for sexual minorities throughout most of the world?

Some related questions follow: What have been the influences of mass communication on social justice for sexual minorities? What are the effects of media presentations on personal identities? Are gay and lesbian citizens portrayed objectively and fairly in the media? Finally, when will gays come to see themselves as a positive identity group, eventually integrating into the larger society and sharing with the rest of humanity?

Certainly, looking at media representations of gay people in the United States, the roles most typically assigned to lesbians and gay males have been devalued ones. Even when sympathy is attached to TV portrayals of gay AIDs patients, the images are often denigrating, limited in both range and content.[11] Although there is some evidence that the media avoid sensationalist language in referring to the AIDs disease, the results of such studies should not be taken to mean that Americans are truly sympathetic to homosexuals, or to homosexuality (Gross 1991). At the very least, media representations have often had a patronizing effect (i.e., trivial portrayals). In reporting on gay and lesbian issues in the news, negative events tend to capture audience attention. There is a preference for events that more or less "fit" audience expectation. The public, according to Denis McQuail (1989), often demands such comforting myths.

Reputed cases of child molestations by gay men get disproportionate attention, for example, compared to coverage of the estimated 1.5 million American families headed by a gay parent (Kirk & Madsen 1989). Often a principle of omission is in operation. What is excluded from the account is often more important than what is included. Consider one of the more annoying habits in journalism: the "canceling out" technique, what newspaper people call "balancing." A discrete positive article about gays or lesbians is often followed by a longer article (with photos) of a sensational murder of a teenaged boy by an unidentified adult male (sexual preference not specified). The message is clear: We may *have* to acknowledge gays, but don't ever forget (facts notwithstanding) that "they" are all really "child molesters."[12] The "good" message is canceled out by the "bad." This double-barreled approach to reporting is common in journalistic treatment of gay and lesbian issues. Normative ideals are presented instead of realities being challenged.

Another problem with newspaper reports is the use of "buzzwords" that subtly slant the news. John Horn believes that such journalistic shorthand (a legacy of TV's inculcating us with a short attention span) can adversely affect public opinion and shift sympathies when preframing a debate (1990: 10). Examples: people with AIDs being called "AIDs victims" or children born with AIDs "those innocent victims" as if other people with AIDs were directly responsible and should feel guilty. The use of shorthand buzzwords is a liability in communication about sexual minorities. Rather than emphasizing commonalities between gays and nongays, such reporting tactics only confirm fears and prejudices, perpetuating separatism and more discrimination.

Kirk and Madsen make an important observation about media access (1989: 77). The primary communication medium allowed gays is print, the forum left over for minorities whose views are not deemed "appropriate and newsworthy" enough for prime-time TV. In addition, gay spokespersons typically have had less access to news media. Kirk and Madsen also suggest that filmmakers continue to incorporate homosexuality into a "melodramatic, black-and-white symbolism for good and evil" (1989: 53). This is especially true of romanticized accounts of "AIDs victims," where an illness metaphor is used to equate disease with sex, sex with sin, and sin with death. Pollution and contagion metaphors remain paramount in media imagery of AIDs.

Lindsay St. Claire (1989: 130), in a challenging article entitled "When is Gender a Handicap?" introduces the concept of "handicapping" to explain the social disadvantages often experienced by women in society. I believe this image-metaphor can be usefully employed with reference to gays and lesbians in many societal contexts.[13]

St. Claire makes the important distinction between "objective disadvantages" and "socially constructed" ones. Beliefs about gender and sexuality, not sex per se or gender per se, account for the limited opportunities and restricted performances. Therefore, what masquerades as inherent disadvantages of the group spring, not from being gay or lesbian, but from cultural beliefs about what it means to be homosexual. When media presentations are degrading, slanted, or patronizing, the result is curtailment of the group's positive social contributions. It is in this sense that gays and women are socially handicapped by media presentations. When sexual minorities buy into the stereotypes, handicapping can result in a self-fulfilling prophesy. Thus, more realistic and sympathetic media *images* of gays and lesbians are to be encouraged since social and cultural representations of homosexuals are believed to provide the source of handicapping beliefs (St. Claire 1989).

A Time of Economic Change/The Metaphor of Sympathetic Victim

Metaphors, we have learned, can be one-sided, hence misleading. Minorities themselves often resort to a negative "victim" metaphor that, while sometimes vividly dramatizing their plight, may not always fully represent the positive gains that are, in fact, being made. A case in point is the growing appreciation in the West that homosexuals are an overlooked market waiting to be tapped. Gays and lesbians are increasingly seen as potential consumers. Modern businesses are likely to wake up to this "new" segment of the population as advertisers discover the hidden potentialities of the "gay market" (McLeod 1991: E1). Consider the recent decision by Lotus, a popular computer company, to offer medical benefits to the partners of its homosexual employers.[14] Perhaps not a sweeping movement for gay and lesbian equality in the United States, it is, nevertheless, certainly a step in the right direction (Associated Press 1991: A3).

One cannot help but see a connection between this hallmark decision and the evolving recognition that gay and lesbian citizens are a growing economic market in the United States. As a nation committed to technological solutions to social problems, it is not surprising that change for sexual minorities is taking place more rapidly in the informationalized arenas of our society.

Witness, too, the recent results from a broad-based demographic survey of homosexuals by a marketing research firm in Chicago (McLeod 1991: E1), described as a "profile that some advertisers may find hard to resist." A major finding of the Chicago survey is that gay and lesbian households tend to be both affluent and educated. Gay male household incomes averaged $51,325 and lesbian ones a not unsubstantial $45,927, the average US household income being only $36,520. Despite the possibility of a conservative backlash, these figures are likely, in the very near future, to speak loudly and convincingly for a pragmatic approach to a minority market estimated at nearly $400 billion! (1991: E5). In the end, the profit motive alone may bring about significant social changes for sexual minorities. The bottom line is probably less concern over humanitarian justice for minorities and more an admission that businesses—through sheer ignorance—have overlooked a potentially lucrative market.

Images, as "pictures of reality," can become so fixed that they take on the meaning of stereotypes that justify unfair practices toward individuals or groups (Real 1989: 129). Media images, however, can and do change. Although there is a lot of talk today about "bisexual chic," overt acceptance of gay men and lesbians seems far removed from this brand of media extravagance. People still fear the promotion of homosexuality as a valid lifestyle (Miller 1989: 215). Most seem to prefer gays portrayed, however sympathetically, as victims. Furthermore, changes in communication patterns in the media do not always translate to better treatment of minorities in terms of social conditions. The "victim" is kept firmly under control in homophobic societies.

The two main mass media roles for gay people, according to Larry Gross (1991: 30), have been the "villain" and the "victim." He claims that portraying lesbians and gay men as healthy, nonstereotypic men and women still poses problems for the way normalcy is maintained in our society. Although the fact that the media have shifted the dominant image of gays from villain to the more passive, but marketable, metaphor of victim does not in itself indicate real equality for sexual minorities. It merely means that a consumer-oriented society is inclined to promote gay liberties that are perceived to create a gay consumer demand (Kirk & Madsen 1989: 76).

Inserting more positive images of gays and lesbians into news and television presentations should bring about changes in how stereotypes are perceived (cf. the movie *Switch*); but McQuail points out limits to the influence of the media as well as the need to view media in their total cultural context (1989). This is a thesis shared by Real in *Super Media* (1989). Many scholars feel that personal contacts between people (if under favorable conditions) do more to reduce prejudice than exposure to positive media content alone. Paradoxically, there is growing evidence that, while media are more sympathetic toward aspects of the gay experience, there is less personal communication between gays and nongays than ever before (Kirk & Madsen 1989).

Culture and communication reciprocally influence each other, and identities are often created out of this complex interaction. Media alone, then, can affect but minor changes if culture is not ready for such changes. Both the media *and* culture help in self-constructions. McQuail (1989: 194) argues that there is usually bias toward consensual values of a society, with "out-groups" receiving differential treatment from the media that bears little relationship to actual numbers or their significance. A general pattern has been to over-emphasize "troublesome groups," not infrequently misrepresenting the facts about them in the process. Furthermore, McQuail accepts the fact that this sort of media bias may be more or less inevitable (1989: 156).

The media, according to this "cultural norms theory," constitute a collective response to social deviance in general. The mirror metaphor (media reflecting consensual values of society) tends, however, to absolve media creators and their audiences of any responsibility for ameliorating the social condition of sexual minorities. The implication is that media merely passively mirror myths and stereotypes rather than actively aid in their construction and transmission (Real 1989: 251). Even though media have been guilty of systematically distorting information about homosexuality, they do offer at least the potentiality, not only for symbolic annihilation of this subordinated group, but for its liberation as well.

Kirk and Madsen (1989: 162), in *After the Ball: How America Will Conquer its Fear and Hatred of Gays in the '90s*, detail a fairly comprehensive public relations campaign for presenting a better public image of homosexuals through specific communication strategies. They suggest the following media tactics: *desensitization* (presenting gays as normal people), *jamming* (juxtaposing typically perceived opposing ideas, e.g., gay Christians) and the more long-term goal of *conversion* (trying to cancel out negative with positive images).

Anything that reinforces revulsion is not persuasive communication. Gay marches, they argue, are a case in point. Mostly presented in the media as "freak shows," marches are designed to visually shock rather than edify, thus are to be avoided. Likewise, they remind the reader that too much emphasis on so-called "gay culture" may translate negatively: "They are not like us and deserve therefore to be punished as different" (1989: 183). Rather, emphasis should be on gays gaining fundamental freedoms: constitutional rights and equal protection under the law—in other words, basic fairness and justice. Civil rights should be the goal, not simply sexual rights. Much remains, however, in trying to integrate homosexuality into an equitable legal framework in this country. *After the Ball*, in spite of its sometimes histrionic tone, remains a significant book about the importance of image for gay people.

Strategies of Social Creativity/Beyond the Stereotypes

Despite real strides in overcoming oppression in places like Sweden, gay people worldwide have been relatively unsuccessful in educating the nongay public about gay issues. Part of the difficulty surely lies with the media presentations of gays and lesbians. Sensationalism (reputed gay child molestation themes) and romanticism (dying AIDs "victims"), respectively, are media images that, although less than edifying, apparently still sell. The AIDs crisis, which has the potentiality to virtually overshadow all other concerns in the gay social and political agenda, certainly has complicated this issue, even if lately media response in the United States appears somewhat more sympathetic.

The myth of the composite portrait still lingers in the minds of many people. Stereotypes about lesbians and gay men seem not to go away. Most researchers stress the role of minorities in siphoning away potentially threatening accumulations of unrest in the established orders. Barry Adam has called this function "the lightning rod" theory (1978: 28–29). Stigmatized people serve as "lightning rods" for the discontent and aggression that ebb and flow with historical ups and downs. What has been dubbed the "moral panic" function of the media in policing so-called deviance is similar to this sociological metaphor. Hence, the economic insecurities of the 1980s paralleled the revival of racism, the Ku Klux Klan, anti-Semitism, the neo-Nazis, and an anti-gay backlash.

Ultimately competition is over political and economic control of goods and resources (Adam 1978). Political access usually remains the monopoly of the nonstigmatized. The politics of homosexuals as social strangers translates into restricted life opportunities. The ideal goal would be to educate the dominant society to accept a degree of diversity in lifestyles (as in cultures), while avoiding the more ego-destructive myths that dehumanize people and, in so doing, seek new substitutes for the older scapegoat functions that minorities have traditionally performed. Certainly, a key to understanding a lot of behavior is identity, the framework for making sense of our feelings about self and society.

Both nongays and gays are guilty of using the metaphor of closet to symbolize and justify exclusion or exclusiveness, respectively. When gays argue for a separate culture, they inadvertently perpetuate the stranger role. By emphasizing differences, many of which do not exist, they are in essence giving societal justification for more separateness, hence more discrimination based on differences. Although anthropological evidence suggests there are more similarities than differences in the human family, this straightforward idea has not found much philosophical support in the present decade (cf. the contemporary emphasis on "educational particularism" on American campuses). Gay scholars, too, have some responsibility in clarifying their positions on this unfortunately still controversial matter of gay culture.

It is argued here that a closet mentality, rather than providing a common ground of communication between homosexuals and heterosexuals, tends to erect barriers to social interaction and ultimately contributes to the stranger status common to gays as a group in many societies. A *Newsweek* article (March 12, 1990: 23), for example, claimed that there is widespread disagreement within the gay community (read, communities) over how to live "outside the closet." I quote: "Should gays pursue their own *countercultural lifestyle* in such urban ghettos as San Francisco's Castro district, or *assimilate* into the dominant *straight culture?*" (my emphases). I believe this dichotomous choice is a gross over-simplification.

This model of cultural change (no doubt with oblique reference to liberal sociology and anthropology) is largely an inappropriate metaphor of change for groups that are not, in fact, *culturally* distinctive! Can you culturally assimilate a group that is already a part (albeit a closeted part) of an existing culture? This question reiterates the need *not* to confuse the construct of "society" with that of "culture," hence mistaking social changes for cultural change. Lifestyle differences may indeed sometimes exist among segments of the gay and lesbian communities, but not cultural differences per se. A culture based simply on sexual preference would be perplexing at best. Issues of sexuality, race, gender, and social class are, according to Miller (1989: 179), often complex and intertwined, making easy generalizations about identity and culture somewhat suspect. Hence, the reference in the magazine article to "straight culture" is incorrect. Nongay individuals in our society may dominate both the political and social scenes, but the culture is shared by both groups![15]

Henri Tjafel's model of social change may offer a way out of this conceptual dilemma (1978, 1984). For groups where power and status have an important bearing on social identities, Tajfel argued that dominated groups will develop collective strategies to try and create more positive social identities for themselves. Ultimately, the real issue is over *social participation*.[16]

Members of minority groups, then, are motivated to achieve a positive identity through adopting the "best" features of the high-status group (unfortunately, labeled "assimilation"); creating new and positive images of self and group ("social creativity"); and, finally, challenging the power relationship itself through resistive strategies (what he calls "social competition"). I believe that homosexuals in American culture are primarily characterized today as trying to create new and positive images. Therefore, gays and lesbians are in stage two of "social creativity." Tjafel's model, as it does not imply the creation of a separate culture, seems to work more efficiently than the older cultural change models. *Social creativity* is related only to the desire of the group for a better self-image and, subsequently, public image. A separate identity, as was pointed out in chapter 5, can exist without a separate culture just as identity itself need not always correspond with sexual orientation.

The next step for gay and lesbian citizens is to decide what kinds of social changes are possible for social strangers in homophobic cultures. Changes for sexual minorities may have to come primarily through restructuring interpersonal relationships between gays and nongays and altering societal relationships through political persuasion. Only then will the elimination of institutionalized homophobia take place. At present, however, American law treats a significant portion of our population "differently, unequally, and unfairly" (Rivera 1982: 332). In summary, the social stranger, to paraphrase Goldman (1989), is a "pedagogical metaphor" that challenges us to address our biases about sexuality and invites us to adopt more open-minded views of the unfamiliar, whether socially, culturally or *sexually* alien to our world views.

Principal Points

Using the closet metaphor, this chapter examined the role of homophobia, with its denial of cultural legitimacy and social participation, in creating a category of social stranger for sexual minorities. The metaphor of closet is an apt image of the constant insider-outsider dilemmas that face homosexuals in society. The author's Swedish research was described in order to illustrate how groups with externally imposed identities learn to cope positively with domination. The major debate today is still over social exclusion or social inclusion. The concept of handicapping reveals limits of media influence while raising an important question of how gays—presently "sympathetic victims"—might eventually be integrated into the larger society. Is the notion of a shared humanity still only a utopian dream for sexual minorities throughout most of the world?

Notes

1. Part of this text adapted from a chapter written in 1983 for a sociology textbook: Thomas K. Fitzgerald, "Homosexuality: the Myth of the Composite Portrait" in R. C. Federico and J. S. Schwartz, eds. *Sociology* 216–21. Reading, Mass.: Addison-Wesley. Permission to use this material granted by McGraw-Hill.

2. Herek (1985) has reminded us that gender roles are differentially sanctioned for men and women, have different consequences for the advantaged and the disadvantaged, and are viewed differently by persons of different ages, races, and social circumstances.

3. This outlaw role is similar to La Fontaine's (chapter 3) nonperson category. As "person" is society's confirmation of self, homosexuals in many cultures—lacking such validation of their personhood—pay a heavy psychological price as far as identity is concerned. Harsh metaphorical images, such as nonperson and cultural outlaw, often offend liberal sensibilities because of their stark, negative connotations. Thus, I have chosen here to employ the more neutral concept of social stranger (cf. Gudykunst & Kim's [1984] concept of cultural stranger) even though, as a pedagogical metaphor, it has some limitations. "Social stranger" is used here to mean social outsider

rather than "foreigner," or "one unacquainted with the culture." Therefore, the social stranger is a person having the quality of not fitting in socially, or one who is *perceived* to be different from the norm.

4. A high-risk group would surely be gay teenagers. At a New York City counseling service, Judy Folkenberg (1989) found that half of the gay adolescents had been emotionally or physically abused—mostly by family members! Apparently some parents vented their own negative feelings on their homosexual children.

5. Herek is not totally happy with the metaphorical medical imagery suggested by the label "homo-*phobia*" and questions the automatic assumption that prejudice toward gays is always based on phobic fears rather than institutionalized, learned hostilities (1985: 145). He suggests that prejudice may be less an individual problem and more a social one. These different approaches carry with them different strategies for combatting stereotypes.

6. James Weinrich points out that arguments involving nature are difficult to evaluate scientifically (1982: 203). When animals do something we humans like, we call it "natural"; when it is something we do not like, we call it "animalistic."

7. Gallup polls in 1989 showed some improvement in attitudes, due possibly to the responsible way that gays and lesbians handled the AIDs crisis, which some believe may have led to a new respect for the gay community. At the same time, incidents of violence against gays rose sharply in some areas ("The Future of Gay America," *Newsweek*, March 12, 1990: 21–27).

8. Combinations may include celibacy, with or without a particular identity; bisexuality, with homosexual or heterosexual identification and matching social behaviors; or exclusive identity, with sometimes corresponding sexual behaviors, as "straight" or "gay." Gender identity does not always inform us about actual social or sexual behaviors (Plummer 1981; Troiden 1985).

9. William Paul (1982b: 373) makes the valid point that the contest for recognition and control, as far as media coverage is concerned, is vastly uneven when you compare the New Right and its resources with the so-called invisible minorities.

10. Compare this brilliant observation: "When gays, for example, publicly protest for equal treatment under the law, including the right to teach and the recognition of homosexual marriages, they are not only saying, 'I'm different and I'm proud of it.' They are also saying, 'I should be treated as if I'm the same as everyone else'" (Meyrowitz 1986: 133).

11. Despite the overall anti-gay climate that prevails, the AIDs crisis made the media wake up to the existence of gays and lesbians in American

society (Miller 1989: 295). Even negative stereotypes can produce a degree of sympathy for individuals and groups previously shunned (cf. the American Playhouse production of "Longtime Companion," September 29, 1991).

12. Kirk and Madsen report that only about 10 percent of all detected child molesters are, in fact, gay (1989: 43).

13. The other side of this negative metaphorical image of handicap is the occasional "positive handicap," where the outsider role actually becomes a source of strength. Consider Thomas Cowan's (1988: 1–3) celebratory book, *Gay Men and Women Who Enriched the World*, which introduces the novel idea that these extraordinary men and women enriched the world, not in spite of their sexuality, but probably because of it. The argument: Some gay people, having had their worth as persons denied, nonetheless confronted society and, in so doing, gained self-confidence and strength of character. The outsider perspective proved useful for a number of these individuals, allowing them to emerge as interpreters of culture and communication mediators.

14. A.T. & T. has had a nondiscriminatory policy for all its workers since 1975; the Xerox Corporation recently instituted a policy of prohibiting discrimination based on sexual orientation, and U.S. West Communications is considering benefits for domestic partners on the same par as legal spouses (Deutsch 1991: E4).

15. Concerning the debate over same-sex marriage, a thoughtful letter to the editor appeared in *Out/Look* (no. 8, Spring 1990: 6), which gives an insider's point of view on this issue of gay culture: "The dangerous undercurrent . . . is the idea that homosexual America is a culture unto itself—fundamentally different and thus fundamentally separate. Gay and straight Americans learn in the same schools, worship in the same churches, work for the same corporations, grow up in the same families. Homosexuals are no more a distinct culture than the poor, the elderly, or the left-handed. I am not merely squabbling about the semantics of the word 'culture.' The point is this: We gay Americans are *not* fundamentally different. To argue otherwise can lead at best to a 'separate but equal' status" (Tom Chatt, California).

16. Neil Miller (1989: 9) maintains that gay and lesbian individuals are becoming "mainstream Americans" as they learn to reconcile their lives with their roots, their families, and many of the essential values of the larger culture. His is a book about finding one's place in society, as it portrays gays and gay life on a continuum, with individuals and groups from time to time at different points along its progression (1989: 303).

8

○ Metaphors and Scientific Discourse in Social Gerontology

As it is, the outdated metaphors and negative stereotypes that surround the concept [aging] are a hindrance to creative thinking about the possibilities for later life.

—John Bond and Peter Coleman, *Aging in Society*

Image-metaphors have been used throughout this book to illustrate and highlight concepts, ideas, and debates in the culture-communication dialogue. Nowhere is the use of metaphor better exemplified than in research on gerontology, the study of aging. Contemporary images of the elderly, however, have changed so dramatically over the years that even to try to summarize different points of view, using now-discarded metaphors, is problematic. In the following summaries of aging and the aged in other cultures, readers may react negatively to some of the representations. Probably not because such portrayals are incorrect. Such metaphorical imagery, from our modern twentieth-century perspective, simply strikes us as inept, quaint, and a little threatening at some level. With this warning in mind, let us turn to a consideration of metaphors and scientific discourse in social gerontology.

Aging As Metaphor/Changing Images

Metaphor, a way of expressing one thing in terms of another, has always played an extensive role in the culture-communication dialogue. According to Lakoff and Johnson (1980: 4), metaphors help to structure how we perceive reality, how we think, and what we do.

More than merely figurative speech—always rooted in cultural and social experiences—metaphors carry culture-bound assumptions about our everyday lives. What a culture values, then, will frequently be metaphorically expressed. Thus, metaphors are potentially powerful intellectual tools.

As cultural values change, so will the metaphors that represent those aspects of experience also change. Pervasive in scientific language, metaphors tend to highlight certain cultural values that we experience collectively (Lakoff & Johnson 1980: 66). Studies of the elderly in different cultures have been replete with such imagery: from the more static disengagement images of old age; to the more neutral dramaturgical metaphors suggesting role competence and onstage activity; finally, to the contemporary building metaphors that emphasize positive self-constructions. From the point of view of the elderly themselves, for the most part these have been negative images of aging and the aged. Considerable changes, however, have occurred in this regard in the past few years.

Although studies of the elderly abound in metaphorical representations, metaphors in scientific discourse have some serious limitations. In general, this book considers negative as well as positive uses of "metaphors of identity" as these relate to discussions of culture and communication. The present chapter, in particular, is concerned with the effectiveness of metaphor in scientific discussions of the last phases of adulthood.[1]

Metaphorical images are cultural signs which sometimes illuminate "truth" about a subject but also can contribute to a certain amount of social illusion. Like other cultural signs and symbols, Berger argues that metaphors may serve ideological purposes rather than contributing to human betterment (1990). Where the media is a factor, misleading emotional imagery can have adverse political consequences, for example, when overly romanticized images of elderly support systems result in government policies that exacerbate rather than address social problems (Sokolovsky 1990a). There is, then, need to look at both the historical and cultural contexts of metaphorical conceptualizations of any social phenomenon. A major goal of the present chapter is to consider the changing metaphors of aging, trying to unravel their social and cultural meanings. What metaphors have been used in scientific discourse in social gerontology? How have these image-metaphors changed over time, as well as in different social or cultural contexts?

The Cultural Context of Aging and the Aged

Discourse in social gerontology, claims Sokolovsky (1990b: 3), is fairly recent, often incomplete, and sometimes little more than "sentimental nonsense." In the last twenty-five years, however, a characteristically anthropological approach to aging and the aged has developed that promises to give us a broader, more "inside" (emic) view of this last phase of adulthood (Clark & Anderson 1967; Fry 1981; Keith 1985; Kaufman 1986; Myerhoff 1978a; Meyerhoff 1978b; Myerhoff & Simić 1978; Sokolovsky 1990b).

Age is a significant ingredient of personality development, another important context for examining human identification. Ethnographic studies have suggested that each culture defines what is appropriate behavior for the elderly. Therefore, we need to keep in mind the distinction between the biological fact of age and the social construction of the aging process. Furthermore, we need to investigate some of the ways that the media are transforming this biological potential into new social patterns. Media attention for the elderly population is a fairly recent phenomenon about which we know relatively little.

As metaphors often are used to facilitate communication between scholars and lay readers, these cultural signs have been frequently employed to shed light on this profoundly existential aspect of our existence. It has been argued that people tend to act in terms of their intuitive understandings of deeply felt metaphorical images that correspond to emotional feelings of what best fit their perceptions of reality. Discourse in social gerontology cannot escape image-metaphors. To give the reader some historical perspective, we might briefly consider the anthropological investigations of this subject in other cultures.

The anthropological study of aging (Myerhoff 1978b; Myerhoff & Simić 1978; Fry 1981; Counts & Counts 1985b; Keith 1985; Sokolovsky 1990b) has focused on cultural comparisons (Do all people in all cultures define "old" in the same way?), as well as the consequences of social change for the elderly (Is growing old a social asset or a social liability?). There has been considerable interest in cultural strategies and solutions that different elderly groups have devised to handle basic human problems (What happens, for example, when older persons are placed in segregated facilities?).

The topic of gender and aging has become a lively consideration of scholars of social gerontology (What are the sex differences in aging?) Ethnicity, as it relates to culture and health, continues as a concern in this ongoing dialogue (Is ethnicity always a positive resource for the elderly?). Sociologists and anthropologists have long been interested in age differences and their relationships to social organization (How does age affect membership in social groupings?). To a lesser extent, more recent research has begun to inquire into the identity of elderly persons, focusing on how people maintain a sense of continuity and meaning in face of inevitable biological changes (Myerhoff 1978b; Matthews 1986; Kaufman 1986; Hazan 1990a). In short, cross-cultural studies of aging have contributed to a better understanding of the meaning of "old" in cultural context, have exploded some of the myths about this group, and have looked at the consequences of age for the cultural construction of a sense of personhood, or identity.

Definition may be the most obvious cultural influence on the aged. According to Keith (1985: 240), the most common criteria for assigning people to the category "old" in all cultures are functionality and chronology. In a sample of world cultures, it was found that not all people have an explicit definition of old age, 62 percent lacking such categorization.[2] A recent reconsideration of more modern evidence suggests that the use of chronological age may no longer be the most useful way of defining the later stages of human aging (Bond & Coleman 1990b). When the label is used, "immobility" is most often the key to how the elderly are treated. It is the frail elderly, almost everywhere, that are viewed as troublesome to society (Logue 1990: 350).

Social role, then, becomes crucial in defining an older person's place in society. Decline in strength and health can result in the elderly being considered "burdens" on society. Hence, most old people will try at all odds to prevent being labeled "nonfunctional" and will continue tasks no matter how trivial or degrading. In preindustrialized societies, according to Glascock (1990: 52), totally dependent elderly are sometimes referred to as "the already dead" or "the over-aged"; and stark metaphors, such as "the sleeping period," were applied to their condition.[3] Although we react to such image-metaphors with mild disgust, ethnographers have long recognized that throughout much of the world the socially "defunct" are often classified with the dead (Counts & Counts 1985a: 12). "Excessive longevity" (survival beyond one's ability to make positive contributions to society), according to Barbara Logue (1990: 353), is universally devalued.

When elderly people can no longer actively participate in family and community events—at least in nonindustrialized societies—they may be forsaken, abandoned, even killed (Glascock 1990: 43–56). In terms of treatment for the elderly, clearly there are cultural contexts that favor this group and those that do not. Some type of functional definition, therefore, is resorted to based on changes either in social or physiological status. Consequently, it is increasingly recognized that there is likely to be more than one phase of old age. It is the "old-old" that are the least likely to have social protections in society (Logue 1990: 359).

Cultural definitions of these different stages of "oldness" have resulted in different social treatments. Most societies make a distinction between *intact* old and *decrepit* old, between the active and the totally dependent elderly. The concept of cultural centrality (a measure of how involved in the culture individuals are, based on the ability to perform social roles) becomes crucial in explaining an older person's place in society. When social performance is in jeopardy, definition of a person's status may change dramatically. Like ethnicity, gender, class, and sexual preference, age is just another way by which people can be stratified in a society. When an individual's "communicative performance" is compromised because of age, the consequences can be devastating.

This "dark side of aging" has been examined in rich ethnographic detail in the excellent Sokolovsky edition (1990b), *The Cultural Context of Aging.* Judith Barker systematically explored the distinction between decrepit and intact elders in the little-known Western Polynesian island of Niue (1990: 295–313). There she found considerable differences in the treatment of the very frail and the more physically intact elderly. By our Western cultural standards, frail old people on Niue were not receiving the kind of attention the author expected they would or should, especially given the central Polynesian values that typically stress the importance of the elderly as respected community figures. She asked why.

The decrepit elderly are spoken of as "the gray fish of the land," using the graphic metaphor of the *mutumutu-fonua,* or the "ritually unclean." The Niuean explanation for the "neglect" of "the nearly dead" is based on the cultural premise that the decrepit old are those in transition between this world and the twilight world of ghosts. Therefore, they are feared as any malevolent or foreign intrusion— similar, the author points out, to Mary Douglas's notion of "matter out of place" (quoted p. 312). Thus, treatment of the elderly in Niue is not simply a means of relieving younger people of an economic burden (there is no such treatment of young persons who are mentally incompetent, for example), but a sensible precaution against ghostly contamination. After the death of such persons, the community shows both deference and grief appropriate to the status of an elderly Polynesian.[4] The anthropological approach gives us a more comprehensive view of the reality of aging in its total cultural and social contexts.

Andrei Simić has used a now familiar image-metaphor of the aging process (1978, 1990). His argument is that aging should be regarded as a kind of career, in which some fail and some succeed, in varying degrees, in achieving the goals set out by their culture. Contrasting the stereotypical American ethos of individualism, generational independence, and self-determination with the Yugoslavian world view stressing kinship and intergenerational symbiosis, Simić concluded that the American desire for complete independence can cause feelings of isolation for older Americans (1990: 89). For the Yugoslavs, even in death, generational continuity is preserved and perpetuated in elaborate mortuary customs. The dead in Yugoslavia are honored in ways unimaginable in the United States. Thus, the Yugoslav deceased continue to exert a strong psychological presence among the living. Aging, in this context, is viewed metaphorically as a career that builds "upon the present and past for future payoffs" (1990: 80).

Looking at the construction of personhood among another contemporary group of elderly, Haim Hazan researched "adjustment problems" of elderly Jews in a comparative study of old-age homes in Israel and England (1990a: 263–276). Using a situational-contextual analysis, being concerned with how nursing homes maintain social strategies of "exclusion" or "inclusion," he focused on three dimensions of selfhood for the elderly: the mental, the socio-cultural, and the physical (1990: 268). The dichotomy of categorizing the old as "fit" and "unfit" was handled quite differently in the two home settings.

The old-age home in Israel, for example—favoring members with élite, influential backing—placed an emphasis on physical fitness to the extent of excluding all disabled residents. The elderly Jewish residents in the London home, by contrast, lacked all hierarchical ordering of human beings into the fit and unfit. As Hazan puts it: "[T]he participants did not adopt somatic yardsticks to erect social divisions" (1990a: 272). The division of the old into the categories fit and unfit left the frail and dependent with disgrace and indignity in the Israeli situation. In the London home, however, there was more care and unconditional help for all residents regardless of illnesses and disabilities. One group, then, erected rigid boundaries of exclusion based on physiological, social, and mental differences. The other, by contrast, tried to blur these categories by adopting a stance of social inclusion.

A major theme of this provocative article is that identity must be viewed in its social context rather than merely in reference to an individual's life history, especially in an artificially constructed "home" environment where cultural values, to some extent, are suspended in favor of social realities. The author recognized a gap between culture and the aged self in this ethnographic example, which suggests that the self is reconstituted through cultural classifications "based on a newly acquired balance between the desirable and the attainable" (1990a: 276). This approach is not the usual view of personhood generated by *culture* precisely because it looks at the aged self in more dynamic *social* interactions. This thesis is in keeping with the conclusions of the present book, which has emphasized social realities over cultural determinism.

Jay Sokolovsky makes a similar plea in his research report "Aging, Ethnicity, and Family Support" (1990a: 207). He argues that there is a tendency to over-romanticize ethnic support systems and the ethnic family structure in general. Although ethnicity can certainly be a positive resource for some elderly persons, women with a traditional ethnic sex-role identity—contrary to sentimental expectation—were found to have higher levels of psychological distress. Considering the impact of social factors on the ethnically different, he points out how family support networks may work for males but be socially disastrous for females. His conclusion is that unrealistic and sentimental views of the strength of ethnic culture can have unfortunate effects for certain members. Using the metaphor of culture as a guiding map rather than a rigid set of rules for human action, culture is seen as providing a framework for categorizing older people. Actual social experiences, however, are often more crucial in determining human adjustments.

We turn to Sweden for a splendid example of a national program that promotes the independence, integrity, and meaningful participation of the aged in community life. Bruce Zelkovitz (1990: 163–180) argues that capitalist welfare states have tended to perpetuate social inequalities by segregating the elderly, while at the same time trying to ensure that basic needs are at least minimally met. He labels this policy toward the elderly "reproductive."

Sweden is a country with about 8.3 million citizens and the most populous of the five Nordic nations with the largest percentage over sixty years of age. A capitalist country (90 percent private ownership) having a standard of living 30 percent higher than the United States, Sweden has no homeless citizens and no slums; health care is universal and relatively inexpensive (1990: 165–67). Rather than being labeled "reproductive," Sweden's aging policy should be called "transformative," argues Zelkovitz, because it is a policy that actively creates positive social changes for the elderly in Swedish society.

The principles of self-determination, active participation, and meaningful environments for older Swedes are geared toward increasing democratization and integration of Swedish society. A government official put the sentiment this way: "In the U.S., isolated people create possibilities. In Sweden, we create the networks that create possibilities" (1990: 169–70). These "networks" embody cultural values that stress less separation between groups in society, including both physical and status separation. The term *transformative*, from the viewpoint of the aging recipients themselves, further connotes a more open and flexible future. With less limitations linked to class, physical disabilities, ethnicity, sex, or culture, elderly people in Sweden are empowered with more human potential (1990: 176).

Changing Metaphors/Aging as Identity Transformation

Social gerontology, until recently devoid of much theory development, has utilized guiding metaphors that have both helped and hindered our understanding of the aging process (Marshall 1985: 251). Typically, metaphors reveal more about feelings than fact. They are likely to be incomplete and always culturally specific. As John Bond and Peter Coleman (1990a: 281) have demonstrated, outmoded metaphors of aging can become hindrances to creative thinking about the changing possibilities of later life.

Older metaphors of aging placed heavy emphasis on cultural, social, or situational influences on elderly individuals. Suggested in this mirror metaphor was an image of people more or less passively "reflecting" cultural prescriptions appropriate to a given age. Furthermore, it was assumed that, as people aged, they gradually disengaged from society, becoming increasingly socially isolated. As our understanding of culture increased, so gradually did our appreciation of some of the complicated relationships between aging and culture. Culture has come to be seen as a potential human resource subject to both interpretation and misinterpretation. In this model, individuals can manipulate, interpret, and reinterpret culture throughout the life course. Ethnographic studies of aging have begun to challenge both the disengagement notion and its guiding metaphors.

One of the major challenges to the older perspective on aging has come from cross-cultural research on gender and aging.

Anthropologists have concluded that a person's gender is not biologically fixed and, contrary to cultural ideology, has compensatory functions that often vary by sex. Aging poses different cultural challenges for men and women in different cultural contexts. For women, onset of age in many cultures often signals the lifting of cultural taboos on social interactions. The expanded activities of elderly Maori women was cited in chapter 6 as an example that countered the older disengagement idea (Counts & Counts 1985a: 3). Although both men and women undergo changes in their behavior as they age, society's expectations vary by sex. Men typically experience a move from more to *less* social activity, women often the reverse (1985a: 7). As women age, traditional gender rules seem to relax.

Old women apparently age with less difficulty than old men. The explanation may lie in the distinction between "ascribed" versus "achieved" social identities. Simić and Myerhoff (1978: 238) believe that women, with their more ascribed identities, learn greater skills in establishing social relationships. Men, with more achieved identities, experience in aging a diminished ability to fulfill the cultural ideals of machismo, work, and achievement and, therefore, may suffer from a sense of role alienation. An interesting, if unproven, supposition.

Catherine Coles documents an intriguing case of changing power for older women in urban Nigeria (1990: 65–66). In this country, the passage from middle to old age brings increased freedoms from restraint and reserve in female behaviors. Older women, for example, can voice their opinions more freely. They have considerable power and authority in kinship matters, work, and community affairs. Paradoxically, a woman may portray herself as prematurely old in order to escape the burdens that traditionally accompany role behavior for a younger female. In this case, the passage from middle to old age is actually speeded up—and by choice!

The most widely accepted approach to aging and the aged in social gerontology today is, according to Marshall (1985: 255), the "life course perspective," which most often utilizes an interpretive or hermeneutic methodology. Rather than emphasizing the normative and deterministic role of culture, this model typically has employed a career metaphor. Because aging can involve the output of effort and energy, it is conceived of as a kind of *work*, hence the rationale for using this imagery. Older people are pictured as actively shaping their own roles and negotiating their own careers. This image-metaphor contradicts the concept of growing old as simply "a series of losses to be endured" (Myerhoff & Simić 1978: 240).

The concept of old age as career, argues Victor Marshall (1985), is a natural outgrowth of a more humanistic approach to human behavior that has become increasingly characteristic of contemporary social science. The message in this scientific dialogue is that age status is situational rather than fixed, achieved rather than ascribed. Aging is seen as a period of purposeful participation rather than the inevitable isolation suggested by the mirror metaphors that characterized earlier studies. The inflexible disengagement metaphors, then, have been replaced with less deterministic images of the aging process. Marshall suggests that a common metaphor in social gerontology is the dramaturgical metaphor that places emphasis on the playing of roles that are negotiated in "careers" over the life course (1985: 265). This emergent "life course perspective," he reasons, pictures individuals as socially constructing (negotiating) the life course.

Rather than a blueprint of human action, culture becomes merely the framework that people can use to guide human behavior. Throughout this book, culture has been viewed metaphorically as a sort of map, the goal of human behavior ultimately being a journey (performance = communication) and identity, from an individual or a group perspective, acting as compass, piloting or steering the journey.

Studies of aging and the aged, we repeat, abound in metaphorical representations. Today we have extended the life course perspective and, to some extent, may have replaced the dramaturgical metaphors. Using building metaphors to accentuate negotiation and self-construction, it is assumed—rightly or wrongly—that people can construct and transform their own selves. The new buzzword is "transformation." The guiding metaphor of aging for the 1990s is that of *transforming identities* for adaptation, growth, and survival. Caution is merited, however, in drawing firm conclusions in this area.

Over the past twenty-five years, there seems to have been a noticeable evolution of metaphorical imagery in research studies in social gerontology. Although assuming a variety of forms in different cultures, aging has been viewed metaphorically using the more static mirror image of the individual passively reflecting society (cultural disengagement theories); as well as the more action-oriented dramaturgical metaphors that have suggested acting out "roles on a stage" (fashioning a career, if you will); and, finally, the contemporary, elastic building metaphors that, correctly or incorrectly, conclude that individuals are in control of their own destinies, constructing or transforming their own selves.

Sharon Kaufman's *The Ageless Self: Sources of Meaning in Late Life* nicely illustrates this research genre (1986). Assuming that mental health is dependent upon a continuous sense of self, Kaufman asked an elderly sample how they viewed themselves. This research necessarily became an inquiry into identity because the focus was on how old people maintain a sense of continuity and meaning that helped them to live with changes in life. The theme of this very readable book is that being old is not, per se, a central feature of the self, nor necessarily the primary source of meaning for the elderly. Rather, old people emphasize the continuity of life by maintaining "the ageless self" amid changes across the life span (1986: 13). This is essentially the common-sense adage, "As you become old, you are simply more of the same." Personal identity, being stronger than age as such, may persist throughout life. Hers, however, is not a static understanding of self-development.

Kaufman also viewed the self as an interpreter of experience. From this perspective, individual identity is revealed by the pattern of symbolic meaning that characterizes each individual's unique interpretation of experience. Culture only provides a person with a "frame" for making sense of and interpreting his or her own life within the larger society. "Identity is not frozen in a static moment of the past," Kaufman (1986: 14) stressed:

> Old people formulate and reformulate personal and cultural symbols of their past to create a meaningful, coherent sense of self, and in the process they create a viable present. In this way, the ageless self emerges: its definition is ongoing, continuous, and creative.

With age comes a steady extension in the self-concept, with ever-widening contexts for self-expression.

She collected fifteen in-depth life histories (from her sample of sixty urban, white, middle-class Californian elderly over seventy years old) in order to study the relationships among old age, personal reflection, and identity.[6] In the descriptions of their lives, she felt that people create themes which explain, unify, and give substance to their perceptions of social experience. Themes become "explanation markers" that emerge as individuals relate their life stories. This idea is similar to Elizabeth Stone's notion of the function of family stories as "explanation myths" (1989: 100).

Kaufman (1986: 26) considers these themes, or "reformulated experiences," to be the "building blocks of identity." But, how do themes operate in shaping identity? Isolating social factors, Kaufman (1986: 72) concluded that themes are subjective interpretations of one's cultural heritage as well as interpretations of personal experience. Themes are ways in which old people formulate their identities to create symbols of continuity. An important methodological question remains. Where did these themes come from: societal expectations, the culture, or from the author herself? "Building" metaphors, as guides to gerontological research, may be more of a hindrance than a help in understanding this complex process.

Using both the concept of culture as an interpretive enterprise and the idea of identity development as a dynamic ongoing process, Kaufman nonetheless offers a new perspective that suggests that successful aging takes place—at least, with a middle-class, white urban American sample—when individuals symbolically connect meaningful past experiences with current circumstances. By looking at themes from respondents' stories, she could see how old people attempt to cope with their losses, creating new meanings as they reformulate and "build" viable selves in this lifelong process. The conclusion is that the elderly in this sample do not define themselves as old but rather maintain an ageless self that transcends life-span changes by providing continuity and meaning to experience (1986: 161).

Millennium as the "Metaphor of the ₁Future"

We stand at the dawn of a new era, claim Naisbitt and Aburdene (1990: 16), authors of *Megatrends 2000*. The millennium is the pre-eminent metaphor of the future. A rosy picture of telecommunications supporting an economic boom and "technology empowering the individual," this image-metaphor suggests a triumphant global economy in the 1990s. The shift, the authors (1990: 181) add, is as much economic as cultural.

Employing the contemporary building metaphor, Dychtwald and Flower (1989), in *Age Wave: Challenges and Opportunities of an Aging America*, make equally optimistic predictions for the future of the elderly in America. No longer evoked are the disengagement images of aging. Considering the challenges and opportunities of an aging society, the authors preferred a guiding metaphor emphasizing individual growth, development, and, above all, positive changes for the elderly—truly a rising tide of enthusiastic change.

The theme of the book is straightforward: Postindustrial and information societies, especially America, pose new challenges for the rapidly expanding elderly population. Why is this necessarily so? The so-called "baby boomers" (seventy-six million born between 1946 and 1964) will become the dominant concern of American business and popular culture (1989: 13). In July of 1983, for example, the number over the age of sixty-five surpassed the number of teenagers in America. We are no longer a nation of youths. An information society, argue Dychtwald and Flowers (1989: 11), makes children an increasing economic hardship. The first wave of boomers will hit retirement around 2011. The authors predict a future dominated by the political and economic concerns of an elderly population (1989: 59). When a few thousand people share an opinion, read a book, or cast a vote, they concluded (1989: 18), this is an interesting fact. When seventy-six million do so, it is a revolution—a veritable "age wave."

In the not-so-distant future, the concept of "old" may be extended to include individuals 90, even 100 years old (1989: 39). As people live longer, the elderly will fashion new patterns of love, marriage, and family. They will alter the physical environment and work patterns to suit their special needs. Ultimately, it is predicted, older Americans will help to create a new society. A flexible identity for this "new wave" generation will no doubt emerge to match the social and cultural changes that are taking place in this last stage of adulthood. These are some of the utopian challenges and opportunities of an increasingly aging America.

The upbeat economic argument proposed in *Age Wave* sounds seductively plausible. As of 1989, those fifty and above owned 77 percent of the financial assets in America, 80 percent of all the money in U.S. savings-and-loan institutions, and accounted for 40 percent of the total consumer demands (1989: 269). American elderly indeed seem on a "tidal wave" of success! Not all social and economic predictions, however, have come to the same conclusions. Yankelovitch also predicted a cultural revolution "transforming the rules of American life" (1981: 36). Writing eight years before Naisbitt and Aburdene, he argued that this "new life" was, at best, risky. The core of the cultural revolution, wrote Yankelovitch (1981: 39), is the "self-fulfillment contradiction," the mismatch between the goals of the American quest for self-fulfillment and the means we will have to achieve these goals.

Yankelovitch felt that the Me generation is too preoccupied with its own needs and wishes. The negative side of the age wave optimism is cultural narcissism. Although a valid quest for positive identity in the 1990s is a noble goal, he fears that we may not have learned the proper strategies to overcome the inherent contradictions of such a visionary quest. Furthermore, claimed Yankelovitch (1981: 50), the economic realities of 1981 were "not hospitable to the self-fulfillment goals." Self is not some sort of private, autonomous, limitless, culture-free entity. Such a fallacy, he argued, is destructive to both the individual and society. The self is embedded in both culture *and* the economy. The goals of self-fulfillment may be severely limited in a fluctuating economy. Americans, he concluded (1981: 90), will be called upon to make considerably more changes to accommodate to new economic realities: "The decades ahead will be a time of harsh economic realities and the troubled conflicts of a society in change."

How can one explain the seemingly contradictory and polar images of optimism and pessimism without recourse to metaphors? Elizabeth Stone suggests that metaphors carry important unconscious messages that help us to deal with our deepest emotions and feelings (1989: 99–100). Because metaphors, like story, speak to the unconscious, they help us to "believe emotionally." Metaphors, she states (1989: 101), are versatile in this capacity precisely because they provide the foundation on which we can add our own perceptions and modifications. Above all, metaphors reveal things that the individual researcher may not be consciously aware of. Metaphors of aging and the aged, whether optimistic or pessimistic, can potentially help or hinder research interpretations.

Economic Realities, Metaphors, and the Media Challenge

It has been said that we are living in the age of aging. As far as many elderly are concerned, we are indeed living in a new era. By the year 2000, persons 65+ are expected to represent 13 percent of the U.S. population. This percentage may climb to 21.8 percent by 2030 (Fowles 1988: 2). As of 1980, the elderly made up almost 6 percent of the world's population. The 1990s will surely see dramatic and positive changes for older people worldwide (Sokolovsky 1990b). It is argued in this book that metaphors (especially those from ethnography that may have adequately pictured the vulnerability of old people in preindustrial contexts) do not totally capture the complex realities of the elderly in modern, information-based societies.

The massive explosion of telecommunications in many parts of the globe has meant the end of traditional social roles based exclusively on age. Neugarten has studied the ways society (mostly American society) transforms biological time into social time (Meyrowitz 1986: 274). She has promulgated the now widely accepted concept of an "age-irrelevant society." To summarize her argument: The lines that previously distinguished between old and young are blurring in American society (read, Western society). Age has lost a lot of its traditional meaning as many older Americans engage in activities only a few years ago considered inappropriate.

Age, then, is becoming less important as a basis for social differentiation as older people become more economically secure. Neugarten and others agree that Americans, on the whole, are less appalled at the prospects of growing older than we once were and that the cultural meaning of aging has changed, at least in Western, media-dominated societies (Gelman 1990: 53). Older individuals in contemporary societies have potentially different identity configurations. The question is why.

As we have shown, identity (the academic metaphor for self-in-context) obviously comes from face-to-face interactions, or interpersonal communications. In today's post-industrial, information societies, identity is also a product of interpersonal interactions *and* media interactions (Real 1989: 8). This constitutes a major difference between modern and preindustrial societies. What has been the influence of this mediated culture on how the elderly are viewed in contemporary societies? Media is just one type of communication defined by Real as "social interaction through messages" (1989: 33–34). This social interaction creates, expresses, and reflects culture. Furthermore, in the modern world, "the media today provide a near-total environment in which we live rather than specific stimuli causing only specific behaviors" (Real 1989: 253). The notion of media occupying a significant place between ourselves, others, and mediated experiences is itself a metaphor inviting the use of additional metaphors to characterize the role played by the media in transforming roles and identities for the elderly in modern societies.

Since the so-called telecommunication revolution, culture is something more or less shared by all people. Socialization, based on chronological age, Meyrowitz (1986) has brilliantly argued, is becoming less and less marked. Electronic media have led to a general break in the passages of the life-course. A sense of self, or identity, naturally develops through multiple avenues, including influences as far-ranging as modernization, migration, economic changes, and the like. Not denying these other explanations, Meyrowitz (1986: 52) has suggested that the merging of social roles and information systems through the widespread use of the electronic media—especially television—may account for some major shifts in role behavior, including socialization for appropriate roles of the elderly. The gist of this challenging treatise is that media change affects role change: both "roles of affiliation" (group identity), as well as "roles of transition" (socialization). Both concern us in our discussions of aging and identity in the culture-communication dialogue.

Meyrowitz further claimed that merging informational worlds for different age groups encourages egalitarian forms of interaction (1986: 64). In short, television offers new perspectives from which to gain a reflected sense of self. Media offer previously isolated groups, such as the aged, new forms of social engagement (Meyrowitz 1986: 181). What is the real challenge of media presentations as they potentially affect the lives of the elderly?

Many communication scholars have found that stereotypes of aging and the aged are reinforced by the media. *Stereotypes* (over-simplified opinion or belief) can become obstacles to effective communication between people of different ages when combined with individual or collective prejudice. Because mass media today circulate symbolic images to wider audiences than ever before, they can be severely damaging to our relationships with other people—what Featherstone and Hepworth refer to as their "symbolic stigmatization" effect (1990: 218). The media, then, can have negative as well as positive outcomes on the identities of older people.

Freimuth and Jamieson (1979: 1–38) have systematically explored the ways in which media perpetuate distorted views about the elderly and, thus, act to impede productive interpersonal communication for this group. Stereotypes, they argue, deny the elderly social supports, sometimes prevent confirmation of full personhood, and can become self-fulfilling prophesies. Until recently, old people typically appeared in advertisements for pain relievers, digestive aids, laxatives, and denture formulas (1979: 13). When they considered the fact that television commercials have about sixty seconds to develop an idea, this tendency to stereotype became even clearer (Freimuth & Jamieson 1979: 24).

Other common negative images of older people appear in the contexts of humor (jokes about the aged), in language usage ("old biddy" remarks), and in various forms of fiction,[7] for example in children's books where the elderly are often pictured as "unexciting and unimaginative" (1979: 23). Sadly, Freimuth and Jamieson

(1979: 14) concluded that, on the whole, the American public has not been very critical of the media's projections of older persons. The "identificatory tags" of aging (body image, physical traits, and competencies) have, for the most part, been negatively portrayed in the American media.

Older people universally want to be seen as people integrated and involved, both within their families and in the community—not as decrepit dependents. However, until recently the reality has been a case of media invisibility. The population over fifty-five was simply not well represented in advertising, marketing, and television. Fortunately, today there are some notable exceptions to this depressing picture. On American television, signs of change include such popular shows as the "The Golden Girls" (NBC), Jessica Fletcher in "Murder She Wrote" (CBS), and Andy Griffith's portrayal of the "cool" lawyer in "Matlock" (NBC): "[T]hese popular shows may be the vanguard of a new trend—one that accurately and sensitively mainstreams older characters into everyday television programming." (*Modern Maturity* 1991: 86)

There are, then, increasingly positive role models for the elderly; at least, this is the case in modern societies. Stereotypes for this group, nevertheless, are still widespread and continue to be reinforced by communication media in the United States. One might ask: How have the elderly fared in television presentations in other cultures?

The case study method, combined with content analysis, has provided communication researchers with an appropriate means of answering questions about the interactions of culture and the media. Using the concept of "symbolic type," Hazan analyzed a media presentation of older people on Israeli television (1990b: 77–84). He found the old symbolically pictured as "defenseless potential victim." In a youth-oriented society, such as Israel, argues Hazan, the elderly are allocated to a marginal, almost invisible place in society and treated as "objects of ridicule," "heralds of death," or else "objects of collective guilt." Hazan believes that the media message exonerates the nonaged viewer from assuming full personal responsibility for their older kin.

He concludes that the old are, thereby, socially "excommunicated" from Israeli society. This alienated position as social stranger, he further claims, is justified by the media. Hazan used a guiding mirror metaphor to explain how cultural values are reflected via the broadcast media.[8] His is essentially a "culture norms" approach, which suggests that media act as standards of behavior as well as enforcers of social norms. When people do not live up to these cultural standards, they may be treated as social strangers, since validation of personhood ultimately depends on social recognition of identity.

A minor problem with this interpretation is that stereotypes can and do change as societies change. Since the media—always a part of culture—to some extent reflect social and economic realities, these stereotypes are likewise dependent on social, political, and economic factors. The media change according to changes in these specific social areas (Wilson & Gutierrez 1985: 103). Certainly the media have responsibility for educating the larger society about the elderly population. As Michael Real (1989: 129) has consistently stressed, the power of media is not absolute but negotiable.[9] His argument is a valuable one in pointing out the complexity of media change for particular groups in society.

A significant social factor is clearly the economic position of the elderly. The aging minority—at least, this is the case in many Western societies—has become a potential consumer. Profit motive alone, then, should help bring about the demise of negative media portrayals of the elderly. According to Wilson and Gutierrez (1985: 234), the media will increasingly seek diversity in age groups, as well as in cultural and social fashions, devising new ways to capitalize on differences that will "sell." We have witnessed how the U.S. economic boom may well be related to the proliferation of telecommunications. This relationship is expected to increase dramatically between the years 2010 and 2030, when the baby boom generation reaches age sixty-five (Fowles 1988: 2). Social issues, including economic ones, ebb and flow; but certainly one of the major concerns of the 1990s will be the elderly and their position in contemporary societies.

Consumer marketing, until recently, shied away from the older population. This situation has dramatically changed in most Western societies in more recent times (Bond & Coleman 1990b). As the elderly population is growing rapidly (the over-eighty group the fastest), business is increasingly targeting the fifty-five and older group for special attention (McCauley 1990). Growth areas in "senior marketing" include, among others, the expanding convenience services for the aged. In the United States at least, it would appear that the mature market will be served.[10]

For example, a Washington-based consulting firm recently conducted research on older workers and concluded that the elderly in the workforce are just as flexible about hours and duties as younger workers, have lower turnover and absenteeism, and are often better salespeople than younger staff members (*Modern Maturity* 1991: 88). Much of this consumer-oriented research has clear and profound implications for understanding aging and identity. Factors contributing to positive self-images for the elderly, such as size, accompanying political strength, and sheer economic clout, should bring about significant changes that eventually may eliminate aging as a culturally pejorative concept. At least, this may be so in Western contexts. It is difficult, however, to know which explanation best accounts for such a complex and interacting process of change.

To sum up our present argument, metaphorical images—whether media-bound, research-based, or merely products of the larger cultural belief system—can promote positive or negative policies toward aging and the aged. The older metaphors of "role exit," or disengagement, left the elderly with more or less nonperson status, whereas the more active and contemporary building metaphors of aging stress social involvement and continued social interaction. The essential pedagogical message is how to make the elderly "stranger" more familiar, hence more acceptable in society. As hopefully this chapter has demonstrated, the transition to old age need not be a transition to a state of social decay. It is possible for the old to make healthful and wholesome adaptations to the aging process while retaining rightful and respectful positions in society (Fitzgerald 1977c). This perspective suggests that with age can come an enriched and expansive view of self.

Principal Points

Considering aging as metaphor, this chapter looked at personal chronology as another significant context for understanding identity, the academic metaphor for self-in-context; compared different cultures and their treatment of the elderly; considered the social constructions of aging and the aged; and, finally, looked at identity transformations—how identity changes with changing image-metaphors. A major debate in the culture-communication dialogue has been over what aging was like in other times and other places and where it might be going in the future. The media challenge, as response to economic realities, was considered with futurist predictions of the millennium, the pre-eminent metaphor for the future. Although progress was noted, caution is merited in drawing too rosy a conclusion based on current metaphors of aging and the aged.

Notes

1. Howard Becker (1986: 86) has claimed that metaphors work only if they are fresh enough to attract our attention; hence, he argues against the use of "tired metaphors" in social science writing. The issue in the present discussion, however, is the effectiveness of image-metaphors in the formulation of research ideas on aging and the aged, not their grammatical "freshness."

2. Among so-called primitive people, capabilities and change in physical characteristics are less frequently used as the basis for a definition of "old," most likely because they did not live long enough to become physically incapacitated (Glascock and Feinman 1981: 13–32).

3. Neil Henderson (1990: 317) employs the evocative metaphor of "the long goodbye" to describe Alzheimer's disease, a type of dementia responsible for destroying brain cells that leaves the patient in a "liminal" state, i.e., psychologically and socially neither in one category or the other.

4. The old are often viewed as powerful because they are seen as effective communicators with the influential dead (Keith 1985: 243). An unusual ethnographic twist: Among the Vanatinai (Papua, New Guinea), it is believed that elders who thought themselves poorly treated while living can, in the afterlife, return and bring misfortune upon the offenders (Lepowsky 1985: 167).

5. Recent evidence suggesting that aging adults show improvement in job performance poses a severe paradox for the parallel conclusion that supervisors often rate older workers as slightly less effective than younger ones (Bond and Coleman 1990a: 283). Images get in the way of reality.

6. Concerning minorities and aging, John Bond and associates have questioned Erik Erikson's "ego integrity" notion (the idea that the last stages of aging typically give meaning and order to one's life) as an assumption that always holds true for all minorities, even for the modern elderly in general (1990: 27).

7. Exceptions to the generalization of negative portrayals of the elderly in magazine accounts include two splendid journals, *Modern Maturity* and *Choices*, both which picture older citizens in a wide variety of upbeat social encounters.

8. Real feels that there are problems in the use of the mirror metaphor for media analysis since this metaphor suggests a vision of social reality that is rarely a perfect reflection (1989: 250).

9. Although there have been sharp reductions in negative stereotyping of the elderly in American society in recent times, the contrasting images of old age, Barbara Logue (1990: 363) argues, do not always work to the

advantage of the elderly. The ultimate evil of medical progress may be the prolonging of life when there are only declining benefits in doing so, especially for the elderly themselves.

10. A more pessimistic view is found in Susan Crowley's suggestion that the "beauty myth" is the modern "sin of aging" (1991: 2). She argues that a beauty obsession, which reflects the larger societal biases against women, often translates into age discrimination because women are bombarded with commercial messages that success must be equated with beauty.

9

◯ Communication: Identity, Community, and Survival

Any culture is primarily a system for creating, sending, storing, and processing information. Communication underlies every thing...Culture can be likened to an enormous, subtle, extraordinarily complex computer. It programs the actions and responses of every person, and these programs can be mastered by anyone....

—Edward T. Hall and Mildred Hall, *Hidden Differences*

The Future/Communication and "Cultural" Competence

As early as 1982, John Naisbitt claimed that the information society had become a reality. Although we continue to think we are living in an industrial society, stated Naisbitt, we have already changed to an interdependent economy based on the creation and distribution of information; "satellites have turned the earth inward upon itself" (1982: 12). To be successful in this information society, he reasoned, Americans will need to be trilingual: fluent in English, Spanish, and the computer.

Along the same lines, the most recent prediction is that, worldwide, we can expect to see a renaissance of language and cultural assertiveness (Naisbitt & Aburdene 1990). Cultural diversity is "in"; monoculturalism passé, predict Naisbitt and colleague. Although the "discourse of futurology" has from time to time confused culture and identity, Naisbitt and Aburdene (1990: 129) recognize that, despite the leveling of culture by modern media, there will be a corresponding accent on tradition, symbolic or real, and identities—whether religious, cultural, national, linguistic, or racial (1990: 147).

Cultural differences, where these indeed exist, are important. Unfortunately, there is the tendency today to misinterpret and overinterpret such differences. So-called cultures are described in strokes so broad that *non-cultural* differences, for example, communication styles and social behavior, often are not fully explained.[1]

This book has consistently argued that linguistic and cultural assertiveness need not imply more cultural diversity. Paradoxically, the compensatory need to assert distinctive identities, most likely due to mediated communication influences, parallels the homogenization of cultures throughout the world. Strictly speaking, then, it is not always culture that is at issue, but *identities*—with or without matching cultures. This was essentially the lesson of chapter 5.

Communication between diverse groups, whether social or cultural in origin, remains essential for our global survival. Acceptance of different lifestyles, sexual minorities, and ethnic interest groups (as well as different cultures) will be the ultimate challenge of the identity of the future. Furthermore, those who predict the future see the basic building blocks of society shifting from the traditional family to individuals and individual relationships. As science and technology gain ascendancy, we are likely to substitute intense interpersonal relationships for traditional social institutions (religion and extended family) as a way of anchoring our sense of self.[2]

This shift to a more introspective, particularized locus of responsibility for self helps to explain the prominence of the "psychic shelter" function of identity in modern times. It has long been observed that by changing the locus of identity to the personal, a heavy burden is placed on individual persons which ultimately contributes to our contemporary narcissistic tendencies (Fine 1986). Social identities take on special functional significance for humans trying to cope with the "flood of imagery" produced by the mass media and other communication networks, leaving us sometimes "over-whelmed by superficial messages and undigested cultural elements" (Lifton 1970: 318).

In our world of seemingly constant change, the creative person constantly tries to discover and rediscover self, to remodel identity in a never-ending quest for meaning. The postmodern, electronic transformation of our society to a new "cyberculture" will require persons with flexible identities that can effectively bridge the past and future. Robert Lifton felt that human minds create imagery and mythology in order to sustain a coherent sense of self. Some essential questions: What types of cognitive skills make for the most effective interpersonal or intercultural communicator? How are the mass media related to the shaping of this unique human identity? In short, what type of identity will best serve human beings in recapturing a sense of community in a world made up of so many disparate cultural and quasi-cultural parts?

Applegate and Sypher have argued persuasively that "good communication is appropriate communication" (1988: 50). Behavioral strategies are tailored to particular goals for effective communication. However, a laundry list of skills most likely to produce effective communication may not be the best way to approach the problem, inasmuch as the correlates are likely to be more situationally specific.[3] There are recognized dangers in using too strict a performance model of communication. Roloff and Kellermann caution that the focus should be on the dynamics of the decision-making process itself rather than solely on characteristics of the performers (1984: 215). For one thing, participants and observers in a communication encounter often view the interaction from quite different perspectives. In any case, one would have to be acutely aware of culture, society, and the communication context in which judgments of competence are made (Powers & Lowry 1984: 57).

Employed in this book is the concept of "cognitive flexibility"— not a static personality type, but one that bends with changing situations. Using the tripartite adaptive-growth (performance) model, effective communication, whether involving cultural or social competencies, engages the individual in at least three separate adaptive dimensions: motivation, knowledge, and the ability to perform situationally appropriate roles. Identity, as the bridge between culture and communication, must be flexible, then, in order to assure a degree of communicative competence.

One basic function of communication is to effectively control the environment; hence, competence becomes a reflection of social skills (knowledge) and social outcomes (performance), as well as, naturally, some desire (motivation) for acting out these skills. In this integrative model, behavioral flexibility means essentially adaptation in face of situationally variable environments (Sypher 1984: 110). Henry Treuba (1990: 123) gives an example of the educated Mexican-American who, rather than choosing between Chicano culture or the mainstream American one, maintains flexibility by developing bicultural skills in "code-switching" between the two contexts.

Self-concept helps to reinforce and affirm the core symbols of a society (Collier & Thomas 1988). As these core symbols change, communicative competence is challenged. Identities are validated, then, to the extent that they facilitate adaptive behavior. Communication is judged effective when individuals can deal effectively with psychological stresses. View of self ("self-monitoring," to use the current in-word) becomes crucial in communication situations. Identity, the academic metaphor for self-in-context, is an important key in explaining communicative competence. Metaphors of identity, too, have shed light on the way identity functions in changing societies.

Metaphors Revisited/The Quest for Identity

The construct of identity (abstract, multi-dimensional, always complex) has been expressed throughout this volume using a variety of metaphors—some old, some new—to highlight different aspects of the identity pool. One should note that metaphors, as images of the "good society," have changed considerably over time; thus, there is constant need to scrutinize the use of such imagery in scientific discourse. We shall examine metaphors in the context of the contemporary culture-communication dialogue.

Certainly, image-metaphors abound in academic descriptions of identity.[4] Metaphors often provide emotional "feeling tone" to otherwise literal, scientific jargon. By the same token, we have learned that metaphors are time-bound and context-specific, therefore difficult to interpret unless judged in reference to specific historic and social backgrounds. Like other aspects of culture and language, metaphors change with changing circumstances (Sacks 1979).

Arden King (1977: 106–117), one of the participants in a special volume (Fitzgerald 1977) on cultural and social identity, described the seventies using the metaphor of the labyrinth. He pictured human beings moving from one uncompleted labyrinth to another in the quest for identity. Furthermore, King suggested that this type of identity might be an entirely different phenomenon from the identity processes of the past.

Those familiar with the literature on identity will see in King's labyrinth an immediate similarity to Robert Lifton's "protean style of self-process" (1970). Proteus was a Greek god who continually changed shapes rather than committing himself to any single form. "Protean Man" was Lifton's metaphorical image of the then-modern construal of self. He traced the lack of a sense of connection in society to historical dislocations. The response to this confusing array of "identity fragments" ("identity confusion," to use Erikson's terminology) was believed to be a new psychological style of coping characterized by restless exploration, experimentation, and flux—with rapid shifts in identification and belief. This protean self, claimed Lifton (1970: 31), was no less than a new consciousness of self in history. But, was Lifton's protean identity really a new functional and psychological process?

Like other end-of-the-sixties social theorists, Lifton (1970: 331) may have been overly optimistic in his easy assumption that the youth movement, and its accompanying drug revolution (the "chemical aid to expanded consciousness"), would automatically yield an "extraordinary range of possibility for man's betterment" and eventual survival. Today, this position sounds sentimental and naive. Lifton's thesis (1970: 37) that we maintain psychological equilibrium through shifting identities and by compartmentalizing beliefs and identifications may be true, in varying degrees, at all periods of history. Humans are never perfectly adjusted to the environment and rarely in a state of equilibrium in the first place. Hence, identity— exaggerated in times of social and cultural dislocations—always performs the universal psycho-social function of helping us cope in particular contexts, especially in changing circumstances. Identity, as mediator between culture and communication, informationally links individual with environment.

Culture and communication are crucial to our understanding of how human beings achieve a sense of community. It has been argued that community depends on effective communicating. *Community* and communication, according to Glenn Tinder (1980: 131), are both fundamentally matters of sharing. Authentic community implies a collection of people that share and exchange ideas freely, the ultimate goal no doubt being a communicating global society. Although community as romantic metaphor, in the end, may be largely unattainable, community of some sort can come about only through serious attempts at interpersonal and intercultural communication. As a starting point, commitment to global communication, as suggested in this book, calls for more cultural *and* social awareness. The identifying self becomes highly significant in communication encounters.

Hence, the representation of self as essentially "personified agent," one who makes choices and manages human affairs, is the powerful image-metaphor presented in this volume (Knowles & Sibicky 1990: 603).[5] Emphasis is on individual motivation, goal-striving, and strategic actions that, hopefully, can yield improved interpersonal and intercultural communication. Using these building metaphors of identity, the ultimate goal is to rise above cultural limitations (ethnocentrism, sexism, and racism, to name a few), using our identity potential to enhance rather than restrict our lives. What is this "adaptive self" that we are fashioning for an emerging world culture?

Adaptive-Growth Model/The Flexible Identity

In this book, culture has been treated as the "frame" in which people derive a sense of who they are, how they should act, and where they are going. Identity is an important adaptive, mediating process between culture and communication. Essentially, identity gives people a sense of direction, especially in times of social and personal disunity. We have used the following metaphor: the map = culture; the journey = communication; the compass = identity. Despite its limitations, this guiding metaphor, similar to Kohut's notion of identity as the organizer of personality, places emphasis on the executive role of identity in facilitating individual adaptation and growth. Potentially, then, identity aids in human adaptation and human survival.

Adaptation, according to Ellingsworth, was the predominant concept of the 1980s, defined as "changes that individuals make in their affective and cognitive identity as well as in their interactive behavior as they deal with a new cultural environment" (1988: 259). Although culture—not always, but to a large extent—gives us our sense of who we are, identity is fundamentally the problem-solving tool for daily coping in particular environments. The individual, after all, is the action unit of culture. We speak figuratively when we say that cultures help people to cope. Individuals, through cognitive processes like identity, use cultural and social knowledge to communicate more effectively. Such proficiencies ultimately can be related to organizational success, business and trade matters, relocation experiences, and international communications, as Harris and Moran have extensively described (1989: 23–24).

We need to be more aware of the diversity of cultures and subgroups, even if some of them—strictly speaking—lack cultural authenticity. In other words, we need to know why and how communication most effectively occurs, taking into account factors such as race, ethnicity, gender, sexual preference, and religion—as well as culture itself. Approaches to learning about different cultures, or identity groups based essentially on *social* distinctions, have followed two opposing points of view: the "communication-as-problem" approach and the "communication-as-learning/growth" approach

(Kim & Ruben 1988: 30). For this text, I have adopted an adaptive-growth (performance) model for explaining identity change.

The problem approach typically has focused on role shock, language barriers, cultural and social fatigue—in short, what anthropologists call "culture shock." These constitute largely adverse reactions, both physically and psychologically, to social and cultural dislocations, or having to adjust to ways of life different from one's own. This anthropological rite of passage recently has been questioned by Herdt and Stoller (1990: 39), who suggest that the negative aspects of culture shock are too often exaggerated in fieldwork accounts.

The learning/growth approach, as originally proposed by Adler (1987), views the experience in the broader context of intercultural learning and individual growth. Focus is on the positive rather than negative consequences of the learning experience. Adjusting to human differences becomes a challenge for future behavioral flexibility. Correspondingly, image-metaphors parallel the contemporary emphasis in the social sciences on the social construction of reality.

Culture shock, in this scheme, is seen as normal in situations of learning new cultural and social knowledge, even leading to greater degrees of self-awareness and personal growth. As viewed by Kim and Ruben (1988: 305), culture shock is a crucial stage in the learning process, at the very heart of the cross-cultural experience. It becomes "an experience in self-understanding and change." Culture shock, one might say, is an integral and inevitable part of the process of becoming more intercultural, multicultural, or simply more attuned to diversities of various sorts whether strictly "cultural" or not. Kim and Ruben list five phases of the experience (1988): contact with newness, disintegration (the normal culture "shock" experience), reintegration, and a final stage where differences become understood, even cherished.

Identity, then, is an essential step in this "stress-adaptation-growth" process (Kim and Ruben 1988: 308). Persons faced with diversity, and its accompanying "psychic dislocations," will act to restore harmony by restructuring the internal communication system. A certain amount of psychological disintegration, as argued above, is both normal and expected, a prelude to further psychological growth. People have their prior expectations reorganized and then move beyond their own psychological limitations. The consequences include the development of identities more sensitive to cultural and social differences, more open to new forms of reality.

Becoming intercultural or multicultural is seen as a process of *reaching beyond culture* for "full blossoming of our uniquely human adaptive capacity" (1988: 315). Identity aids in making the individual psychologically flexible in diverse and changing environments. Harris and Moran refer to this same process as achieving "cultural synergy" (1989: 11): building upon cultural and social differences, then integrating such differences into a single whole to arrive at a common goal of mutual growth. They propose detailed, culturally specific, strategies for the accomplishment of this goal.

When it comes to learning new knowledge, human beings have an enormous capacity for growth and adaptation. As we open ourselves to new awareness, adjusting the self accordingly, our identities can become increasingly flexible.[6] Identity, after all, is uniquely human—potentially adaptive and transformative for those who accept the challenges of growing beyond previous expectations. Although there are surely limits to such transformative metaphors, they at least suggest the possibility for positive as well as negative outcomes from the individual's point of view.

Reaching Beyond Culture/Self in the 1990s

"These days questions of *culture* [my emphasis] seem to touch a nerve because they quite quickly become anguished questions of *identity* [my emphasis]," states Renato Rosaldo in *Culture and Truth* (1989: ix). Certainly the United States, as a nation, can be characterized by its "irreversible pluralism," but that pluralism is today more than cultural pluralism (Hoopes & Pusch 1980: 3). Although we need to learn to recognize, appreciate, and respect cultures and cultural differences where they genuinely exist, there are important social, psychological, structural, and symbolic similarities and differences that also have to be understood.

Diversity becomes the raw material out of which we learn to create new elaborations and transformations in the communication process. This emphasis on *diversity* generally has been seen as positive. It is often assumed that cultural diversity is "good" and should be preserved. Focusing on how culture, identity, and communication are interrelated causes us to view groups differently from the ways we have conceptualized them in the past. What are the characteristics of diversity in an emerging world culture? Are all cultures equal? Do we want to preserve behavioral patterns demonstrated to be ineffective (no longer functional) in a changed environment? How do we achieve a more relevant identity for our contemporary information society? What are the complex, often contradictory, relationships among identity, community, and survival?

First of all, we must recognize that diversity is more than cultural diversity and comes from differences in age, gender, class, physical fitness, race, and sexual orientation—incidently, all more or less characteristics shared by groups previously neglected by the social sciences. Culture surely helps to delineate identity groups, but identity groups do not always constitute separate cultures (Hoopes & Pusch 1980: 3). Identity, although not equally experienced by all individuals within a group, has become the critical focus around which many minorities in the 1990s have polarized—I believe, at least in part, because of increased media attention. Even if we can agree that ethnic and racial stratifications, as a case in point, are not always culturally grounded, ethnic identity—one type of human identification— remains a political force to be dealt with in the present century.

Ethnic nationalism is often an appeal for redress of presumed inequalities based on ethnic identity (Fox, Aull & Cimino 1978: 124). To assume, however, that each group—*because* it is different— constitutes a different culture may be a serious error. Rather than being lumped into the wastepaper-basket category of culture, each group may need to be explained differently. The real challenge is to find ways of communicating with individuals and groups that may be different in a variety of ways from our own, at the same time going "beyond culture." How can this awareness of the various non-cultural dimensions of life be best understood and implemented?

Anya Peterson Royce's *Ethnic Identity: Strategies of Diversity* systematically explored the changing images of ethnicity and identity (1982). No longer was ethnicity defined solely on the basis of overt cultural features, such as appearance, dress, dance, and language. This was the major conclusion of Royce's carefully crafted book. Rather, the objective emphasis on visible cultural traits has given way to more subjective definitions of self. In short, people often feel different regardless of the degree of cultural distinctiveness. There is a symbolic rather than real quality about the identity base in modern times. A group may even maintain ethnic cohesion and identity without a cultural base whatsoever (cf. Lumbee Indians). Gaining social and cultural competence, then, is clearly more than learning only the visible aspects of a culture.

Royce preferred the term "style" over the more conservative implications of the label "tradition." Style is flexible; tradition is static. For her, the essence of the "new ethnicity" is the room to maneuver, to make flexible and strategic choices. The key to understanding many groups today is not so much in recognizing past needs, argued Royce, but in appreciating current ones. The new ethnicity is not revitalization of static past traditions but the conscious discovery of a group's common interests. It is more identificational and less traditional in cultural orientation. American society, as well as many contemporary Western societies, must be conceptualized as a multi-layered system made up of residential, physical, age, class, race, and gender considerations—none of which, necessarily, presumes separate cultures. Culture and identity are not isomorphic. Royce's early analysis skillfully moved us "beyond culture" to the subtleties and complexities of identification.

Multiculturalism and the Educational Debates

Tensions between diverse groups in the United States have recently crystallized around the debates over what should be taught to whom in the schools. Paraphrasing Sollors (who is quoting Josiah Royce), one may evoke the metaphoric symphony of American pluralism, but the real question is which instrument will be played? (1986) This image-metaphor epitomizes the contemporary multicultural debates. In a nutshell, the issue is one of power. Who ultimately will control what is taught in the American school system? For many, the debate is over how to preserve a sense of an American community to which all diverse groups might ultimately belong. As Diane Ravitch (1990: 4) points out, in her excellent summary article "Multiculturalism: E Pluribus Plures": "It is not necessary to denigrate either the one or the many." Pluralism, of course, is a positive value in American society; but public education, she argues, has as its primary purpose the creation of a national community, "a definition of citizenship and culture that is both expansive and inclusive."

   The debate, as Ravitch (1990: 2–4) has brilliantly demonstrated, has polarized between two educational extremes: On the one hand, the "particularists," with intellectual roots in a separatist ideology, propose an ethnocentric curriculum to raise the self-esteem and academic achievement of children from racial and ethnic minority backgrounds. By contrast, the "pluralists" argue that racial and ethnic minorities should simply become a part of the larger American culture.[7] The pluralist argument is that the effects of "particularistic multiculturalism" are mostly counter-productive. Ravitch, in fact, calls particularism "a bad idea whose time has come." The demand for "culturally relevant" studies, it has been claimed, detracts attention from the real needs and interests of school children. The public function of education, so the argument goes, exists to teach general skills and public knowledge needed to survive in American society—not a world view that rejects this common culture.

Unfortunately, debates that frame arguments either for or against are rarely adequate. Both sides of this discussion, from time to time, take on an excessively self-righteous tone. This may be especially the case when academic dialogues are articulated in a modern media context. Is there not some middle ground in the balancing of unity or diversity?

Although scholars have typically skirted around the issue of multiculturalism—not squarely facing up to its ultimate implications—John Edwards (1985: 109) states unequivocally that multiculturalism, a British term that once stood for "pluralism," and national unity may be largely incompatible. Part of the heated rhetoric (unsupported discourse) derives from our intellectual heritage of *cultural relativism*, which states that all cultures are valuable and worthy of support—an idea, he argues, that may present more problems than it solves. "Social evolution involves judgment, evolution, repudiation and change" (1985: 114). Extreme forms of relativism easily lead to a position without objective standards. Edwards (1985: 116) reminds us, however, that anti-relativism presents its own set of problems. Rather than relativism or anti-relativism, Edwards favors some sort of liberal pluralism as a more natural social process. As does this book, he advocates keeping identity and culture (ethnicity) conceptually separate.

Edwards argues that ethnic groups are more "mainstream" than generally believed. Furthermore, ethnic groups themselves generally desire change (1985: 107). He supports the notion that ethnic revivals are largely a romantic view of the past and, as such, disguise harsh realities. There simply is no hard evidence, he states (1985: 101), that people en masse wish to escape modernity, least of all ethnics themselves. Minority parents do not want minority studies for their children so much as a good basic education in science, history, and geography.

Unfortunately, today's debates in the culture-communication dialogue represent examples of contradictory rhetoric often supported by the media's attention to so-called "balanced" coverage. "Symbolic ethnicity" is rampant in mass media reproductions. Whether real or not, these images can be very powerful indeed. Consider the nostalgic movie *Dances With Wolves* with its over-romanticization of American Indians of yesteryear. Similarly, ethnicity is typically glorified in media presentations in the name of community as romantic metaphor.

A national culture and identity are often viewed with suspicion, almost as if they were threats to ethnic consciousness.

Minorities no doubt need a feeling of closeness that comes with group identity; and, when accused of falsely pretending to be different culturally, they will react as if this unity were in jeopardy. Jean Jackson gets at the heart of the multicultural debates with this penetrating question (1989: 139): Is there a way to talk about "making culture" without "making enemies"? She believes that what we need are more neutral terms (*culture* is rarely a value-free word these days) to describe ethnic (minority) resurgence that "neither overly romanticizes nor denigrates the process"—a process she nicely but, perhaps simplistically, refers to as "inventing culture."

In the battle over control of information in this mediated society of ours, certainly we could use better models and metaphors to analyze, in non-derogatory langauge, the contemporary phenomenon of group assertiveness. A major problem with Jackson's position, however, is its tendency to equate culture and identity. Part of the difficulty, then, remains purely semantic. Groups claiming to "invent culture" are today mostly asserting identity in the name of culture! Current evidence surely favors identity over culture (Edwards 1985; Keefe, et al. 1989; Roosens 1989; Spindler & Spindler 1990). *Metaphors of Identity* is a book that attempts to solve the dilemma of "making culture" or "making enemies" by separating culture and identity. Self-conscious group awareness refers mostly to identity; culture—invented or not—may have little to do with it! Having a separate identity may be a noble—more importantly, a functional thing to do—whether groups can authenticate a corresponding culture or not. If culture is the logic by which we give order to our worlds, then something is "out of sync" when groups use mainstream logic to bolster rhetoric about nonexistent cultures.

Ironically, the battle to preserve ethnic cultures becomes the very thing that may doom certain minorities to academic failure (Foley 1991: 66). The question is whether well-meaning supporters of cultural diversity are, in fact, preventing minorities from effectively functioning in the mainstream culture. Unfortunately, what is often forgotten during the so-called debates over multiculturalism is the welfare of the children being taught. If the school goes against mainstreaming, Edwards (1985: 118) has argued convincingly, education ultimately may be seen as limiting children's chances in life.[8] This is a strong statement.

Arguing much the same point, Mosgrove (quoted in Edwards 1985: 120) stressed that multiculturalism is valuable if it promotes sympathy for other groups, but schools must be "open windows onto wider worlds." Basically, education can open doors to employment opportunities. Continuing with this didactic metaphor, the culture debates today threaten to close these metaphorical doors or windows. A distinction between public versus private educational goals can be crucial in avoiding convoluted thinking in this emotionally charged debate. The role of the school, a public institution, is primarily to transform cultures in contact. It would seem that all of us have a duty to assume a national identity with common public goals, without this loyalty necessarily implying the wholesale destruction of private social or cultural behaviors that retain positive psychological meaning for individuals or groups.

A simple example might illustrate this distinction between *public* versus *private* dimensions of education. At the public level, it can be argued that we must integrate, i.e., share in a common set of assumptions about society. All nations, to my knowledge, expect group loyalty and public patriotism. Allowing for gradual change, schooling inevitably must support the values of the dominant culture. Private sentiments, however, are another matter. Moslems in Great Britain, for example, may make accommodations to public cultural arrangements without repudiating private cultural beliefs and practices. The Salmon Rushdie affair, nevertheless, showed how easily this distinction can be discarded.

Although these conclusions remain controversial, the dialogue itself suggests that increased tolerance for diversity often goes hand-in-hand with increased social fragmentation. The contemporary resurgence of minority consciousness is glorified in the name of community as romantic metaphor. Inherent contradictions remain in the debates over the role of the school in maintaining group identities. Ultimately, the result of over-enthusiastic approval of so-called multiculturalism, we are reminded (Edwards 1985: 136), can have the reverse effect of forcing people into a stance of less awareness, less tolerance for ethnic or other differences.[9] In the end, education becomes regressive rather than progressive. Tolerance for diversity, Edwards argued, should not be equated with the active promotion of diversity in its original form. The issue, as articulated in chapter 5, is really one of social participation rather than cultural exclusiveness. Separating identity from culture may be one way out of this dialectical dilemma.

Acknowledging the widespread inclination today to confuse cultural issues with social ones may be the real key to understanding the so-called multicultural debates. Michael Prosser (1989: 197) believes that Ward Goodenough, a cognitive anthropologist, was responsible for defining "subjective culture" as human cognitive processes, thereby reducing culture to each individual behavioral reaction. With such an elastic definition, everything humanly experienced by any individual becomes a part of this subjective culture—no doubt, a case of "idealism gone to seed" (quoted, p. 197).

Although not dealing directly with the cultural debates in American institutions of higher education, George and Louise Spindler (1990) make the important observation that cultural minorities, regardless of numbers now or in the future[10], are largely defined by what they refer to as the "American cultural dialogue," a historically stable national character which includes a constellation of value orientations that constitutes our American culture. Even when minorities share mainstream cultural values, many today want to retain separate group identities. This was essentially the conclusion of my Fulbright research (chapter 5). Cultures change while identities frequently persist, precisely because each fulfills different and important functions for the individual or society.

The central tensions between such groups, according to the Spindlers (1990: 53), are not over values per se but over power and participation between "those who are carrying on the central dialogue and those who are excluded from it and who would like to be full participants." The Spindlers argue convincingly that no group in America is entirely outside the American cultural dialogue, no matter how exclusive (1990: 39). In short, they call for an educational system (curriculum) that would include all of these diverse elements—*within* a common national culture.

Thus, they would agree with Edwards that cultural assimilation—an unpopular idea today—is taking place, and has always taken place, in America. Ethnicity is simply being "reshaped" in the process. Although "[t]he balancing of assimilation and preservation of identity is constant and full of conflict," the Spindlers (1990: xii) attribute the changes to no less than achievement of success in American society, in fact "a necessary corollary to full participation." Unfortunately, many other cultural theorists have tended to romanticize culture rather than deal with contemporary social changes and adaptations.

Today we can observe the virtual creation of so-called cultural identities that often have no separate cultural supports. Despite the fact that groups today want to retain strong group identities, we have seen how it is possible to have change that renders cultures virtually obsolete. The Spindlers (1990: 23) recognized that there is no significant association between self-ascription (identity) and the expression of the value orientations that they identify with the "American cultural dialogue." Culture and identity are not always the same. What seems most relevant today is identification, not cultural placement.

What we are witnessing, in fact, are dramatic exhibitions of identities based on ethnic/gender/sexual preference at the same time that we are clearly seeing more and more media-induced cultural homogenization of American (read, Western) societies. This is one of the central themes of *Metaphors of Identity*. The Spindlers (1990: 80) would no doubt agree with the conclusions of this chapter which suggest, as they do, that the so-called culture debates (specifically, "diatribes about cultural literacy")—rather than any true appreciation or celebration of diversity—constitute "a rejection of increasing cultural diversity of America."

Just as there are negative implications from the abuses of culture, there are also both positive and negative subsets to the identity construct itself—whether based on ethnicity, sexuality, minority status, or the existential sense of personhood. We identify with something primarily because it gives us stability, "roots." From the individual's point of view, identity really is a fairly deliberate effort to effect a more satisfactory self-image. This is the psychic shelter function of identity mentioned earlier, especially in societies perceived as alienating or without psychological anchor.

From the individual's point of view, the positive side of identity is self-growth, self-actualization, through our relationships with others in the human family.[11] On the negative side, however, are the more familiar narcissistic tendencies of our times: an unwholesome focus on self-gratification for individuals and the horrendous consequences of nationalism for groups. To over-emphasize narrow cultural or personal identity is to work against interpersonal and intercultural communication, the result being a form of narcissistic self-indulgence or group-indulgence.

We may well need to preserve identities and sometimes culture—at the same time, hopefully avoiding the manipulative aspects of a zoo mentality, which keeps people culturally "pure" as specimens for our curiosity rather than for the integrity that cultural diversity can bring to the communication process. Universally, we have need to affirm our solidarity with other human beings, regardless of differences. To be sure, not all divergent groups have communication problems to any marked degree. Furthermore, sensitivity to diversities need not imply a fixed endorsement of every type of behavior no matter how much temporary psychological security it offers the individuals concerned. Reaching beyond culture, how do we maintain the positive aspects of human identity: the celebration of diversity and the re-affirmation of our common humanity, a sense of being part of a larger community? What type of personality will be socially and psychologically more adaptive for survival in a global society?

Flexible Identity and the Global Person

The information society has brought us closer to a global culture (Featherstone 1990). In this emerging world culture, there must be understanding and appreciation of "fundamental differences" between groups (with emphasis on diversity) but, equally, a recognition of "fundamental similarities," cultural universals that can link us to a common humanity (Brown 1991). The tendency today has been to exaggerate human differences, when in reality we generally are more alike than different.[12] We need to maintain an openness to new meanings—whether social, cultural, or sexual in origin—increasing our knowledge of similarities and differences that can help us avoid misunderstanding and miscommunication. Too much concentration on differences among groups can obscure our real similarities.

In a society emphasizing global communication, the ideal would be a person[13] able to successfully adapt and communicate in a variety of challenging situations; able to move in and out of social, cultural, and mixed gender encounters with relative ease; able to handle diversities of many sorts—in short, a "mediating," psychologically secure personality that believes in the common unity of humankind, one flexible in face of social changes.[14] Condon and Yousef (1975: 252)), however, caution against what they call the "myth of the universal communicator," the idea that a universal type can really be generalized across all cultures except in the broadest of terms.

Although such concepts sound overly grand, empirical evidence suggests that people can, in fact, become more "empathic," i.e., less judgmental about other people (Pusch, et al. 1980: 91).[15] Several concepts have been employed to typify this cognitively flexible identity of the future. Since Peter Adler first argued for "the multicultural person," one socially and psychologically committed to the unity of all human beings, some of the terms used to describe this "new" personality type have included the following: "international," "universal," "communitarian," "communal," "transcultural" and "cosmopolitan," to name only a few (Prosser 1985: 71).

Harris and Moran refer to the global manager of the future as the cosmopolitan (1989: 9): "a sensitive, innovative, and participative leader, capable of operating comfortably in a global or pluralistic environment," whether in an organizational context, in terms of intercultural performance, or with minorities of diverse cultural, social, and sexual orientations. The cosmopolitan person, they have argued, may be a more relevant identity for the future.[16] Emphasizing global communication, this book has sought to understand the emerging world culture through an examination of how communication and culture interact. I prefer the term "global," rather than "multicultural" or "cosmopolitan," because the latter terms today carry associations that go beyond their original meanings.

The culture-communication dialogue, with its increased awareness of social and cultural identities and communication skills, places emphasis on building upon cultural and social differences for mutual growth and enrichment of humanity. The *global person* can learn to relate to people of diverse backgrounds, objectively respecting diversity and tolerating ambiguity—hence, contributing to more effective interpersonal and intercultural communication. Identity, in this equation, becomes crucial since developing such awareness is a process of looking inward, being more knowledgeable about self-in-context, and reaching beyond personal limitations to the ultimate goal of becoming more pan-human. Identity is the key to this human puzzle.

Community as Romantic Metaphor/Media Effects

If adaptation was the construct of the 1980s, the building metaphors of construction and transformation characterize the 1990s. The culture-communication dialogue has introduced the image of a global person who constructs and transforms self and, in the process, creates community. What are the positive and negative challenges to these notions of identity transformation and community as romantic metaphor for an idealized self-in-society? Furthermore, how do these image-metaphors relate to the new communication technologies?

Our modern understandings of community, as typified in the romantic image of the ancient Greek city-state, Glenn Tinder (1980: 79) calls "reflections on a tragic ideal" and, more importantly, considers them questionable as a viable community ideal in our modern, communication-driven world. Suggested in the expression "romantic metaphor of community" is the notion of a "perfect unity" (social solidarity) brought about by rational human beings more or less totally in control of their destinies. Appealing and simple, this romantic ideal is intellectually suspect (1980: 125). Our metaphors of American idealism may delude us about community, creating some irresolvable tensions in the process.[17] Although an ancient idea (this dream of unity that "promises both self-realization and an end to loneliness"), it is still only an ideal, or "romantic dream," claims Tinder (1980: 2). In fact, community has become the romantic metaphor of our times.

We live in a world of seeming paradoxes. On the one hand, we talk and write endlessly about our efforts to establish community but are daily faced with both perplexing and contradictory evidences of the extremes of "anti-community" (Wilkinson 1988). Social theory has continued to be concerned about "loss of community" (Scheff 1990). Although certainly the ideal of community still strongly moves us, we apparently live in a universe not favorable to this utopian vision.

Ours is a world made up of various factions (political, economic, social, racial, gender, and so on), the opposite of a true community because factionalism rejects the larger society in favor of closed societies. In the name of community, particular groups today uncompromisingly defend their own turf while stubbornly refusing to consider joining larger associations. Such groups use the romantic metaphor of community to enhance "compulsive intolerance" of others who do not belong to their particular factions (cf. the extremes of educational particularism as a case in point). This may be too exclusive a definition of community.[18]

In an intriguing article entitled "The Secret History of Self-Interest," Stephen Holmes (1990: 272–74) grapples with this irrational psychological need of human beings to exhibit "compulsive intolerance" and concludes that factionalism ("not so much a symptom of arrogance but insecurity") is deplorable because loyalties in such groups are too narrow to qualify as real community. Authentic community is ultimately a "sharing and exchanging" in a communicating global society, as Tinder has eloquently argued (1990). The ultimate goal is not particular communities (private communities are a contradiction of terms) but a community that embraces the entire human race. Challenges to this utopian, romantic ideal are everywhere evident in today's world. We use the rhetoric of community but, rather than trying to achieve a global citizenship, prefer to strike a pose of particularism and exclusiveness. Such ethnic or group resurgences—in reality, identity assertions—are often the antithesis of community.

We seem, in fact, content with our romantic illusions. Nostalgia in the contemporary world has become big business (Davis 1981: 219). Rosaldo has pointed out the ironic contradictions of an "imperialist nostalgia" (1989: 87): the curious phenomenon of modern-day people's longing for what they themselves have already destroyed. Nowhere is this idea better illustrated than in the debates over what constitutes culture today. Anthropologists and tourists, Rosaldo (1989: 69) suggests, are paradoxically the ones who most mourn the passing of cultures they themselves have helped to transform. At the same time, those unfortunate people who have had their human and natural environments destroyed are mystically "codified" and "deified" in the aftermath (cf. the American Indian as symbol of lost innocence). This tendency to overly romanticize visions of bygone, harmonious societies remains a paradoxical challenge to the goal of achieving a more encompassing, all-inclusive world order.

The romantic notion of community as a "small, isolated and harmonious unit" may need to be abandoned, or at least reworked, in the modern context of an information society (Prosser 1985: 25). As technology looms large in the debates over "effects," we must make some guarded inferences about the relationships between modern-day communication technologies, culture, and community. Is technology really causing the disappearance of community, or are we simply witnessing different types of community based on the potentialities of the new media technologies? (1985: 27). As Americans are especially given to exuberant confidence in the capacity for technological control, the effect which technology may have on culture and social discourse is an issue worthy of review in the context of the culture-communication dialogue.

In *Communication Tomorrow*, E. W. Brody (1990) makes the important distinction between the new technologies and the new media,[19] although the debates in this ongoing dialogue have tended to talk rather loosely about mass media and their "effects" (influences) on culture and communication. What are the opportunities, as well as problems, presented by the new communication technologies in an information age? A number of studies have decried the homogenizing effects of the modern media.

Do mass media account for the destruction of cultural diversity, replacing it with cultural sameness or "mass culture"? The answer seems to be both yes and no. The concept of diversity *within* mass culture has been supported by American studies since the 1970s, reports George Lewis (1981: 202). Some media are agents of change and diversity, while others are less so or not at all. Increasingly, audience perception is recognized as an important part of this complex equation (Katz 1981). The persistent characterization of mass communication (mediated communication) as metaphorically mirroring or molding society may be too simple-minded. Joseph Turow suggests that there is a problem in using "mass communication" as an "umbrella term" to accommodate all issues of media consequences (1990: 481). Media select and frame cultural knowledge; but audiences interpret, whether in an intended or unintended manner. Certainly we need greater precision in our definition of effects. This is Elihu Katz's sensible warning (1981: 265).

In these old debates in new contexts, it has been argued (Brody 1990: 25) that communicators can probably overcome the major barriers erected by the new technologies, new media, and new audiences; but information, in order to have social value, must be accessible and applicable. For example, in *The Information Gap: How Computers and Other New Communication Technologies Affect the Social Distribution of Power*, Siefert and associates offer serious caveats to any optimistic hope that the new media will be an instant panacea for social inequalities worldwide (1989: 193). In the discourse on futurology, information is ideally free-flowing and equally distributed; but, given the social, economic, political, and social disparities in evidence today, it may be naive to ignore the "information gaps" (1989: 8). They further argue that the new communication technologies not only do not address the inequalities but often introduce new ones. A "technology of surveillance," for example, is the negative side of computers and telecommunications.

Along the same lines, researchers have asked: "Can the new technology strengthen a democratic society?" (Downing 1989: 154–162). Attempts to answer this complex question have ranged from touting the possibly "liberating and empowering" effects of technology to warning of almost total "citizen exclusion"—that is, glaring disparities between the information haves and have-nots. Sometimes those most in need of information have less access to the media. Likewise, there is increasing evidence of widening gaps between gender and income groups in this same regard (Jansen 1989; Murdock & Golding 1989).

Chris Arterton (1987), in *Teledemocracy: Can Technology Protect Democracy?*, takes a more sanguine view of the idea that a communication revolution can transform our politics. Examining a number of "teledemocracy" projects (Alaska's Legislative Teleconferencing Network, Berke Community Television, North Carolina's OPEN/net, and the Quabe interactive system in Ohio, among others), he raised similar questions about access, information gaps, limits of cost, and lack of citizen participation in such projects. In the end, he concluded, one must be content with "incremental improvements" rather than expect "utopian" results. Over time, experiments, such as Electronic Town Halls, can have significant cumulative effects leading to more effective media for public discussion and dissemination of information. Certainly, then, the possibilities exist that communication technology can be harnessed to stimulate and improve the political dialogue between government and governed. If "teledemocracy" does not offer total and instant "empowerment of the people through technology," Arterton would argue that it can offer us "improvements in democracy" (1987: 204).

The atomization of society, as well as some inevitable loss of community, can be found in media effects; but, consensus-building through media formats is also a common theme in the contemporary culture-communication dialogue. The media can be used to strengthen shared national values, traditions, and identities. At least in much of the Western world, the media have encouraged joint space ventures, medical research projects, business and development efforts, as well as a host of positive educational enterprises. Computers can even give older adults, for example, a way to participate in contemporary culture while acquiring a new network of emotional peer supports, although at present such "electronic communities" are limited to those who can afford computers (Furlong 1989: 245). Another promising positive use of media is CHESS ("Comprehensive Health Enhancement Support Systems"), a PC-based network designed to help high-risk people examine their lifestyles and reduce risks for developing or transmitting diseases, e.g., AIDs (1989: 153). Allowing television coverage of courtroom activities has even been called a "format for justice" (Altheide 1985: 244).

An intriguing theory about how we experience "a shared humanity" through media channels is presented by Anderson and Meyer (1988: 113). The nature of mass media (they prefer the term "mediated communication") is that the media provide a set of experiences that become part of our common "currency of exchange." Thus we potentially share in one another's lives through such channels. Participation in these experiences can be seen as communal activity, giving us some common goals for social interaction (1988: 115).

In an age of television, for example, images mediate larger and larger amounts of life's experiences. David Altheide gives the excellent example of the power of the visual portrayal of international peace through the Olympic Games (1985: 243). By linking people across national boundaries, there is at least the potential for better global community-building. For an opposite point of view, see Margaret Archer's (1990) more pessimistic appraisal of "user-friendly technology."[20] To the extent that media serve as experiences for a shared humanity, theoretically they should liberate and empower, rather than restrict, human activity.

In reviewing the following debates, we have sometimes vacillated between extremes. The predominant opinion today is that the media are indeed powerful forces in society; but, as we have observed, the question itself may be too simplistic (Dennis 1989). Any final conclusion in this continuing debate over whether the media have big or little effects may have to await future research for clarification. Our old-style theories of *media effects* may be less than totally adequate for the explanatory task. Debates such as this one cannot be easily resolved. In the culture-communication dialogue, different scholars start out with radically different conceptions of the role of effects; and each side in the debate probably sees the other as essentially unmovable. To some extent, solution to the question of media effects can be found only in the metaphor of the half-empty/half-full glass: Being both, it can be persuasively argued either-or, depending on one's emphasis.

Technology, of course, can enslave or enhance human life. As Everette Dennis (1989: 89) has reminded us, more information is not necessarily better information; and the future of our information society will not be determined by technology alone, but by humans who shape the communication industry and its audiences (1989: 196). In the end, however, we may learn as much by studying community as by considering only the individuals in it. Genuine community can be found, not only in face-to-face relationships, but in mediated communication brought about through mass media channels. Technology and community may not be so antithetical after all. There is certainly as much potential in a communication-based community today as there was in previous attempts at creating the elusive romantic metaphor of community.

Principal Points

This chapter has considered the quest for meaningful self-process in an emerging world culture. Using the adaptive-growth (performance) model, this more speculative discussion examined the concept of the global person and asked how such a flexible identity structure relates to the notions of communication and "communicative competence" as guides for future transformations of self. The novel idea of community as romantic metaphor was pursued in light of the contemporary culture-communication debates over media effects. The real challenge is to recognize both the strengths and weaknesses of the media, in order to more effectively use these important channels of contemporary communication.

Notes

1. Edelstein and associates (1989: 43) propose a theory of "the problematic situation" which supports a *situational* rather than a cultural interpretation of communication. What seems to be cultural, they argue, is often better accounted for by reference to situational differences.

2. John Naisbitt predicted compensatory humanizing responses to technological development (1982). The human side of high tech, such as the self-help movement, is part of what he has called the "high touch" balance, without which people might well reject the new technology.

3. Scholars (Sypher 1984: 103–127, Prosser 1989: 300) interested in "intercultural skills" have suggested some of the following characteristics of a "competent communicator": more responsive to others, tolerating ambiguity, showing empathy, and remaining "open" in personal communication styles. In short, one able to move in and out of cultural/social groups with relative ease. The ability to perceive and to accept a wide variety of things about others is reflected in the term "cognitive complexity" (here called "cognitive flexibility"). This *"flexible" identity* is assumed to possess certain basic knowledge of situational demands.

4. For an excellent review of some of the more distinctive metaphorical representations of self in the psychological literature, see Knowles and Sibicky (1990).

5. Building metaphors that utilize a "personified agent" model suggest conscious control over human destiny; but much of culture is, in reality, accidental, unconscious, and unplanned (compare the idea of "cultural slippage"). In support of the American romantic temperament, our image-metaphors of identity often imply human agencies in total control of communication and culture.

6. An extreme example of this flexibility theme can be found in the so-called "atomic bomb maidens" of Japan. Lifton says that the survivors of

a nuclear disaster need nothing less than a new identity in order to come to terms with a post-disaster world (1970: 155).

7. Diane Ravitch points out an obvious, but often overlooked, fact that "the unique feature of the United States is that its common culture has been formed by the interaction of its subsidiary cultures" (1990: 2). We are one common culture today fashioned from a multicultural base. To confuse the diversity of this base with its evolving future leads to an unwholesome polarization. It is important, she adds, that we preserve a sense of an American community to which we can all belong (1990: 4).

8. John Edwards (1985: 128), however, denies any profound influence from the schools. He argues persuasively that "real-life contexts tend to dwarf what goes on in school." Education, in spite of the heated debate, is unlikely to appreciably alter self-perceptions or the progress of cultural pluralism.

9. Censorship is an important issue in the debates over multiculturalism which can act to inhibit artistic creativity. A London musical hit was canceled in New York, when American Equity barred Jonathan Pryce from the lead role, on the grounds that it was "an affront to the Asian community" for a Caucasian to play the part ("Miss Saigon Pulled Out of Broadway After Ethnic Row," *The Daily Telegraph*, Thursday, August 9, 1990: 6). Racial prejudice was allowed to gain ascendancy over creative freedom. In actual fact, the play afforded ethnic minorities an opportunity to find much-needed work. The American attitude was viewed in Great Britain as "counter-productive, racist, and narrow."

10. Mainstream American academics worry a lot about future numbers. It is probable that by the year 2000, so-called minorities will constitute about one-third of the total U.S. population; but, as the Spindlers point out (1990: 15), the actual number of people who exhibit behaviors, aspirations, beliefs, and values that place them in the mainstream culture is higher than such statistics would suggest. Many minorities have, in fact, acquired mainstream cultural values, or wish to, while claiming separate identities.

11. Anthony Storr, in *Solitude: A Return to the Self,* argues that solitude is one important means of achieving a sense of belongingness, and that the capacity to be alone is an aspect of emotional maturity often overlooked by psychologists, who currently overemphasize intimate personal relationships as the only road to mental health (1988: 92).

12. Often the things that most divide people today are not *cultural* differences, per se, but age, sex, and class barriers that we feel less inclined to acknowledge.

13. Albert Einstein is said to have remarked, when asked what he thought about the future: "The future? Of course I am interested in the future.

It is where I plan to spend the rest of my life!" (quoted in Edelstein, et al. 1982: 139).

14. Robert T. Moran (Harris & Moran 1987: 63) metaphorically symbolized the flexible personality, quoting Scott Peck's example of a seventeenth-century Japanese samurai, who developed the art of handling two swords at the same time: Like a successful communicator, "[s]killed internationalists are hard to find because not many are willing to work hard to handle two swords at the same time."

15. This broad perspective is emotionally appealing, but sometimes the logic behind such typologies fails to be convincing when sociocentric assumptions about classes, races, sexes, and people of different sexual preferences have to be made more or less *out of context*. Obviously, then, correlates of the global personality are hard to generalize across cultures, not to mention from one unique situation to another!

16. Harris and Moran (1987: 47) mention that the antonym for the cosmopolitan, or global type, is the social alien, or "stranger" (cf. chapter 7).

17. Robert Snow (1983: 159) points out that the TV dramatization of "The Autobiography of Miss Jane Pittman," for example, was pure fiction. For the sake of drama, our romantic culture allows—even encourages—such distortions.

18. In explaining social dislocations as far-reaching as nationalism, Thomas Scheff (1990: 14) comments on the notion of "pseudo-bonds," i.e., sects, cults, and other "exclusive" groups that furnish only the semblance of community. Metaphorically, he describes them as cancer cells, self-reproducing and entirely dedicated to their own survival rather than serving the larger system of which they should be a part.

19. The so-called "new media," based largely on technologies developed just over the past five decades, refers to the more interactive communications, including primarily six forms: microcomputers, teleconferencing, teletext, videotext, interactive cable television, and satellite communication, none of which figures extensively in contemporary information delivery systems, Brody points out (1990: 259). The not-so-new media are still our primary concern when talking about media effects on culture and communication.

20. A negative effect of television, and media in general, is the tendency to distance individuals from the demands of human relationships. The act of mediated interaction with inanimate objects was graphically portrayed in the movie *Sex, Lies, and Videotape*.

10

◯ Limits of Metaphor in the Culture-Communication Dialogue

Our comprehension of an idea fades in direct proportion to the loss of metaphorical effectiveness. In this sense the metaphor *is* the meaning. To restore the fullness of meaning, it is frequently necessary to conceptualize the metaphor again.

—Thomas Owens, *Metaphor and Related Subjects*

Guiding Metaphors/A Question of Aptness

This last chapter addresses the question of metaphorical effectiveness in scientific discourse and summarizes major theoretical debates in the culture-communication dialogue. Since this book has used metaphor as the organizational frame for dialogic analysis, a brief review of the aptness of metaphor in science is included, which considers its strengths and weaknesses as a tool for studying culture, identity, and communication. Identity, as the book's primary conceptual focus, has been defined as "the academic metaphor for self-in-context." The contexts for identification were examined, though not exhaustively, chapter by chapter in order to show the many sidedness of this complex idea. In other words, each chapter has emphasized, through a review of image-metaphors, different aspects of the contextual dimensions of identity. The debates that emerge, along with their guiding metaphors, are woven into the discussion of metaphorical effectiveness in the text that follows.

Metaphors, we have discovered, are ubiquitous in academic descriptions of identity (Knowles & Sibicky 1990). It is no longer a question of whether or not scientists use guiding metaphors as frameworks for interpreting meaning in the culture-communication dialogue. In the broadest sense, all scientific models, or theoretical paradigms, are metaphorical, mediating devices for connecting causal ideas. The paradigm has been viewed in this book as a class of sign-images that can reveal hidden meanings and relationships, allowing the reader at some level to make better sense of complex patterns (Lakoff & Turner 1989: 99). In research on culture and communication, then, metaphor may lead a theorist to construct theoretical ideas in quite specific ways, sometimes contributing to a degree of simplification. We often unconsciously reduce complex realities to too few of its parts. This is the blindmen-and-elephant story revisited. Focusing on only one aspect of identity leads to the failure to see the whole in its many-sidedness. When image-metaphors are overused, either too many or too few interpretations become possible. How do we deal with the multi-dimensionality of reality when metaphor tends to highlight certain aspects of the whole while obscuring others?

Some appreciation of the "intent" (function) of metaphor is surely called for. Karsten Harries makes the important observation that metaphors may not have the same function in philosophy, poetry, or scientific texts (1979b: 167–68). Scientific discourse, she argues, has "a commitment to objectivity, a commitment that demands that we try to free ourselves from the limitations of forms of expression that tie us to a particular perspective." If the intent of science is to be systematically precise, the use of metaphor in such texts always carries the risk of false conclusions. Quoting others, she reminds us that what distinguishes metaphor is not meaning per se, but usage. Another way of expressing the same idea: the intent of science and, say, poetry are quite different, resulting in different uses for various figures of speech, including metaphor.

Although metaphors have achieved unprecedented importance as guiding images for researchers of identity, culture, and communication, the use of such figurative devices in scientific discourse is, nevertheless, restricted. Metaphoric images are rarely unambiguous. People everywhere are responsive to context.[1] Metaphor, then, must be judged as to its effectiveness in specific contexts. Everyone from time to time uses metaphors to conceptualize ideas; but metaphor, whether in art or science, can both limit as well as extend what one observes.

Metaphor, though probably essential to many kinds of social discourse, must be carefully selected to fit the demands of a particular situation (Owens 1969). Metaphors are highly localized and particular; they "tell the truth but not the whole truth," to quote Thomas Owens (1965: 70). Meaning is not always evident in metaphorical image or statement. Some metaphors, then, are more apt than others, more or less effective for the intended communication. One may best illustrate this phenomenon of metaphorical aptness by quoting Wayne Booth's near-classic description of the catfish metaphor. When a small Southern public utility company was battling a giant competitor in court, the lawyer deliberately accused the latter, evoking the especially colorful image of "gutting a catfish." Good metaphors, Booth (1979a: 55) reminded the reader, are "active" (appropriate to context), "concise" (metaphors "say more with less"), and "audience appropriate." The catfish metaphor, while perhaps less effective in another setting, was perfect for this Deep South audience! Booth's pragmatic argument was that lawyers are paid to invent such figures of speech (1979a: 56). Metaphors must always be judged, then, with reference to context and intent.

The Hardware-Software Metaphor and the Biological Basis of Self

In the culture-communication dialogue, certainly one of the most neglected contexts for understanding identity has been the biological basis of selfhood. Since Plato's original conceptualization of mind as "pilot" of the "body ship," there have been numerous metaphorical attempts to represent the complex relationships between body and mind. Communication scholars have long been concerned with nonverbal communication, which has obvious relevance for the understanding of identity (Knapp 1972). In recent times, however, the debate of central concern to psychologists and anthropologists (namely, the question of "One-in-Many-Selves") has been largely ignored in the culture-communication dialogue even though this issue, I believe, has profound implications for the communication sciences (Knowles & Sibicky 1990).

First formulated by William James, essentially the One-in-Many-Selves paradox is the question of self-pluralism and the seeming contradiction between empirically verified "many selves" and the common-sense notion that most human beings, nevertheless, manage to maintain a sense of personality continuity (unity). The reader will recall that this debate was more or less resolved in chapter 2 in favor of an illusion of wholeness, which appears to be a functional necessity for human adaptation and survival. Again, communication processes are essential for a full understanding of this argument.

Consider the virtual craze in American psychiatric circles over the "discovery" of self-pluralism and its ultimate implications for the psychiatric condition known as multiple personality. In a cogent counter-response, British psychiatrist Aldridge Morris (1989) argued that multiple personality, as a psychiatric disorder, is grossly overdiagnosed in the United States—in all probability because of excessive and irresponsible media exposure. He feels that neurological studies do not support the notion of different selves capable of continuously recreating themselves. He claims that there is not a single, unequivocal case of MP (multiple personality) in the British literature! Rather, he tries to balance the American excesses by getting his clients to accept and take responsibility for "many aspects of one personality." Borrowing the metaphorical distinction between hardware (brain) versus software (mind), Aldridge-Morris makes the point that American psychology today may be too preoccupied with the former rather than the latter, thereby ultimately contributing to the spiraling numbers of diagnosed cases of multiple personality in the United States.

Communication scholars might well profit from a more careful evaluation of the effects of mediated communication on self-ascriptions as these are presently discussed in the contemporary debates over unitary versus multiple selves. The brain may indeed have plural capacities while the mind still demands an illusion of wholeness necessary for effective enactment of self and other in social and cultural contexts. Equally important questions have emerged from the culture-communication dialogue: What is a person? How have metaphors contributed to this debate. What have been some of their limitations?

"Homo Duplex" and the Issue of Person Status in Other Cultures

The problem arises when we assume that there has to be something concrete to which identity always refers. Just as we have seen how the traditional picture of a unified mind has been challenged by empirical evidence, similarly there may not be a single answer to the question, What is a person? (Glover 1988: 61). Looking at identity in historic context suggests that diverse cultures have conceptualized this idea quite differently. The major historical debates over the nature of "the person" clearly demonstrate that our Western concept of the autonomous individual is both historically and culturally variable. Likewise, self evolves over time and, hence, will not be the same in the future. "Person" and "nonperson" have been represented metaphorically using a moral career analogy. The attempt of "homo duplex" to reconcile individuality with sociality constitutes the human dialectical dilemma. Social communication, it can easily be observed, is intimately dependent on how different cultures define person.

The African tortoise metaphor was borrowed and employed in chapter 3 to highlight the duality of imagery between public self and private self, so consistently represented in cultures around the world. Metaphors, in such contexts, provide organizing images of this dual-level reality. However, as a form of "social code," metaphors can be "particular" or "global" in reference (Crocker 1977: 42). Every perspective may require a metaphor, explicit or implicit, for its organizational base; but such metaphors will differ from culture to culture. Futhermore, there is always the problem of translation when doing cross-cultural comparisons. With transdisciplinary abstractions like identity, no single metaphor fully enables us to comprehend this multifaceted phenomenon. A major weakness of ethnographic descriptions, in the culture-communication dialogue, in fact, has been with the use of one set of cultural metaphors to describe another, quite different, culture.[2]

Certainly, there have been observed weaknesses of metaphorical representations of identity in anthropological research. As cultural signs, metaphors can have more than one referent—more than one meaning—and may be variously interpreted by different people. Metaphoric ambiguity is often heightened in cross-cultural comparisons, precisely because such figures of speech can project their own logic onto the concepts with which they may be less than totally compatible. Not only is there potential bias in translating concepts from one culture to another, but the mismatch of metaphors across cultures can produce considerable misrepresentation.

A case in point was Harriet Rosenberg's (1990) account of the difficulties of using "feminized" metaphors in cross-cultural research on aging (see chapter 1). Metaphors typically used in an American cultural context to describe "caretaker" were found to be ethnographically incorrect in Africa, where both men and women share this role, forcing her to conclude that a feminized metaphor, such as mothering, is hard to express in ungendered language. Although effective metaphors possess the power of providing new insights and new meanings to social realities, they alter with changes in time and place. Metaphors call for constant refinement to be maximally effective in cross-cultural contexts.

Image-metaphors as Culture-Communication Models

There are both productive and unproductive modes of communication (interaction). Culture and communication models of identity were the subject of chapter 4, the purpose being to examine and critique major paradigms to demonstrate the importance of the principle of contextualization. This book employed an integrative, adaptive-growth model (with three mutually interacting conditions: knowledge, motivation, and ability symbolically linking intentions and communication) which suggests how identity, as a crucial psychological mediating process, is always situated in culture and social relationships, but ultimately realized in communicative performance. This *performance model* attempted to reconcile the subjective and objective approaches with a theoretical perspective convergent and integrative, interpretive and functional, all at the same time. Mediation images have been used in the culture-communication dialogue to highlight aspects of this phenomenon. Metaphor, one of the psychic processes used by human beings to organize and interpret a changing sense of self, is rarely easy to interpret.

A splendid example is Dorinne Kondo's (1990) brilliant analysis of identity in a Japanese workplace, which she entitled *Crafting Selves*. By implication, the modern-day Japanese worker is seen as actively in control of self-in-context. Power, gender, and discourse are the subject matter of this intriguing treatise on constructed selves. A careful reading of this book, however, makes clear that the Japanese self is "crafted" by and in specific historic, economic, and social circumstances.

Much cultural and psychological behavior, it should be noted, is less purposeful than our building metaphors imply. In spite of the active-voice in Kondo's original title, she demonstrated clearly that selves, in reality, are crafted in processes of work and within designated fields of power. Furthermore, Kondo (1990: 301) criticizes generalizations derived from the Japanese mainstream culture, which suggest a harmonious image of "automation-like workers happily singing the company song." Stereotypical portrayals of "the Japanese" are challenged in this powerful book about identity-in-context.

Metaphors call attention to certain phenomena and evoke certain responses but, like other aspects of culture and language, change with changing circumstances (Davidson 1979: 43). Using metaphorical description in scientific analyses is like asking the reader to share in a personal opinion. Although literal descriptions have their limitations, metaphorical ones need constant scrutiny; this is Chris

Crocker's (1977: 64) sensible warning. In the most absolute sense, the research models in the culture-communication paradigms, as pointed out, are themselves metaphors. Thomas Owens (1969: 79) mused:

> [T]here always exists the possibility that some as yet unformulated model might have greater explanatory power than an existing model. And this fact, more than any other, identifies models as metaphors.

Thus, when judging the elegance of research models, one must of necessity consider the effectiveness of their guiding metaphors (Brown 1987).

Metaphors abound in media presentations, where image-metaphors serve a kind of "pictorial function" in explaining certain cultural domains (Ricoeur 1979: 141). Ofttimes, reification of metaphor is at the root of the confusion. Concepts are sometimes presented in the text without full recognition that they are, in fact, basically metaphorical. For example, with the pervasiveness of television in our lives, some researchers of this important medium have committed "metaphorical leaps," where television is actually seen *as* American culture (Piccirillo 1990: 15). The analogy between media and culture can be carried too far. Robert Snow's book *Creating Media Culture* (1983), although certainly not the only offender in this regard, serves as a good example of a not-so-splendid metaphorical usage.

Using a dubious language analogy, which suggests that media have a grammar and syntax, *Creating Media Culture* literally equates culture and language—by extension, media and culture. Snow reifies his metaphor. The fact that film and other media can be characterized metaphorically as having a "language" (format/perspective) of their own does not make them a culture in their own right (1983: 209).

Metaphorically equating language and culture, Snow assumes that the media are a culture with a separate and analyzable language, thereby jumping from human interactions, to language, to the creation of a culture, without a theory to explain how this happens. The image-metaphor alone carries the argument. Do the media really tailor information according to such nebulous linguistic criteria; or do human beings, influenced by media formats, create culture out of these perspectives? (1983: 213). How effective is such a metaphor for understanding media influence?

Certainly metaphorical images are never totally free from ideological manipulations, and their interpretations are often subject to misuse. Jim Applegate (1990: 1-2), in an address to members of the "Rhetorical & Communication Theory Newsletter," fears that the use of "distorted metaphors" in current discourse about communication can result in a distortion of the rich complexities of the communication process, ultimately cheapening the process and threatening the credibility of the discipline. Metaphors defining communication as operationalized norms of etiquette (the metaphor of communication as game), those that focus solely on form rather than content, and metaphors that emphasize public relations and advertising as an achievement of consensus are, according to Applegate, metaphorical conceptions that distort unequal power relations and eventually create "flawed reality."

Metaphors are here to stay, both in art and science. As useful guides to spark imagination, they can suggest significant relationships and clarify context but should be viewed as problematic at several levels. The warning offered in this volume is to use such figurative speech freely and imaginatively, but with caution.

Media and Changing Metaphors of Ethnicity and Identity

Chapter 5 was fundamentally concerned with the culture-society debate revisited. Representing a case where identity is still alive in a modern urban setting, this identity did not, however, involve the maintenance of a separate culture. There is often today a wide gap between everyday social realities and rhetoric about culture. How can people maintain *social* ways of doing things that make them "different" without being of a different, hence separate, culture?

It has been suggested that the new media promise a somber future in which cultural identity will be swept away by the rising of a standardized culture (Rogers & Balle 1985). Like the futurists (who do not totally deny standardization by the media, hence predict more "cultural assertiveness"), both approaches tend to confuse culture and society, social changes with culture change—ultimately assuming a sameness between identity and culture.

Culture change and social changes are not always identical, and to confuse the two leads to serious misinterpretations of communication (Carroll 1988: 136). It was suggested in chapter 5 that identity—in large part due to media influences—loses its place-defined quality and, in form and function, begins to act independently of culture per se. The basic conclusion is that identity has important functions that transcend culture as such. Culture certainly is being standardized by the media in many parts of the globe. At the same time, identities are increasingly asserted. The resulting paradox is "cultural" identities without corresponding cultures. This argument raised the practical question of how best to nurture strong national identities, while still recognizing the psychological need for various minorities to retain symbolic "cultural" identities, with or without authentic culture. As education should enhance our commonalities, emphasis on dubious cultural specialness was seen to add to communication problems. An ethnographic example from the South Pacific, using the ubiquitous metaphor of place, illustrated how generation, migration, and the media contributed to changes in both culture and identification, thus challenging some of the positive implications of cultural revivals.

In fact, Carroll had argued earlier that trying to "preserve a culture" is an idea bound to fail because cultures must be renewed by communication exchanges that do not simply depend on human will (1988: 141). This thesis is shared by the present author and is a major conclusion of chapter 5, which not only distinguished culture change from social changes, but posited a functional difference between identity and culture. Metaphors of ethnicity and identity, with radical restructuring of social life and social performance by electronic media, literally change from one generation to another.[3]

Certainly, too much concern with culture, cultural revivalism, and exclusive identity may have negative consequences for second-generation children of immigrants. Unintended or not, the contemporary minority cry for "subjective culture" may be more than counter-productive for the next generation: perpetuating a culture-of-poverty image or, at the very least, resulting in a kind of patronization of the minority, which actually may prolong social conflicts and delay progress in the name of reputed cultural distinctiveness. Yet, as ethnic identity still has important psychological functions to play, it has been argued in this book that identity should be nurtured without falling into the trap of assuming a separate culture. The implications of this line of research are extremely significant for the culture-communication dialogue.

Metaphors of Masculinity/Metaphor Analysis
and Changing Male Images

Metaphors, according to Karsten Harries (1979a: 72), are fundamentally about reality. Many people think that metaphors say more than language can say alone; therefore, it is believed that they transcend what language may not capture. Metaphors, then, have some undeniable strengths as well as unavoidable limitations. One of their strengths is that metaphors invite us to pass beyond the mere image itself (1979a: 79). However, inherited metaphors can easily become obstacles to self-understanding. We sometimes cling stubbornly to metaphors about self that are no longer effective. This is especially true when considering gender as a personal context for understanding identity. Today's modern male is literally trying to create his own metaphors to fit the changing circumstances of his life.

Looking at a variety of cultures, chapter 6 considered the meaning of traditional masculinity as an oppositional identity and, using the metaphor of voyage as "pathways to manhood," traced some contemporary transformations of this gender identity, including a consideration of androgyny (a problematic metaphor) in other cultures. Evidence was presented of media-influenced changes in masculine imagery, both in Western and non-Western contexts. Image-metaphors can stabilize meaning in too permanent a fashion. On the other hand, metaphors may literally help to create something new altogether (Harries 1979a: 71). They may be thought of as a model for changing our way of looking at things, of perceiving the world. How is this self-transformation accomplished?[4]

Metaphor analysis is the current psychological technique for examining old metaphors and exchanging them for new ones. The reason we do this is in order that "we can examine and exorcise the 'ghosts' of our socialization so that we can freely choose meanings out of which we want to live our lives and express them through metaphor" (Deshler 1990: 296). The aim is, of course, to create new metaphors that better suit our changing lives. Image-metaphors, with their emotional nuances (or feeling tone), are powerful devices for capturing, quickly and intuitively, more than can be said in scientific language, offering new meanings and suggesting new relationships (Booth 1979a: 52).

What are the cultural meanings that are communicated through metaphors? Both the intended and unintended consequences of metaphorical images that have guided one's life are reexamined in such an analysis. This conscious use of metaphor as a type of problem-solving illustrates how individuals can reframe conflicts in terms of new analogies. Metaphor analysis, then, offers some promise for personal identity transformations. Unfortunately, there is sometimes a dark side to image-metaphors.

Insider-Outsider Issues in the Metaphor of Closet

Figurative language can create metaphoric visions that can have both positive and negative effects (Harries 1979a: 71). Metaphor often presents a one-sided view of reality. The closet metaphor has long symbolized the stigmatized status of homosexuals in homophobic societies. Examining this closet metaphor, chapter 7 considered the role of homophobia, with its denial of cultural legitimacy and social participation, in creating a category of social stranger for sexual minorities. The metaphor of closet may be an apt image of the constant insider-outsider dilemmas that face homosexuals in society.

The author's Swedish research was offered as illustration of how groups with externally imposed identities learn to cope with domination. Major debates still revolve around issues of social exclusion or inclusion, but the metaphors used to designate these processes often carry multiple referents, hence are interpreted differently by different individuals and groups. We need to be ever-vigilant about the uses and abuses of such metaphorical representations.

Although the development and maintenance of personal identity for gays and lesbians cannot be divorced from the background of a largely repressive heterosexual world, this dialectic is more complex and contradictory than our "metaphors of identity" allow for at this time. In a strange twist of events, homophobic societies may actually help create a quasi-"cultural" status for homosexuals where, I think, there would be no need for such exclusiveness if homosexual persons were given full social equality. The real danger is that identity can be a defensive "master status" that, being exclusive and self-perpetuating, becomes psychologically and socially self-defeating.

Despite contemporary rhetoric (unsupported discourse) about gay culture to the contrary, my research with these so-called cultural outlaws in Scandinavia led me to the conclusion that most gays and lesbians do not really want to separate themselves from the rest of humanity, but prefer to communicate in the larger cultural arenas shared by gays and nongays alike. Too much emphasis on "gay culture" and exclusive sexual identity can translate negatively for sexual minorities seeking fundamental human rights. However, both nongays and gays are guilty of using the closet metaphor to symbolize and justify exclusion and exclusiveness, respectively. Metaphor is always partial, dictating certain associations while denying others. Image-metaphors, then, are rarely free from ambiguity.

When gay males and lesbians argue for a separate culture, for the retention of a closet mentality, they inadvertently perpetuate a stranger role, the metaphor of social stranger being the most accurate image-metaphor for contemporary gays in America. By emphasizing differences, most of which do not exist, they give societal justification for more separation and discrimination. Social scientists have some moral responsibility in clarifying this still controversial matter of *culture* versus *identity*. We need to get beyond rhetorical metaphors which divide, rather than unify, people.

Unfortunately, we continue to use the old models of culture change, with their not-so-oblique reference to a philosophy of cultural relativism, to explain societal changes taking place in the area of same-sex behavior. Culture change models, and their accompanying metaphors of identity, may be inappropriate for groups that are, in fact, not culturally distinct. The concept of handicapping was introduced in chapter 7 to reveal some of the limits of media influence on the acceptance of homosexuals, at the same time raising the question of how gays and lesbians will eventually be integrated into the larger society. We then shifted to a very different context for looking at identity in the culture-communication dialogue: aging as metaphor.

Metaphors and Scientific Discourse in Social Gerontology

Aristotle is said to have described metaphor as "midway between the unintelligible and the commonplace" (quoted in Lodge 1988: 112). Certainly, by now the reader should appreciate how complex image-metaphors can really be. Despite the wonderful richness of such imagery, they are often limited and restrictive.[5] Already mentioned is the fact that metaphors are time-bound and context-specific, variable from culture to culture. This insight was dramatically evident in the chapter on aging and identity. Nowhere is the use of metaphor better exemplified than in research on social gerontology. Our metaphors of aging or the aged have so drastically altered over the years that even trying to summarize earlier points of view, using now-discarded metaphors as guides to understanding, proved problematic.

Considering aging as metaphor, chapter 8 looked at personal chronology as yet another significant context for understanding identity in the culture-communication dialogue. I tried to compare different cultures and their treatment of the elderly, considering both the social constructions of aging and the accompanying identity-transformations. I had to accomplish a delicate transition here. The major anthropological debate has been over what aging was like in other times and other places. Modern gerontological interests, however, have been concerned more with the assessment of its future status.

The culture-communication dialogue has given some attention to identity transformations in this last stage of adulthood, emphasis being on changing metaphors as these relate to changing circumstances of older persons. The most widely-accepted approach to the elderly population in social gerontology today is the "life course perspective," which typically has employed a career metaphor, with older people pictured as actively shaping and negotiating their own destinies.

Communication scholars have been primarily interested in media challenges to the aging population. Thus, analyses of media presentations of older people were presented, and responses to economic realities were considered with futurist predictions of the millennium, the pre-eminent metaphor of the future. Consumer-oriented capitalism, aided by the media, may be undermining age-based identities and promoting more acceptance for this population. Older metaphors of disengagement tended to leave the elderly with more or less nonperson status, whereas the more active and contemporary building metaphors of aging, by contrast, have stressed social involvement and continued social interaction.

Obviously, then, metaphor depends on conventional knowledge and cultural values. Without an adequate ethnographic knowledge of the culture from which the elderly population is drawn, it is virtually impossible to understand its metaphors, especially with regard to such abstract ideas as identity and communication. We then turned our attention to a more speculative endeavor: What type of identity will best suit us in the future?

The Global Person and Community as Romantic Metaphor

Jack Solomon (1988: 22), in *The Signs of Our Time*, argues that metaphor, as one type of cultural sign, is steeped in ideological presuppositions. One needs to learn to read the signs (metaphors) around us so that we can free ourselves from their hypnotic grasp. Certainly, image-metaphors can serve ideological purposes rather than contributing to human improvement. It is surely an error to think that we can totally eliminate cultural metaphors and their potential influence on us; but, at minimum, we can reflect on their implications, strengths, and inadequacies. As we have learned, many scientific perspectives that describe identity require metaphor(s) to organize them. Guiding metaphors, or organizing metaphors, lie at the heart of much research on identity. Some metaphors, however, are better scientific models of reality than others (Brown 1987).

What have been the effects of technology on culture and social discourse? Chapter 9 made some guarded inferences about the relationship between modern-day communication technologies, culture, and community. The mass communication perspective has drawn heavily on both anthropology and the communication sciences. Is technology causing the disappearance of community, or are we witnessing different types of community based on the potentialities of the new media technologies? These have been frequently asked questions in the culture-communication dialogue. Our metaphors of American idealism may have deluded us about community, which we tend to see as a dream of unity that "promises both self-realization and an end to loneliness" (Tinder 1980: 2). This largely romantic response to the process of modernization has profoundly affected our understanding of community itself.[6] Community has become the romantic metaphor of our times.

Related to this imperfect understanding of community is our elusive quest for meaningful self-process (identity) in an emerging world culture. Using an adaptive-growth model, the concept of the global person was examined in some detail. Furthermore, it was asked how such a flexible identity structure relates to better "communicative competence" as a guide for future transformations of self. Communication between diverse groups, social or cultural, will surely be essential for our global survival. Acceptance of diverse lifestyles, sexual minorities, and ethnic interest groups will be the ultimate challenge of this identity of the future.

Electronic transformation of our society to a new cyberculture will require persons with flexible identities that can effectively bridge the past and future. In short, we will be forced to construct identities that help us to improve our communication skills. Using our identity potential to enhance rather than restrict our lives, we should be able to rise above cultural limitations (ethnocentrism, sexism, racism, and the like). The media can be harnessed to strengthen shared national values and identities, with unifying effects for both individuals and society. We live, however, in an information society where the dominant metaphors of the times themselves quickly become obsolete (Toffler 1990: 86). Thus, we seem in perpetual search for a new "vocabulary of identity."

What are the characteristics of diversity in this emerging world culture? Do we really want to preserve everything that today is being labeled "cultural"? How do we achieve a more relevant identity for an information society? These are just some of the issues in the contemporary culture-communication dialogue. In chapter 5, it was argued that the constructs, culture and identity, should not be confused. We tried to move the reader *beyond culture* to the subtleties of identity. This conclusion brought us full-circle to the heart of the contemporary debates over so-called multiculturalism (What should be the role of the school in maintaining group identities?), a heated and polarized argument between the particularists and the pluralists.

I deliberately avoided tackling these thorny issues, so central to the educational dialogue, in earlier chapters because of our modern tendency to immediately choose sides and defend turf. Certainly, polarization can quickly gain ascendancy over sane debate. There may yet be some middle ground in the balance of unity or diversity. The public-private distinction was suggested as crucial for a full understanding of the dynamics of these complex educational processes. Acknowledging the widespread inclination today to confuse cultural issues with social ones may be an important key to understanding the multicultural debates.

The central tensions between groups do not seem to be essentially cultural but originate in inequalities over power and participation in society. More and more, groups are trying to invent cultures through identity assertions. Thus, there is a strong temptation today to see what one wants to see when positing black and white, male or female, gay and straight "cultures." The metaphors that have fueled this debate are themselves ripe for misinterpretation. Words like *assimilation*, for example, suggest to some a kind of cultural genocide of the strong against the weak. The reality is surely more complex.

Perhaps a more benign image-metaphor invokes the call for more "voice" from minorities who feel they do not yet belong to the mainstream culture (Gergen 1989, 1991). Considering the heated debates over multiculturalism, Gergen makes the sensible suggestion that we need to shift our focus from principles and abstractions to the participants themselves (1991: 257). When you do this, he argues, you are more likely to hear the voices of these diverse participants, without having to automatically reject the rhetorical message that is so often contradictory.

Although well-meaning, the insistence on the invention of "subjective cultures" for separate minorities may be counter-productive for the next generations, who hopefully will not have to retreat to the securities of a ghettoized existence, an underclass, or a racial defense in order to have a voice in society. When (if) various minorities ever achieve true social equality, one wonders if these "cultures," so glibly talked about today, will vanish?

Media-induced cultural homogenization of American society (read, Western) is a present reality that cannot be denied. At the same time, we are witnessing dramatic exhibitions of ethnic/gender/sexual preference identities. One cannot ignore the resurgence of minority consciousness in modern times. The essential issue may not be culture, or even cultural diversity, but the need to assert identities of various sorts, the need to have one's voice heard. Many of the so-called cultural debates, rather than celebrating diversity in American life, may constitute "a rejection of increasing cultural diversity in America," as George and Louise Spindler have so eloquently suggested (1990: 80).

The information age is here to stay. Paraphrasing Everette Dennis (1989: 196), the future of our information society will not be solely determined, in any case, by technology alone but by humans who shape the communication industry.[7] Genuine community can be found, not only in face-to-face relationships, but also in mediated communication brought about through mass media and its supporting technology. Community and technology, then, are not necessarily opposed. We can and should be more reflective in how we interact with and utilize the existing media. The real challenge is how to take more control over electronic media rather than merely succumbing to them. There is as much potential, then, in a communication-based community today as there was in previous attempts at creating the elusive, romantic metaphor of community.

To return to where we began, we have seen how metaphors are intimately tied to social experiences, cultural knowledge, belief, and value. Metaphorical images have played a central role in media presentations (Berger 1990), and the creative power of such figurative language has been justifiably acknowledged. David Lodge (1988: 80) wonders, however, if anything that offers to explain so much can possibly be useful—even if metaphor is always, to some extent, "true." Metaphors of identity certainly can be "expressive" and "persuasive" (Crocker 1977: 53; Fernandez 1974). They can also be restrictive and limiting (Sacks 1979). The important thing is to learn to recognize that we constantly use image-metaphors and that metaphor is still indispensible to science. However, as Richard Brown (1987: 103) has sanely suggested, we need to learn how to appraise and use them to maximum advantage.

Principal Points

By way of summary, this last chapter considered some of the strengths and weaknesses of using metaphor as a scientific tool for studying culture, identity, and communication: How effectively have cultural and social meanings been communicated through image-metaphors in the culture-communication dialogue? Guiding metaphors are ubiquitous in scientific descriptions of identity, the academic metaphor for self-in-context. In order to judge the aptness of metaphor in this dialogue, then, these figures of speech had to be assessed in reference to specific contexts. Metaphoric ambiguity was seen to be heightened in cross-cultural comparisons. Metaphoric descriptions, subject to subtle ideological manipulations, remain problematic in scientific discourse. When judging the elegance of research models, the effectiveness of their guiding metaphors must be carefully evaluated.

Notes

1. Communication scholars have had some difficulty in getting a firm grasp on this elusive notion of context. Anderson and Meyer claim that some media studies have tended to ignore context altogether (1988: 27).

2. Metaphors (similes) are culturally specific. Many Pacific Islanders identify themselves by reference to a particular environmental feature, e.g., the human body may be described as "like" a clamshell (Pomponio 1990: 53).

3. Having said this, I do not mean to imply that such identities are insincere or inauthentic. Culture may sometimes be; but identities, if still functional, are "real."

4. Consider Wheelwright's emphasis on the etymology of the term metaphor: meta (change) and phora (motion), suggesting the image of "change in motion" that nicely captures the dynamic function of metaphor in social contexts (quoted in Fernandez 1977: 104).

5. Consider this quote: "Metaphor is the dream work of language and, like all dream work, its interpretation reflects as much on the interpreter as on the originator" (Davidson 1979: 29).

6. Richard Brown thinks that we inherited the assumption that the self should be manifested most fully in community from the ideal of the Greek *polis* (1987: 49).

7. Everette Dennis (1989: 41) believes that today's media, almost by default, do what family or school have done in the past. The media are becoming quasi-public institutions in today's information world.

REFERENCES

Abound, Frances E., and Diane N. Ruble. 1987. "Identity Constancy in Children: Developmental Processes and Implications." In T. Honess & K. Yardley, eds. *Self and Identity* 95–107. London & New York: Routledge & Kegan Paul.

Adam, Barry D. 1978. *The Survival of Domination.* New York: Elsevier.

Adler, Peter S. 1987. "Culture Shock and the Cross-Cultural Learning Experience." In L. F. Luce & E. C. Smith, eds. *Toward Internationalism* 24–35. Cambridge, Mass.: Newbury.

Aldridge-Morris, Ray. 1989. *Multiple Personality: An Exercise in Deception.* Hove & London: Lawrence Erlbaum Associates.

Alexander, Jeffrey C., and Steven Seidman. 1990. *Culture and Society: Contemporary Debates.* Cambridge & New York: Cambridge University Press.

Alford, Richard D. 1988. *Naming and Identity: A Cross-Cultural Study of Personal Naming Practices.* New York: Harper & Row.

Allis, Sam. 1990. "What Do Men Really Want?" *Time* (Fall): 80–82.

Almaguer, Tomas. 1989. "What's Love Got To Do With It?" *Out/Look*, no. 5 (Summer): 80–85.

Altheide, David L. 1985. *Media Power.* Beverly Hills: SAGE.

Anderson, James A., ed. 1990. *Communication Yearbook/13.* Newbury Park: SAGE.

Anderson, James A., and Timothy P. Meyer. 1988. *Mediated Communication: A Social Action Perspective.* Newbury Park: SAGE.

Applegate, James L., and Howard E. Sypher. 1988. "A Constructivist Theory of Communication and Culture." In Y. Y. Kim & W. B. Gudykunst, eds. *Theories in Intercultural Communication* 41–65. Newbury Park: SAGE.

Applegate, Jim. 1990. "R & CT Chair's Address to Membership." *Rhetorical & Communication Theory Newsletter* (Fall): 1–2.

Archer, Margaret S. 1990. "Theory, Culture and Post-Industrial Society." In M. Featherstone, ed. *Global Culture: Nationalism, Globalization and Modernity* 97–119. London & Newbury Park: SAGE.

Arterton, F. Christopher. 1987. *Teledemocracy: Can Technology Protect Democracy?* Newbury Park: SAGE.

Asante, Molefi Kete, and William B. Gudykunst, eds. 1989. *Handbook of International and Intercultural Communication.* Newbury Park: SAGE.

Asimov, Isaac. 1963. *The Human Brain: Its Capacities and Functions.* New York: New American Library.

Associated Press. 1991. "Firm OKs Benefits for Gay Couples." *Greensboro News & Record* (Saturday, Sept. 7): A3.

Barker, Judith. 1990. "Between Humans and Ghosts: The Decrepit Elderly in a Polynesian Society." In J. Sokolovsky, ed. *The Cultural Context of Aging* 295–314. New York: Bergin & Garvey Publishers.

Barnlund, Dean C. [1975] 1989. *Public and Private Self in Japan and the United States: Communicative Styles in Two Cultures.* Yarmouth, Maine: Intercultural Press.

Becker, Howard S. 1986. *Writing For Social Scientists.* Chicago & London: The University of Chicago Press.

Bell, Alan P., and Martin S. Weinberg. 1978. *Homosexualities: A Study of Diversity Among Men and Women.* New York: Simon & Schuster.

Bell, Alan P., Martin S. Weinberg, and Sue K. Hammersmith. 1981. *Sexual Preference: Its Development in Men and Women.* Bloomington: University of Indiana Press.

Bellah, Robert N., Richard Madsen, William M. Sullivan, Ann Swidler, and Steven M Tipton. [1985] 1986. *Habits of the Heart: Individualism and Commitment in American Life.* New York: Harper & Row.

Bem, Daryl, J. 1988. "Putting Persons Back Into the Context." In N. Bolger, et al., eds. *Persons In Context* 203–16. New York & Cambridge: Cambridge University Press.

Bem, Sandra L. 1974. "The Measurement of Psychological Androgyny." *Journal of Consulting and Clinical Psychology* 42: 155–62.

Berger, Arthur Asa. 1990. *Agitpop: Political Culture and Communication Theory.* New Brunswick & London: Transaction Publishers.

Bergheim, Laura. 1990. "Pluggies." In N. Mills, ed. *Culture in an Age of Money: The Legacy of the 1980s in America* 83–96. Chicago: Ivan R. Dee.

Bly, Robert. 1990. *Iron John: A Book About Men.* Reading, Mass.: Addison-Wesley.

Bock, Philip K. 1988. *Rethinking Psychological Anthropology*. New York: W. H. Freeman & Co.

Bolger, Niall, Avshalom Caspi, Geraldine Downey, and Martha Moorehouse, eds. 1988. *Persons in Context: Developmental Processes*. New York & Cambridge: Cambridge University Press.

Bond, John, and Peter Coleman. 1990a. "Ageing Into The Twenty-first Century." In J. Bond & P. Coleman, eds. *Aging in Society* 276–90. London & Newbury Park: SAGE.

————, eds. 1990b. *Aging in Society: An Introduction to Social Gerontology*. London & Newbury Park: SAGE.

Bond, John, Roger Briggs, and Peter Coleman. 1990. "The Study of Aging." In J. Bond & P. Coleman, eds. *Aging in Society* 17–47. London & Newbury Park: SAGE.

Bonnemaison, Joel. 1985. "The Tree and the Canoe: Roots and Mobility in Vanuatu Societies." In M. Chapman, ed. *Mobility and Identity in the Island Pacific*, Special Issue *Pacific Viewpoint* 26 (1): 30–62.

Booth, Wayne C. 1979a. "Metaphor as Rhetoric." In S. Sacks, ed. *On Metaphor* 47–70. Chicago & London: The University of Chicago Press.

————. 1979b. "Ten Literal 'Theses.'" In S. Sacks, ed. *On Metaphor* 173–74. Chicago & London: The University of Chicago Press.

Borman, Leonard. 1976. "Self-help and the Professions." *Social Policy* (Sept./Oct.): 46–47.

Brandes, Stanley. [1980] 1988. *Metaphors of Masculinity: Sex and Status in Andalusian Folklore*. Philadelphia: University of Pennsylvania Press.

Brim, Orville G., Jr. 1960. "Personality as Role-Learning." In I. Iscoe & H. Stevenson, eds. *Personality Development in Children* 127–59. Austin: University of Texas Press.

Brislin, Richard W., Kenneth Cushner, Craig Cherrie and Mahealani Yong. 1986. *Intercultural Interactions: A Practical Guide*. Beverly Hills: SAGE.

Brody, E. W. 1990. *Communication Tomorrow: New Audiences, New Technologies, New Media*. New York & Westport, Connecticut: Praeger.

Brown, Donald E. 1991. *Human Universals*. New York: McGraw-Hill.

Brown, Richard. 1987. *Society as Text: Essays on Rhetoric, Reason, and Reality*. Chicago & London: The University of Chicago Press.

Burridge, Kenelm. 1979. *Someone, No One: An Essay on Individuality*. Princeton: Princeton University Press.

Butler, Judith. 1990. *Gender Trouble: Feminism and the Subversion of Identity.* New York & London: Routledge.

Cairns, Robert B., and Beverly D. Cairns. 1988. "The Sociogenesis of Self-Concepts." In N. Bolger, et al., eds. *Persons In Context* 181–202. New York & Cambridge: Cambridge University Press.

Carrithers, Michael, Steven Collins, and Steven Lukes, eds. 1987. *The Category of the Person: Anthropology, Philosophy, History.* Cambridge: Cambridge University Press.

Carroll, Raymonde. 1988. *Cultural Misunderstandings: The French-American Experience.* Chicago & London: The University of Chicago Press.

Cashmore, E. Ellis. 1987. "Shades of Black, Shades of White." In J. Lull, ed. *Popular Music and Communication* 245–46. Newbury Park: SAGE.

Clark, Margaret, and Barbara Anderson. 1967. *Culture and Aging.* Springfield: Charles Thomas.

Cohen, Ted. 1979. "Metaphors and the Cultivation of Intimacy." In S. Sacks, ed. *On Metaphor* 1–10. Chicago & London: The University of Chicago Press.

Coles, Catherine. 1990. "The Older Woman in Hausa Society: Power and Authority in Urban Nigeria." In J. Sokolovsky, ed. *The Cultural Context of Aging* 57–82. New York: Bergin & Garvey Publishers.

Collier, Mary Jane, and Milt Thomas. 1988. "Cultural Identity: An Interpretive Perspective." In Y. Y. Kim & W. B. Gudykunst, eds. *Theories in Intercultural Communication* 99–122. Newbury Park: SAGE.

Collins, Steven. 1987. "Categories, Concepts or Predicaments?: Remarks on Mauss's Use of Philosophical Terminology." In M. Carrithers, et al., eds. *The Category of the Person* 46–82. Cambridge: Cambridge University Press.

———. [1982] 1990. *Selfless Persons: Imagery and Thought in Theravada Buddhism.* New York: Cambridge University Press.

Condon, John C. 1984. *With Respect to the Japanese: A Guide for Americans.* Yarmouth, Maine: Intercultural Press.

Condon, John C., and Fathi S. Yousef. 1975. *An Introduction to Intercultural Communication.* New York: Macmillan.

Counts, Dorothy Ayers, and David R. Counts. 1985a. "Introduction: Linking Concepts Aging and Gender, Aging and Death." In D. A. Counts & D. R. Counts, eds. *Aging and its Transformations* 1–24. Lanham & New York: University Press of America.

_____, eds. 1985b. *Aging and its Transformations*, ASAO Monograph, no. 10. Lanham & New York: University Press of America.

Cowan, Thomas. 1988. *Gay Men and Women Who Enriched the World*. New Canaan, Conn.: Mulvey Books.

Creighton, Millie. 1990. "Revisiting Shame and Guilt Cultures: A Forty-Year Pilgrimage." *Ethos* 18 (3): 279–307.

Crocker, J. Christopher. 1977. "The Social Functions of Rhetorical Forms." In D. J. Sapir & J. C. Crocker, eds. *The Social Use of Metaphor* 33–66. University of Pennsylvania Press.

Cronen, Vernon E., Victoria Chen, and W. Barnett Pearce. 1988. "Coordinated Management of Meaning: A Critical Theory." In Y. Y. Kim & W. B. Gudykunst, eds. *Theories in Intercultural Communication* 66–98. Newbury Park: SAGE.

Crowley, D. J. 1982. *Understanding Communication: The Signifying Web*. New York & London: Gordon & Breach Science Publishers.

Crowley, Susan L. 1991. "The Sin of Aging: Does 'the Beauty Myth' Hinder Older Women's Advancement?" *AARP Bulletin* 32 (9): 2.

Dank, Barry. 1971. "Coming Out in the Gay World." *Psychiatry* 34 (May): 180–197.

Davidson, Donald. 1979. "What Metaphors Mean." In S. Sacks, ed. *On Metaphor* 29–46. Chicago & London: The University of Chicago Press.

Davis, Fred. 1981. "Contemporary Nostalgia and the Mass Media." In E. Katz & T. Szecsko, eds. *Mass Media and Social Change* 219–30. Beverly Hills: SAGE.

De Cocq, Gustave A. 1976. "European and North American Self-help Movements." In A. H. Katz & E. I. Bender, eds. *The Strength In Us* 202–8. New York: New Viewpoints.

De Montefores, Carmen, and Stephen J. Schultz. 1978. "Coming Out: Similarities and Differences for Lesbians and Gay Men." *Journal of Social Issues* 34 (3): 59–72.

Dennis, Everette E. 1989. *Reshaping the Media: Mass Communication in an Information Age*. Newbury Park & London: SAGE.

Dentan, Robert K. 1979. *The Semai: A Nonviolent People of Malaya*. New York: Holt, Rinehart & Winston.

Deshler, David. 1990. "Metaphor Analysis: Exorcising Social Ghosts." In J. Mezirow, ed. *Fostering Critical Reflection in Adulthood* 296–313. San Francisco: Jossey-Bass.

Deutsch, Claudia. 1991. "Gay Issue Becomes Corporate Concern." *Greensboro News & Record*, Sunday (April 28): E1, E4.

Deutsch, David. 1989. "The HIV/AIDs Situation in Sweden." *Social Change in Sweden*, No. 38 (January): 1–10.

Diamond, Neil. [1972–3] 1981. "Play Me." *Love Songs Album*. Universal City, Calif.: MCA Records, Inc.

Dobkin de Rios, Marlene. 1974. "Cultural Persona In Drug-Induced Altered States of Consciousness." In T. K. Fitzgerald, ed. *Social and Cultural Identity*, Southern Anthropological Society Proceedings, no. 8: 15–23.

Doi, Takeo. 1986. *The Anatomy of Self: The Individual Versus Society*. Tokyo & New York: Kodansha International.

Downing, John D. H. 1989. "Computers for Political Change: PeaceNet and Public Data Access." In M. Siefert, et al., eds. *The Information Gap* 154–62. Oxford & New York: Oxford University Press.

Dumont, Louis. 1980. *Homo Hierarchicus: The Caste System and Its Implications*. Chicago: The University of Chicago Press.

———. 1986. *Essays on Individualism: Modern Ideology in Anthropological Perspective*. Chicago & London: The University of Chicago Press.

———. 1987. "A Modified View of Our Origins: The Christian Beginnings of Modern Individualism." In M. Carrithers, et al., eds. *The Category of the Person* 93–122. New York & Cambridge: Cambridge University Press.

Dychtwald, Ken, and Joe Flower. 1989. *Age Wave: The Challenges and Opportunities of an Aging America*. Los Angeles: Jeremy P. Tarcher.

Eccles, John C. 1989. *Evolution of the Brain: Creation of the Self*. London & New York: Routledge.

Edelstein, Alex S., Youichi Ito, and Hans Mathias Kepplinger. 1989. *Communication and Culture: A Comparative Approach*. New York & London: Longman.

Edwards, John. 1985. *Language, Society and Identity*. New York: Basil Blackwell.

Ellingsworth, Huber W. 1988. "A Theory of Adaptation in Intercultural Dyads." In Y. Y. Kim & W. B. Gudykunst, eds. *Theories in Intercultural Communication* 259–79. Newbury Park & London: SAGE.

Erikson, Erik H. [1950] 1963. *Childhood and Society*. New York: Norton.

———. 1968. *Identity: Youth and Society*. New York: Columbia University Press.

Ewing, Katherine P. 1990. "The Illusion of Wholeness: Culture, Self, and the Experience of Inconsistency." *Ethos* 18 (3): 251–78.

Fajans, Jane. 1985. "The Person in Social Context: The Social Character of Baining 'Psychology.'" In G. M. White & J. Kirkpatrick, eds. *Person, Self, and Experience* 367–400. Berkeley: University of California Press.

Featherstone, Mike, ed. 1990. *Global Culture: Nationalism, Globalization and Modernity*. London & Newbury Park: SAGE.

Featherstone, Mike, and Mike Hepworth. 1990. "Images in Aging." In J. Bond & P. Coleman, eds. *Aging in Society* 250–75. London & Newbury Park: SAGE.

Fernandez, James. 1974. "The Mission of Metaphor in Expressive Culture." *Current Anthropology* 15 (2): 119–33.

———. 1977. "The Performance of Ritual Metaphors." In D. J. Sapir & J. C. Crocker, eds. *The Social Use of Metaphor* 100–131. University of Pennsylvania Press.

Fine, Gary Alan. 1987. "One of the Boys: Women in Male-Dominated Settings." In M. Kimmel, ed. *Changing Men* 131–47. Newbury Park: SAGE.

Fine, Reuben. 1986. *Narcissism, the Self, and Society*. New York: Columbia University Press.

Finer, David. 1989. "The HIV/AIDs Situation in Sweden." *Social Change in Sweden*, no. 38 (January): 1–10.

Fitzgerald, Thomas K. 1972. "Education and Identity: A Reconstruction of Some Models of Acculturation and Identity." *New Zealand Journal of Educational Studies* 7 (1): 45–58.

———, ed. 1974. *Social and Cultural Identity: Problems of Persistence and Change*. Athens: University of Georgia Press.

———. 1975. "Maori Attitudes Toward Integration." In B. E. Griessman, ed. *Minorities* 177–80. Hinsdale, Illinois: Dryden Press.

———. 1977a. "A Critique of Anthropological Research on Homosexuality." *Journal of Homosexuality* 2 (4): 385–97.

———. 1977b. *Education and Identity: A Study of the New Zealand Maori Graduate*. Wellington: New Zealand Council for Educational Research.

———. 1977c. "Nutrition and the Aged: A Look at Some Average, Healthy Older Persons." *North Carolina Review of Business and Economics* 3 (2): 3–7.

———. 1979. "Male and Female Identity Among New Zealand Maoris." In A. McElroy & C. Matthiasson, eds. *Sex Roles in Changing Societies,* SUNY Occasional Papers in Anthropology Series (April): 83–87.

———. 1981. "Suicide Prevention and Gay Self-help Groups in Sweden and Finland." *Crisis: International Journal of Suicide- and Crisis-Studies* 2 (1): 58–68.

———. 1983. "Homosexuality: The Myth of the Composite Portrait." In R. C. Federico & J. S. Schwartz, eds. *Sociology,* 3rd ed. 216–21. Reading, Mass.: Addison-Wesley.

———. 1986. "Diet of Cook Islanders in New Zealand." In L. Manderson, ed. *Shared Wealth and Symbol* 67–86. London: Cambridge University Press.

———. 1988. *Aspirations and Identity of Second-Generation Cook Islanders in New Zealand.* Wellington: Dept. of Education.

———. 1989. "Coconuts and Kiwis: Identity and Change Among Second-Generation Cook Islanders in New Zealand." *Ethnic Groups* 7 (4): 259–87.

———. 1991. "Media and Changing Metaphors of Ethnicity and Identity." *Media, Culture & Society* 13: 193–214.

———. 1992. "Media, Ethnicity and Identity." In P. Scannell, P. Schlesinger & C. Sparks, eds. *Culture And Power: A Media, Culture & Society Reader* 112–33. London & Newbury Park: SAGE.

Foley, Douglas E. 1991. "Reconsidering Anthropological Explanations of Ethnic School Failure." *Anthropology & Education Quarterly* 22 (1): 60–86.

Folkenberg, Judy. 1989. "Gay Kids, Mad Parents: Many Young Homosexuals Face Hostility on the Home Front." *American Health* (December): 77–78.

Foote, Nelson. 1951. "Identification as the Basis for a Theory of Motivation." *American Sociological Review* 16: 14–22.

Ford, Clellan S., and Frank A. Beach. 1951. *Patterns of Sexual Behavior.* New York: Harper.

Forgas, Joseph P. 1988. "Episode Representations in Intercultural Communication." In Y. Y. Kim & W. B. Gudykunst, *Theories in Intercultural Communication* 186–212. Newbury Park: SAGE.

Fowles, Donald. 1988. "A Profile of Older Americans: 1988." 19. Washington, D. C.: AARP & AOA.

Fox, Richard G., Charlotte Aull, and Louis Cimino. 1978. "Ethnic Nationalism and Political Mobilization in Industrial Societies." In E. L. Ross, ed. *Interethnic Communication* 113–33. Athens: The University of Georgia Press.

Freimuth, Vicki S., and Kathleen Jamieson. 1979. "Communication with the Elderly: Shattering Stereotypes." 1–38. Falls Church, Virginia: Speech Communication Association, and Urbana, Illinois: ERIC.

Friedl, Ernestine. 1984. *Women and Men: An Anthropologist's View.* Prospect Heights, Illinois: Waveland Press.

Fry, Christine. 1981. *Dimensions: Aging, Culture and Health.* Brooklyn: J. F. Bergin.

Furlong, Mary S. 1989. "An Electronic Community for Older Adults: The SeniorNet Network." In M. Siefert, et al., eds. *The Information Gap* 145–53. Oxford & New York: Oxford University Press.

Gandy, Oscar H. Jr. 1989. "The Surveillance Society Inequalities: Information Technology and Bureaucratic Social Control." In M. Siefert, et al., eds. *The Information Gap* 61–76. Oxford & New York: Oxford University Press.

Gardner, Howard, and Ellen Winner. 1979. "The Development of Metaphoric Competence: Implications for Humanistic Disciplines." In S. Sacks, ed. *On Metaphor* 121–40. Chicago & London: The University of Chicago Press.

Garfinkel, Perry. 1986. *In A Man's World: Father, Son, Brother, Friend and Other Roles Men Play.* New York: New American Library.

Geertz, Clifford. 1973. *The Interpretation of Cultures.* New York: Basic Books.

Gelman, David. 1990. "A Kiss Is Still A Kiss: Changing Norms Give Aging a Better Name." *Newsweek* (March 5): 53.

Gergen, Kenneth J. 1989. "Warranting Voice and the Elaboration of the Self." In J. Shotter & K. J. Gergen, eds. *Texts of Identity* 70–81. London: SAGE.

———. 1991. *The Saturated Self: Dilemmas of Identity in Contemporary Life.* New York: Basic Books.

Gerson, Kathleen. 1987. "What Do Women Want From Men?: Men's Influence on Women's Work and Family Choices." In M. Kimmel, ed. *Changing Men* 115–30. Newbury Park: SAGE.

Gillespie, Andres, and Kevin Robins. 1989. "Geographical Inequalities: The Spatial Bias of the New Communication Technologies." In M. Siefert, et al., eds. *The Information Gap* 7–18. Oxford & New York: Oxford University Press.

Gillette, Douglas, and Robert Moore. 1990. *King, Warrior, Magician, Lover: Rediscovering the Mature Masculine.* San Francisco: Harper.

Gilmore, David D. 1990. *Manhood In the Making: Cultural Concepts of Masculinity.* New Haven & London: Yale University Press.

Gitech, Lenny. 1980. "Gays Around the Globe: The Issue Is Everywhere." *The Advocate*, no. 296 (July): 15.

Gitlin, Todd. 1990. "Blips, Bites and Savvy Talk." In N. Mills, ed. *Culture in an Age Of Money: The Legacy of the 1980s in America* 1–45. Chicago: Ivan R. Dee.

Glascock, Anthony P. 1990. "By Any Other Name, It Is Still Killing: A Comparison of the Treatment of the Elderly in America and Other Societies." In J. Sokolovsky, ed. *The Cultural Context of Aging* 43–56. New York: Bergin & Garvey Publishers.

Glascock, Anthony P., and Susan L. Feinman. 1981. "Social Asset or Social Burden: Treatment of the Aged in Non-Industrial Societies." In C. Fry & Contributors, eds. *Dimensions: Aging, Culture and Health* 13–32. New York: Bergin & Garvey Publishers.

Glover, Jonathan. 1988. *I: The Philosophy and Psychology of Personal Identity.* London: Penguin Books.

Goffman, Erving. 1959. *The Presentation of Self in Everyday Life.* Garden City, New York: Doubleday.

Goldberg, Herb. 1980. *The New Male: From Self-Destruction to Self-Care.* New York: New American Library.

Goldman, Alan. 1989. "Communication Between Strangers: An Intercultural Mandate for the Late Twentieth Century." *The Carolinas Speech Communication Annual* 5: 22–32.

Gonzalez, Christine F. 1989. "Translation." In M. K. Asante & W. G. Gudykunst, eds. *Handbook of International and Intercultural Communication* 484–501. Newbury Park: SAGE.

Greenberg, David F. 1988. *The Construction of Homosexuality.* Chicago & London: The University of Chicago Press.

Greenwald, Jeff. 1990. *Shopping for Buddhas.* San Francisco: Harper & Row.

Gross, Larry. 1991. "Out of the Mainstream: Sexual Minorities and the Mass Media." In M. A. Wolf & A. P. Kielwasser, eds. *Gay People, Sex, and the Media* 19–46. New York: The Haworth Press.

Grove, David J. 1989. "Resolving Feelings of Anger, Guilt and Shame: A Seminar for Mental Health Professionals." [David Grove Seminars, 20 Kettle River Drive, Edwardsville, Illinois 62025].

Gudykunst, William B. 1988. "Uncertainty and Anxiety." In Y. Y. Kim & W. B. Gudykunst, eds. *Theories in Intercultural Communication* 123–56. Newbury Park: SAGE.

_____. 1990. "Diplomacy: A Special Case for Intergroup Communication." In F. Korzenny & S. Ting-Toomey, eds. *Communication for Peace* 19–39. Newbury Park & London: SAGE.

Gudykunst, William B., and Lauren I. Gumbs. 1989. "Social Cognition and Intergroup Communication." In M. K. Asante & W. B. Gudykunst, eds. *Handbook of International and Intercultural Communication* 204–24. Newbury Park & London: SAGE.

Gudykunst, William B., and Tsukasa Nishida. 1989. "Theoretical Perspectives for Studying Intercultural Communication." In M. K. Asante & W. B. Gudykunst, eds. *Handbook of International and Intercultural Communication* 17–46. Newbury Park: SAGE.

Gudykunst, William B., and Stella Ting-Toomey. 1988. *Culture and Interpersonal Communication*. Newbury Park: SAGE.

Gudykunst, William B., and Young Yun Kim. 1984. *Communicating with Strangers: An Approach to Intercultural Communication*. New York: Random House.

Gumpert, Gary. 1987. *Talking Tombstones and Other Tales of the Media*. New York & Oxford: Oxford University Press.

Hall, Bradford "J." 1992. "Theories of Culture and Communication." *Communication Theory*. 2 (2): 50–70.

Hall, Edward T. 1959. *Silent Language*. Greenwich, Conn.: Fawcett Publications.

Handler, Richard. 1989. "Ethnicity in the Museum: A Culture and Communication Discourse." In S. E. Keefe, ed. *Negotiating Ethnicity*, Napa Bulletin, no. 8: 18–26.

Hanna, Judith L. 1986. "Interethnic Communication in Children's Own Dance, Play, and Protest." In Y. Y. Kim, ed. *Interethnic Communication* 176–98. Newbury Park: SAGE.

Harries, Karsten. 1979a. "Metaphors and Transcendence." In S. Sacks, ed. *On Metaphor* 71–88. Chicago & London: The University of Chicago Press.

_____. 1979b. "The Many Uses of Metaphor." In S. Sacks, ed. *On Metaphor* 165–72. Chicago & London: The University of Chicago Press.

Harris, Philip R., and Robert T. Moran. 1987. "Managing Cultural Differences: Instructor's Guide." Houston & London: Gulf Publishing Co.

———. 1989. *Managing Cultural Differences*. 2nd ed. Houston: Gulf Publishing Co.

Harry, Joseph, and Man S. Das, eds. 1980. *Homosexuality in International Perspective*. New York: Advent Books.

Harwood, Irene H. 1987. "The Evolution of the Self: An Integration of Winnicott's and Kohut's Concepts." In T. Honess & K. Yardley, eds. *Self and Identity* 55–76. London & New York: Routledge & Kegan Paul.

Hazan, Haim. 1990a. "The Construction of Personhood Among the Aged: A Comparative Study of Aging in Israel and England." In J. Sokolovsky, ed. *The Cultural Context of Aging* 263–76. New York: Bergin & Garvey Publishers.

———. 1990b. "Victims Into Sacrifice: The Construction of the Old as a Symbolic Type." *Journal of Cross-Cultural Gerontology* 5 (1): 77–84.

Hecht, Michael L., Peter A. Anderson, and Sidney A. Ribeau. 1989. "The Cultural Dimensions of Nonverbal Communication." In M. K. Asante & W. B. Gudykunst, eds. *Handbook of International and Intercultural Communication* 163–85. Newbury Park: SAGE.

Heger, Heinz. 1980. *The Men With the Pink Triangle*. Boston: Alyson Publications.

Henderson, J. Neil. 1990. "Alzheimer's Disease in Cultural Context." In J. Sokolovsky, ed. *The Cultural Context of Aging* 315–30. New York: Bergin & Garvey Publishers.

Herdt, Gilbert H. 1981. *Guardians of the Flute: Idioms of Masculinity*. New York: McGraw Hill.

———, ed. 1984. *Ritualized Homosexuality*. Berkeley: University of California Press.

———. 1989. "Father Presence and Ritual Homosexuality: Paternal Deprivation and Masculine Development in Melanesia Reconsidered." *Ethos* 17 (3): 326–70.

Herdt, Gilbert, and Robert J. Stoller. 1990. *Intimate Communications: Erotics and the Study of Culture*. New York: Columbia University Press.

Herek, Gregory. 1984. "Beyond 'Homophobia': A Social Psychological Perspective on Attitudes Toward Lesbians and Gay Men." *Journal of Homosexuality* 10 (1/2): 1–17.

———. 1985. "On Doing, Being, and Not Being: Prejudice and the Social Construction of Sexuality." *Journal of Homosexuality* 12 (1): 135–51.

_____. 1987. "On Heterosexual Masculinity: Some Psychical Consequences of the Social Construction of Gender and Sexuality." In M. Kimmel, ed. *Changing Men* 68–82. Newbury Park: SAGE.

Hockett, Charles. 1960. "The Origin of Human Speech." *Scientific American* 203 (September): 48; 88–96.

Hofstede, Geert. 1980. *Cultures Consequences: International Differences in Work-Related Values*. Beverly Hills: SAGE.

Hollis, Martin. 1987. "Of Masks and Men." In M. Carrithers, et al., eds. *The Category of the Person* 217–33. Cambridge: Cambridge University Press.

Holmes, Stephen. 1990. "The Secret History of Self-Interest." In J. Mansbridge, ed. *Beyond Self-Interest*. 267–86. Chicago & London: The University of Chicago Press.

Hooker, Evelyn. 1956. "A Preliminary Analysis of Group Behavior of Homosexuals." *The Journal of Psychology* 42: 217–25.

Hoopes, David S., and Margaret D. Pusch. 1980. "Definition of Terms," In M. D. Pusch, ed. *Multicultural Education: A Cross Cultural Training Approach* 1–8. Yarmouth, Maine: Intercultural Press.

Horn, John. 1990. "Media Buzzwords Slanting the News?" *Greensboro New & Record* (Saturday, January 13): 10.

Hotvedt, Mary E. 1982. "Summary and Conclusions." In W. Paul, J. D. Weinrich, J. C. Consiorek, & M. E. Hotvedt, eds. *Homosexuality* 283–91. Beverly Hills & London: SAGE.

Howard, Alan. 1985. "Ethnopsychology and the Prospects for a Cultural Psychology." In G. M. White & J. Kirkpatrick, eds. *Person, Self, and Experience* 401–20. Berkeley: University of California Press.

Humphreys, Laud. 1970. *Tearoom Trade: Impersonal Sex in Public Places*. Chicago: Aldine-Atherton.

Jackson, Jean. 1989. "Is There A Way To Talk About Making Culture Without Making Enemies?" *Dialectical Anthropology* 14: 127–43.

Jansen, Sue Curry. 1989. "Gender and the Information Society: A Socially Structured Silence." In M. Siefert, et al., eds. *The Information Gap* 196–215. Oxford & New York: Oxford University Press.

Johnson, Don. 1989. "The American Male in Transition." *American Health* (January/February): 59–63.

Johnson, J. David, and Frank Tuttle. 1989. "Problems in Intercultural Research." In M. K. Asante & W. B. Gudykunst, eds. *Handbook of International and Intercultural Communication* 461–83. Newbury Park: SAGE.

Johnson, John M., and Kathleen J. Ferraro. 1987. "The Victimized Self: The Case of Battered Women." In J. A. Kotarba & A. Fontana, eds. *The Existential Self in Society* 119–30. Chicago & London: The University of Chicago Press.

Katz, Alfred, and E. I. Bender, eds. 1976. *The Strength in Us: Self-help Groups in the Modern World.* New York: New Viewpoints.

Katz, Elihu. 1981. "Epilogue: Where Do We Stand?" In E. Katz & T. Szecsko, eds. *Mass Media and Social Change* 265–68. Beverly Hills: SAGE.

Katz, Pearl. 1990. "Emotional Metaphors, Socialization, and Roles of Drill Sergeants." *Ethos* 18 (4): 257–480.

Kaufman, Sharon R. 1986. *The Ageless Self: Sources of Meaning in Late Life.* New York: New American Library.

Keefe, Susan Emley. 1989. "Introduction." In S. E. Keefe, ed. *Negotiating Ethnicity*, Napa Bulletin, no. 8: 1–8.

Keefe, Susan E., Gregory G. Reck, and Una Mae Lange Reck. 1989. "Measuring Ethnicity and Its Political Consequences in a Southern Appalachian High School." In S. E. Keefe, ed. *Negotiating Ethnicity*, Napa Bulletin, no. 8: 21–38.

Keen, Sam. 1991. *Fire in the Belly: On Being a Man.* New York: Bantam Books.

Keith, Jennie. 1985. "Age In Anthropological Research." In R. Binstock & E. Shanas, eds. *Handbook of Aging and the Social Sciences.* 231–63 (2nd ed.) New York: Van Nostrand.

Kelley, Raymond C. 1977. *Etoro Social Structure.* Ann Arbor: University of Michigan Press.

Kenny, Michael G. 1986. *The Passion of Ansel Bourne: Multiple Personality in American Culture.* Washington, D. C. & London: Smithsonian Institute Press.

Kilborne, Benjamin, and L. L. Langness, eds. 1987. *Culture and Human Nature: Theoretical Papers of Melford E. Spiro.* Chicago & London: The University of Chicago Press.

Kim, Young Yun, and Brent D. Ruben. 1988. "Intercultural Transformation: A Systems Theory." In Y. Y. Kim & W. B. Gudykunst, eds. *Theories in Intercultural Communication* 299–322. Newbury Park & London: SAGE.

Kimmel, Michael S. 1987a. "Rethinking 'Masculinity': New Directions in Research." In M. S. Kimmel, ed. *Changing Men* 9–24. Newbury Park: SAGE.

———, ed. 1987b. *Changing Men: New Directions in Research on Men and Masculinity.* Newbury Park: SAGE.

King, Arden R. 1974. "A Stratification of Labyrinths: The Acquisition and Retention of Cultural Identity in Modern Culture." In T. K. Fitzgerald, ed. *Social and Cultural Identity* 299–322. Athens: The University of Georgia Press.

Kirk, Marshall, and Hunter Madsen. 1989. *After the Ball: How America Will Conquer its Fear and Hatred of Gays in the '90s.* New York: Doubleday.

Knapp, Mark L. 1972. *Nonverbal Communication in Human Interaction.* New York: Holt, Rinehart & Winston.

Knowles, Eric S. and Mark E. Sibicky. 1990. "Continuities and Diversity in the Stream of Selves: Metaphorical Resolutions of William James' 'One-in-Many Selves Paradox.'" *Personality and Social Psychology* 16 (4): 676–87.

Kochman, Thomas. 1986. "Black Verbal Dueling Strategies in Interethnic Communication." In Y. Y. Kim, ed. *Interethnic Communication* 136–57. Newbury Park: SAGE.

Kohut, Heinz. 1971. *The Analysis of the Self.* New York: International Universities Press.

_____. 1977. *The Restoration of the Self.* New York: International Universities Press.

Kondo, Dorinne K. 1987. "Creating an Ideal Self: Theories of Selfhood and Pedagogy at a Japanese Ethics Retreat." *Ethos* 15 (3): 241–72.

_____. 1990. *Crafting Selves: Power, Gender, and Discourses of Identity in a Japanese Workplace.* Chicago & London: The University of Chicago.

Korzenny, Felipe, and Stella Ting-Toomey, eds. 1990. *Communicating for Peace: Diplomacy and Negotiation.* Newbury Park: SAGE.

Kotarba, Joseph A., and Andrea Fontana, eds. 1987. *The Existential Self in Society.* Chicago & London: The Chicago University Press.

Kushner, Gilbert. 1974. "Discussion," In T. K. Fitzgerald, ed. *Social and Cultural Identity,* Southern Anthropological Society Proceedings, no. 8: 126–33.

La Fontaine, J. S. 1987. "Person and Individual: Some Anthropological Reflections." In M. Carrithers, et al., eds. *The Category of the Person* 123–40. Cambridge: Cambridge University Press.

Lakoff, George, and Mark Johnson. 1980. *Metaphors We Live By.* Chicago & London: The University of Chicago Press.

Lakoff, George, and Mark Turner. 1989. *More Than Cool Reason: A Field Guide to Poetic Metaphor.* Chicago & London: The University of Chicago Press.

Langbaum, Robert. 1982. *The Mysteries of Identity.* Chicago: The University of Chicago Press.

Lattas, Andrew. 1990. "Poetics of Space and Sexual Economies of Power: Gender and the Politics of Male Identity in West New Britain." *Ethos* 18 (1): 71–102.

Lepowsky, Maria. 1985. "Gender, Aging, and Dying in an Egalitarian Society." In D. A. Counts & D. R. Counts, eds. *Aging and Its Transformations*, ASAO Monograph, no. 10: 156–78. Lanham & New York: University Press of America.

Lerner, Max. 1991. "After the Fall: Keeping his Sense of Self Became the Biggest Challenge of Illness." *American Health* 10 (12): 69–74.

Levine, Robert, and Ellen Wolff. 1989. "Social Time: The Heartbeat of Culture." *Anthropology 89/90* 56–59. Guilford, Conn.: The Duskins Publishing Group.

Levy, Robert I. 1973. *Tahitians: Mind and Experience in the Society Islands.* Chicago: The University of Chicago Press.

Lewis, George H. 1981. "Taste Cultures and Their Composition: Towards a New Theoretical Perspective." In E. Katz & T. Szecsko, eds. *Mass Media and Social Change* 201–18. Beverly Hills: SAGE.

Lienhardt, Godfrey. 1987. "Self: Public, Private: Some African Representations." In M. Carrithers, et al., eds. *The Category of the Person* 141–45. Cambridge: Cambridge University Press.

Lifton, Robert Jay. 1970. *History and Human Survival.* New York: Random House.

Littlejohn, Stephen W. 1989. *Theories of Human Communication*, 3rd. ed. Belmont, California: Wadsworth Publishing Co.

Lodge, David. 1988. *The Modes of Modern Writing: Metaphor, Metonymy, and the Typology of Modern Literature.* Chicago: The University of Chicago Press.

Logue, Barbara J. 1990. "Modernization and the Status of the Frail Elderly: Perspectives on Continuity and Change." *Journal of Cross-Cultural Gerontology* 5 (4): 345–74.

Lowenthal, David. 1985. "Mobility and Identity in the Island Pacific." In M. Chapman, ed. *Mobility and Identity in the Island Pacific*, Special Issue, *Pacific Viewpoint* 26 (1): 316–26.

Lukes, Steven. 1987. "Conclusion." In M. Carrithers, et al., eds. *The Category of the Person* 282–301. Cambridge: Cambridge University Press.

Lull, James, ed. 1987. *Popular Music and Communication.* Newbury Park: SAGE.

Lutz, Catherine A. 1988. *Unnatural Emotions: Everyday Sentiments on a Micronesian Atoll and Their Challenge to Western Theory.* Chicago & London: The University of Chicago Press.

Malinowski, Bronislaw. 1939. "The Group and the Individual in Functional Analysis." *American Journal of Sociology* 44: 938–64.

Maltz, Daniel D., and Ruth A. Borker. 1982. "A Cultural Approach to Male-Female Miscommunication." In J. J. Gumperz, ed. *Language and Social Identity* 196–216. Cambridge, Mass.: Cambridge University Press.

Manderson, Leonore. 1980. "Self, Couple, and Community: A Review Article of Recent Writings on Lesbian Women." *Hecate: Lesbian Studies* 6 (1): 67–79.

Marcia, James E. 1987. "The Identity Status Approach to the Study of Ego Identity." In T. Honess & K. Yardley, eds. *Self and Identity* 161–71. London & New York: Routledge & Kegan Paul.

Marcus, George E., and Michael M. J. Fischer. 1986. *Anthropology as Cultural Critique.* Chicago & London: The University of Chicago Press.

Markus, Hazel Rose, and Shinobu Kitayama. 1991. "Culture and the Self: Implications for Cognition, Emotion, and Motivation." *Psychological Review* 98 (2): 224–53.

Marmor, Judd, ed. 1980. *Homosexual Behavior: A Modern Reappraisal.* New York: Basic Books.

Marshall, Victor. 1985. "Conclusions: Aging and Dying in Pacific Societies: Implications for Theory in Social Gerontology." In D. A. Counts & D. R. Counts, eds. *Aging and Its Transformations,* ASAO Monograph no. 10: 251–74. Lanham & New York: University Press of America.

Masters, William H., and Virginia E. Johnson. 1979. *Homosexuality in Perspective.* Boston: Little, Brown & Co.

Matsumoto, David, Harold G. Wallbott, and Klaus R. Sherer. 1989. "Emotions in Intercultural Communication." In M. K. Asante & W. B. Gudykunst, eds. *Handbook of International and Intercultural Communication* 225–46. Newbury Park: SAGE.

Matthews, Sarah H. 1986. *Friendships Through the Life Course: Oral Biographies in Old Age.* Beverly Hills: SAGE.

McAdams, Dan P. 1985. "The 'Imago': A Key Narrative Component of Identity." In P. Shaver, ed. *Self, Situations, and Social Behavior* 115–41. Beverly Hills & London: SAGE.

McCauley, Byron. 1990. "Seniors Marketing Gaining Respect." *Greensboro News & Record* (Monday, March 26): 1; 8–9.

McGuire, William J., and Claire V. McGuire. 1987. "Developmental Trends and Gender Differences in the Subjective Experience of Self." In T. Honess & K. Yardley, eds. *Self and Identity* 134–46. London & New York: Routledge & Kegan Paul.

McLeod, Ramon G. 1991. "Advertisers Discover Gay Market." *Greensboro News & Record* (Sunday, September 9): E1; E5.

McPhail, Thomas L. 1989. "Inquiry in International Communication." In M. K. Asante & W. B. Gudykunst, eds. *Handbook of International and Intercultural Communication* 47–66. Newbury Park: SAGE.

McQuail, Denis. 1989. *Mass Communication Theory: An Introduction.* London & Newbury Park: SAGE.

Mead, Margaret. 1935. *Sex and Temperament in Three Primitive Societies.* New York: New American Library.

Meyrowitz, Joshua. 1986. *No Sense of Place: Impact of Electronic Media on Social Behavior.* New York & Oxford: Oxford University Press.

Miller, Neil. 1989. *In Search of Gay America: Women and Men in a Time of Change.* New York: Harper & Row.

Miller, Ron. 1989. "Beyond Sitins, Setasides: Civil Rights Movement Rethinks its Course." *Greensboro News & Record* (Sunday, December 10): B1–6.

Mishkind, Marc, Judith Rodin, Lisa R. Silberstein, and Ruth H. Striegel-Moore. 1987. "The Embodiment of Masculinity: Cultural, Psychological, and Behavioral Dimensions." In M. Kimmel, ed. *Changing Men* 37–52. Newbury Park: SAGE.

Modern Maturity. 1991. "Older Workers Are Good Workers." (October-November): 88.

Modern Maturity. 1991. "Toward Graceful Aging of TV." (August-September): 86.

Montegu, Ashley. 1972. *Statement on Race: An Annotated Elaboration and Exposition of Four Statements on Race.* Issued by UNESCO (3rd. ed.) New York: Oxford University Press.

Montegu, Ashley, and Floyd Matson. 1983. *The Humanization of Man.* New York: McGraw-Hill Book Co.

Murdock, Graham, and Peter Golding. 1989. "Information Poverty and Political Inequality: Citizenship in the Age of Privatized Communications." In M. Siefert, et al., eds. *The Information Gap* 180–95. Oxford & New York: Oxford University Press.

Murphy, Gardner. 1947. *Personality: A Biosocial Approach to Origins and Structure.* New York: Harper & Brothers.

Myerhoff, Barbara. 1978a. "A Symbol Perfected in Death: Continuity and Ritual in the Life and Death of an Elderly Jew." In B. Myerhoff & A. Simić, eds. *Life's Career-Aging* 163–206. Beverly Hills: SAGE.

_____. 1978b. *Number Our Days*. New York: Simon & Schuster.

Myerhoff, Barbara G., and Andrei Simić, eds. 1978. *Life's Career-Aging: Cultural Variations on Growing Old*. Beverly Hills: SAGE.

Nagel, Thomas. 1975. "Brain Bisection and the Unity of Consciousness." In J. Perry, ed. *Personal Identity* 227–45. Berkeley: University of California Press.

Naisbitt, John. 1982. *Megatrends: Ten New Directions for Transforming Our Lives*. New York: William Morrow & Co.

Naisbitt, John, and Patricia Aburdene. 1990. *Megatrends 2000: Ten New Directions for the 1990s*. New York: William Morrow & Co.

Nash, Betty Joyce. 1991. "The Changing Face of America's Work Force: Diversity Training a Key Element for Company Survival." *Triad Business Weekly/Greensboro News & Record* (Monday, June 17): 1/5.

Nash, Dennison. 1989. *A Little Anthropology*. Englewood Cliffs, New Jersey: Prentice Hall.

New York Daily News. 1991. "Many Moods of Men Today." *The Raleigh News & Observer* (Tuesday, June 25): 2E.

Newsweek. 1990. "The Future of Gay America." (March 12): 20–25.

Ortner, Sherry B., and Harriet Whitehead, eds. 1981. *Sexual Meanings: The Cultural Constructions of Gender and Sexuality*. Cambridge: Cambridge University Press.

Owens, Thomas. 1969. *Metaphor and Related Subjects*. New York: Random House.

Pacanowsky, Michael E., and Nick O'Donnell-Trujillo. 1983. "Organizational Communication as Cultural Performance." *Communication Monographs* 50 (June): 126–47.

Page, Stewart, and Mary Yee. 1985. "Conceptions of Male and Female Homosexual Stereotypes Among University Undergraduates." *Journal of Homosexuality* 12 (1): 109–18.

Parfit, Derek. 1975. "Personal Identity." In J. Perry, ed. *Personal Identity* 199–226. Berkeley: University of California Press.

Paul, William. 1982a. "Minority Status for Gay People: Majority Reaction and Social Context." In W. Paul, et al., eds. *Homosexuality* 351–70. Beverly Hills & London: SAGE.

Paul, William. 1982b. "Summary and Conclusions." In W. Paul, et al., eds. *Homosexuality* 371–73. Beverly Hills & London: SAGE.

Penfield, Joyce, and Mary Duru. 1988. "Proverbs: Metaphors that Teach." *Anthropological Quarterly* 61 (3): 119–28.

Perry, John. 1975. "The Problem of Personal Identity." In J. Perry, ed. *Personal Identity* 3–32. Berkeley: University of California Press.

Peterson, Richard A. 1979. "Revitalizing the Culture Concept." *Annual Review of Sociology* 5: 137–66.

Pfeiffer, John. 1989. "How Not To Lose The Trade Wars by Cultural Gaffes." *Anthropology 89/90* 60–63. Guilford, Conn.: The Dushkin Publishing Group.

Phinney, Jean S., and Mary Jane Rotheram, eds. 1987. *Children's Ethnic Socialization: Pluralism and Development*. Newbury Park: SAGE.

Piccirillo, Mary S. 1990. "An Isocratean Rhetoric of Television." *Communication* 12: 1–18.

Pillard, Richard C. 1982. "Psychotherapeutic Treatment for the Invisible Minority." In W. Paul, et al., eds. *Homosexuality* 99–113. Beverly Hills: SAGE.

Pines, Malcolm. 1987. "Mirroring and Child Development: Psychodynamic and Psychological Interpretations." In T. Honess & K. Yardley, eds. *Self and Identity* 19–37. London & New York: Routledge & Kegan Paul.

Pleck, Joseph. 1987. "American Fathering In Historical Perspective." In M. Kimmel, ed. *Changing Men* 83–97. Newbury Park: SAGE.

Plummer, Kenneth. 1981. "Homosexual Categories: Some Research Problems in the Labelling Perspective of Homosexuality." In K. Plummer, ed. *The Making of the Modern Homosexual* 53–75. London: Hutchinson.

Pomponio, Alice. 1990. "Seagulls Don't Fly into the Bush: Cultural Identity and the Negotiation of Development on Mandok Island, Papua New Guinea." In J. Linnekin & L. Poyer, eds. *Cultural Identity and Ethnicity in the Pacific* 43–65. Honolulu: University of Hawaii Press.

Ponse, Barbara. 1979. *Identities in the Lesbian World: The Social Construction of Self*. Westport, Conn.: Greenwood.

Popper, Karl R., and John C. Eccles. 1977. *The Self and Its Brain*. London: Routledge & Kegan Paul.

Powers, William G., and David N. Lowry. 1984. "Basic Communication Fidelity: A Functional Approach." In R. N. Bostrom, ed. *Competence in Communication* 57–74. Beverly Hills & London: SAGE.

Price, Gail M. 1987. "Empathic Relating and the Structure of the Self: Parallels in Mother-Infant Patient-Therapist Interaction." In T. Honess & K. Yardley, eds. *Self and Identity* 38–54. London & New York: Routledge & Kegan Paul.

Prosser, Michael H. [1985] 1989. *The Cultural Dialogue: An Introduction to Intercultural Communication*. Washington, D. C.: SIETAR International.

Pusch, Margaret D., ed. 1980. *Multicultural Education: A Cross-Cultural Training Approach*. Yarmouth, Maine: Intercultural Press.

Pusch, Margaret D., H. Ned Seelye, and Jacqueline H. Wasilewski. 1980. "Training for Multicultural Education Competencies." In M. D. Pusch, ed. *Multiculturalism* 86–103. Yarmouth, Maine: Intercultural Press.

Quinton, Anthony. 1975. "The Soul." In J. Perry, ed. *Personal Identity* 53–72. Berkeley: University of California Press.

Raphael, Ray. 1988. *The Men From the Boys: Rites of Passage in Male America*. Lincoln & London: University of Nebraska Press.

Ravitch, Diane. 1990. "Multicultualism: E Pluribus Plures." *The Key Reporter* 56 (1): 1–4.

Real, Michael R. 1989. *Super Media: A Cultural Studies Approach*. Newbury Park: SAGE.

Redford, Dorothy Spruill. 1988. *Somerset Homecoming: Recovering a Lost Heritage*. New York: Doubleday.

Redman, Alvin. 1959. *The Wit and Humor of Oscar Wilde*. New York: Dover Publications.

Reid, Thomas. 1975. "Of Mr. Locke's Account of Our Personal Identity." In J. Perry, ed. *Personal Identity* 113–18. Berkeley: University of California Press.

Restak, Richard. 1984. *The Brain*. Toronto & New York: Bantam Books.

Ricoeur, Paul. 1979. "The Metaphorical Process as Cognition, Imagination, and Feeling." In S. Sacks, ed. *On Metaphor* 141–58. Chicago & London: The University of Chicago Press.

Rivera, Rhonda. 1982. "Homosexuality and the Law." In W. Paul, et al., eds. *Homosexuality* 323–36. Beverly Hills & London: SAGE.

Rogers, Everett M. "Inquiry in Development Communication." 1989. In M. K. Asante & W. B. Gudykunst, eds. *Handbook of International and Intercultural Communication* 67–86. Newbury Park & London: SAGE.

Rogers, Everett M, and D. Lawrence Kincaid. 1981. *Communication Networks*. New York: Free Press.

Rogers, Everett M., and Francis Balle, eds. 1985. *The Media Revolution in America and in Western Europe*. Norwood, New Jersey: Ablex Publishing Corporation.

Roland, Alan. 1989. *In Search of Self in India and Japan: Toward a Cross-Cultural Psychology*. Princeton: Princeton University Press.

Roloff, Michael E, and Kathy Kellermann. 1984. "Judgments of Interpersonal Competency: How You Know, What You Know, and Who You Know." In R. N. Bostrom, ed. *Competence In Communication* 175–228. Beverly Hills & London: SAGE.

Roosens, Eugeen E. 1989. *Creating Ethnicity: The Process of Ethnogenesis*. Newbury Park: SAGE.

Rosaldo, Renato. 1989. *Culture and Truth: The Remaking of Social Analysis*. Boston: Beacon Press.

Roseman, Marina. 1990. "Head, Heart, Odor, and Shadow: The Structure of the Self, the Emotional World, and Ritual Performance among Senoi Temiar." *Ethos* 18 (3): 227–50.

Rosenberg, Harriet G. 1990. "Complaint Discourse, Aging, and Caregiving Among the !Kung San of Botswana." In J. Sokolovsky, ed. *The Cultural Context of Aging* 19–42. New York: Bergin & Garvey Publishers.

Rosenberg, Morris. 1979. *Conceiving the Self*. New York: Basic Books.

———. 1987. "Depersonalization: The Loss of Personal Identity." In T. Honess & K. Yardley, eds. *Self and Identity* 193–206. London & New York: Routledge & Kegan Paul.

Rosenberg, Seymour, and Michael A. Gara. 1985. "The Multiplicity of Personal Identity." In P. Shaver, ed. *Self, Situations, and Social Behavior* 87–113. Beverly Hills & London: SAGE.

Rosenberger, Nancy R. 1989. "Dialectic Balance in the Polar Model of Self: The Japan Case." *Ethos* 17 (1): 88–113

Ross, E. Lamar, ed. 1978. *Interethnic Communication*. Athens: The University of Georgia Press.

Roy, Ramashray. 1985. *Self and Society: A Study in Gandhian Thought*. New Delhi & Beverly Hills: SAGE.

Royce, Anya Peterson. 1982. *Ethnic Identity: Strategies of Diversity*. Bloomington: Indiana University Press.

Sacks, Oliver. 1987. *The Man Who Mistook His Wife For A Hat*. New York: Harper & Row.

Sacks, Sheldon, ed. 1979. *On Metaphor*. Chicago & London: The University of Chicago Press.

Sahlins, Marshall. 1976. *Culture and Practical Reason*. Chicago: The University of Chicago.

St. Claire, Lindsay. 1989. "When is Gender a Handicap?: Towards Conceptualizing the Socially Constructed Disadvantages Experienced by Women." In S. Shevington & D. Baker, eds. *The Social Identity of Women* 130–51. London & Newbury Park: SAGE.

Sampson, E. E. 1989. "The Challenge of Social Change for Psychology: Globalization and Psychology's Theory of the Person." *American Psychologist* 44: 914–21.

Sapir, David J., and J. Christopher Crocker, eds. 1977. *The Social Use of Metaphor: Essays on the Anthropology of Rhetoric.* University of Pennsylvania Press.

Scarr, Sandra. 1988. "How Genotypes and Environments Combine: Development and Individual Differences." In N. Bolger, et al., eds. *Persons in Context* 217–44. New York: Cambridge University Press.

Scheff, Thomas J. 1990. *Microsociology: Discourse, Emotion, and Social Structure.* Beverly Hills & London: SAGE.

Schuman, Howard, Charlotte Steeh, and Lawrence Bobo. 1985. *Racial Attitudes in America.* Cambridge, Mass.: Harvard University Press.

Seidler, Victor. 1989. *Rediscovering Masculinity: Reason, Language and Sexuality.* London & New York: Routledge.

Shaver, Philip, ed. 1985. *Self, Situations, and Social Behavior.* Beverly Hills & London: SAGE.

Shield, Renée Rose. 1990. "Liminality in an American Nursing Home: The Endless Transition." In J. Sokolovsky, ed. *The Cultural Context of Aging* 331–52. New York: Bergin & Garvey Publications.

Shore, Brad. 1982. *Sala'ilua: A Samoan Mystery.* New York: Columbia University Press.

Shulins, Nancy. 1991. "Is it Art or Is it Man-bashing?" *Greensboro News & Record* (Sunday, July 14): F–14.

Shweder, Richard A, and Edmund J. Bourne. 1984. "Does the Concept of the Person Vary Cross-Culturally?" In A. J. Marsella & G. M. White, eds. *Cultural Conceptions of Mental Health and Therapy* 97–137. Dordrecht, Holland & Boston: D. Reidel Publishing Co.

Siefert, Marsha, George Gerbner, and Janice Fisher, eds. 1989. *The Information Gap: How Computers and Other New Communication Technologies Affect the Social Distribution of Power.* Oxford & New York: Oxford University Press.

Simić, Andrei. 1978. "Winners and Losers: Aging Yugoslavs in a Changing World." In B. Myerhoff & A. Simić, eds. *Life's Career-Aging* 77–106. Beverly Hills: SAGE.

_____. 1990. "Aging, World View, and Intergenerational Relations in America and Yugoslavia." In J. Sokolovsky, ed. *The Cultural Context of Aging* 89–108. New York: Bergin & Garvey Publications.

Simić, Andrei, and Barbara Myerhoff. 1978. "Conclusions." In B. Myerhoff & A. Simić, eds. *Life's Career-Aging* 231–46. Beverly Hills: SAGE.

Sinclair, Karen P. 1985. "Koro and Kuia: Aging and Gender Among the Maori of New Zealand." In D. A. Counts & D. R. Counts, eds. *Aging and its Transformation*, ASAO Monograph, no. 10: 27–46. Lanham, Maryland, & New York: University Press of America.

Singer, June. 1976. *Androgyny: Toward a New Theory of Sexuality.* Garden City, New York: Anchor Press.

Skevington, Suzanne, and Deborah Baker, eds. 1989. *The Social Identity of Women.* London & Newbury Park: SAGE.

Slugoski, B. R., and G. P. Ginsburg. 1989. "Ego Identity and Explanatory Speech." In J. Shotter & K. J. Gergen, eds. *Texts of Identity* 36–55. Newbury Park: SAGE.

Smith, M. Estellie. 1974. "Portuguese Enclaves: The Invisible Minority." In T. K. Fitzgerald, ed. *Social and Cultural Identity, Southern Anthropological Society Proceedings*, no. 8: 81–91.

Smith, Robert J. 1988. *Japanese Society: Tradition, Self, and The Social Order.* Cambridge & New York: Cambridge University Press.

Snow, Robert P. 1983. *Creating Media Culture.* Beverly Hills & London: SAGE.

Sokolovsky, Jay. 1990a. "Bringing Culture Back Home: Aging, Ethnicity, and Family Support." In J. Sokolovsky, ed. *The Cultural Context of Aging* 201–11. New York & Westport, Conn.: Bergin & Garvey Publishers.

_____, ed. 1990b. *The Cultural Context of Aging: Worldwide Perspectives.* New York: Bergin & Garvey Publishers.

Sollors, Werner. 1986. *Beyond Ethnicity: Consent and Descent in American Culture.* New York & Oxford: Oxford University Press.

Solomon, Jack. 1988. *The Signs of Our Time.* New York: Harper & Row.

Spindler, George, and Louise Spindler (with Henry Trueba & Melvin D. Williams). 1990. *The American Cultural Dialogue and its Transmission.* London, New York & Philadelphia: The Falmer Press.

Spinelli, Eresto. 1989. *The Interpreted World: An Introduction to Phenomenological Psychology.* London & Newbury Park: SAGE.

Spiro, Melford. 1987. "Some Reflections on Cultural Determinism and Relativism with Special Reference to Emotion and Reason." In B. Kilbourne & L. Langness, eds. *Culture and Human Nature* 32–58. Chicago & London: The University of Chicago Press.

Stone, Elizabeth. 1989. *Black Sheep and Kissing Cousins: How Our Family Stories Shape Us.* New York: Penguin Books.

Storr, Anthony. 1988. *Solitude: A Return to the Self.* New York: The Free Press.

Sypher, Beverly Davenport. 1984. "The Importance of Social Cognitive Abilities in Organizations." In R. Bostrom, ed. *Competence in Communication* 103–27. Beverly Hills & London: SAGE.

Szecsko, Tamas, and Elihu Katz, eds. 1981. *Mass Media and Social Change.* Beverly Hills: SAGE.

Tajfel, Henri. 1978. *Differentiation between Social Groups: Studies in the Social Psychology of Intergroup Relations.* London: Academic Press.

_____. 1984. *The Social Dimensions.* Cambridge: Cambridge University Press.

Tamsin, Lorraine E. 1991. *Gender, Identity and the Production of Meaning.* Boulder: Westview Press.

Tan, Amy. 1989. *The Joy Luck Club.* New York: G. P. Putnam & Sons.

Taylor, Shelley E. 1989. *Positive Illusions: Creative Self-Deception and the Healthy Mind.* New York: Basic Books.

Thompson, Edward H, and Joseph H. Pleck. 1987. "The Structure of Male Role Norms." In M. Kimmel, ed. *Changing Men* 25–36. Newbury Park: SAGE.

Tinder, Glenn. 1980. *Community: Reflections on a Tragic Ideal.* Baton Rouge: Louisiana State University Press.

Ting-Toomey, Stella. 1986. "Conflict Communication Styles in Black and White Subjective Cultures." In Y. Y. Kim, ed. *Interethnic Communication* 75–88. Newbury Park: SAGE.

_____. 1988. "Intercultural Conflict Styles: A Face-Negotiation Theory." In Y. Y. Kim & W. B. Gudykunst, eds. *Theories in Intercultural Communication* 213–35. Newbury Park: SAGE.

Toffler, Alvin. 1990. "Power Shift: Knowledge, Wealth and Violence at the Edge of the 21st Century." *Newsweek* (October 15): 86; 90; 92.

Triandis, Harry C. 1978. "Some Universals of Social Behavior." *Personality and Social Psychology Bulletin,* no. 4: 1–16.

Troiden, Richard Russell. 1985. "Self, SelfConcept, Identity, and Homosexual Identity: Constructs in Need of Definition and Differentiation." *Journal of Homosexuality* 10 (3): 97–108.

Trueba, Henry. 1990. "Mainstream and Minority Cultures: A Chicano Perspective." In G. Spindler & L. Spindler. *The American Cultural Dialogue and Its Transmission* 122–43. London & Philadelphia: The Falmer Press.

Turner, Ralph H. 1978. "The Role and the Person." *American Journal of Sociology* 84: 1–23.

Turner, Victor W., and Edward M. Bruner, eds. 1986. *The Anthropology of Experience*. Urbana & Chicago: University of Illinois Press.

Turow, Joseph. 1990. "Media Industries, Media Consequences: Rethinking Mass Communication." In J. A. Anderson, ed. *Communication Yearbook/13* 478–502. Newbury Park: SAGE.

van Baal, Jan. 1966. *Dema: Description and Analysis of Marind-anim Culture*. The Hague: Martinus Nijhoff.

van Dijk, Teun A. 1987. *Communicating Racism: Ethnic Prejudice in Thought and Talk*. Newbury Park: SAGE.

Wallerstein, Immanuel. 1990. "Culture is the World-System: A Reply to Boyne." In M. Featherstone, ed. *Global Culture* 64–65. London & Newbury Park: SAGE.

Warren, Mary Anne. 1980. "Is Androgyny the Answer to Stereotyping?" In M. Vetterling-Brassin, ed. *"Femininity," "Masculinity," and "Androgyny"* 170–86. Totowa, New Jersey: Rowman & Littlefield.

Wax, Murray L., Rosalie H. Wax, and Robert V. Dumont, Jr. 1989. *Formal Education in an American Indian Community*. Prospect Heights, Illinois: Waveland Press.

Weigert, Andrew J., J. Smith Teitge, and Dennis W. Teitge. [1986] 1990. *Society and Identity: Towards a Sociological Psychology*. Cambridge & New York: Cambridge University Press.

Weinberg, Thomas S. 1983. *Gay Men, Gay Selves*. New York: Irvington.

———. 1984. "Biology, Ideology, and the Reification of Developmental Stages in the Study of Homosexual Identities." *Journal of Homosexuality* 10 (3/4): 77–84.

Weinrich, James D. 1982. "Is Homosexuality Biologically Natural?" In W. Paul, et al., eds. *Homosexuality* 197–208. Beverly Hills & London: SAGE.

Weintraub, Karl Joachim. 1982. *The Value of the Individual: Self and Circumstance in Autobiography.* Chicago & London: The University of Chicago Press.

White, Geoffrey M., and John Kirkpatrick, eds. 1985. *Person, Self, and Experience: Exploring Pacific Ethnopsychologies.* Berkeley: University of California Press.

Whitehead, Harriet. 1981. "The Bow and the Burden Strap: A New Look at Institutionalized Homosexuality in Native America." In S. B. Ortner & H. Whitehead, eds. *Sexual Meanings* 80–115. Cambridge: Cambridge University Press.

Wilkinson, Rupert. 1988. *The Pursuit of American Character.* New York: Harper & Row Publisher.

Williams, John E. 1974. "Discussion." In T. K. Fitzgerald, ed. *Social and Cultural Identity,* Southern Anthropological Society Proceedings, no. 8: 118–25.

Wilson, Clint C., and Felix Gutierrez. 1985. *Minorities and Media: Diversity and the End of Mass Communication.* Newbury Park & Beverly Hills: SAGE.

Woodman, N. J., and H. R. Lenna. 1980. *Counseling with Gay Men and Women.* San Francisco: Jossey-Bass.

Yankelovich, Daniel. 1981. "New Rules in American Life: Searching for Self-Fulfillment in a World Turned Upside Down." *Psychology Today* (April): 35–91.

Yaple, Peter, and Felipe Korzenny. 1989. "Electronic Mass Media Effects Across Cultures." In M. K. Asante & W. B. Gudykunst, eds. *Handbook of International and Intercultural Communication* 295–317. Newbury Park: SAGE.

Yum, June Ock. 1988. "Network Theory in Intercultural Communication." In Y. Y. Kim & W. B. Gudykunst, eds. *Theories in Intercultural Communication* 239–58. Newbury Park: SAGE.

Zelkovitz, Bruce M. 1990. "Transforming the 'Middle Way': A Political Economy of Aging Policy in Sweden." In J. Sokolovsky, ed. *The Cultural Context of Aging* 163–80. New York: Bergin & Garvey Publishers.

AUTHOR INDEX

SUBJECT INDEX